The Mobilization of the United States in World War II

The Mobilization of the United States in World War II

How the Government, Military and Industry Prepared for War

by V. R. Cardozier

McFarland & Company, Inc., Publishers
Jefferson, North Carolina, and London

British Library Cataloguing-in-Publication data are available

Library of Congress Cataloguing-in-Publication Data

Cardozier, V. R.
The mobilization of the United States in World War II : how the government, military and industry prepared for war / by V. R. Cardozier.
p. c.m.
Includes bibliographical references (p.) and index.
ISBN 0-7864-0076-5 (lib. bdg. : 50# alk. paper)
1. World War, 1939–1945—United States. 2. United States—Armed forces—Mobilization. 3. Industrial mobilization—United States—History—20th century. I. Title.
D769.2.C33 1995
940.53'73—dc20 94-48001
CIP

Manufactured in the United States of America

McFarland & Company, Inc., Publishers
Box 611, Jefferson, North Carolina 28640

to

Nancy Pattison Fyfe

Table of Contents

Preface

IN DOING RESEARCH for a book on the World War II period, I became fascinated with the phenomenal success of America's mobilization for a war that the nation had struggled to stay out of for so long. When attacked, the entire country rallied to the cause. I found it startling to consider not only the speed with which the military expanded and trained its personnel and the amazing productivity of American industry, but how quickly the government and the entire populace adapted following the attack on Pearl Harbor.

The change was all the more striking because of the widespread antimilitarism that had prevailed in the country. Most people today are shocked to discover how ill prepared the United States was for war in the 1930s, relying for much of the decade on an army comparable in size to that of Portugal, Bulgaria, or the Netherlands. Divisions and regiments were skeletons, scattered about the United States and its territories. Looking back on the starvation of the military between the wars, it is amazing that the Army was able to retain the officers who would become the great leaders of World War II—Marshall, Eisenhower, MacArthur, Bradley, Patton, and dozens of other senior officers whose military talents would prove so vital to victory.

The debate over whether America should become involved in the European war, and to what extent, permeated public discourse for two years before America entered the war, but with the bombing of Pearl Harbor the debate ended and the entire country became dedicated to winning the war. In addition to those who served in the military, citizens at home joined in the war effort in dozens of ways. The most notable was in the production of war materials, for it was America's industrial productivity that made the difference, both in Europe and the Pacific. If the German army had been as well supplied and equipped as the armies of the Allies in the battle for western Europe in 1944-45, the final outcome might have been the same but the Allies would have paid a higher price.

Should the United States have declared war on Germany sooner? Many in England still resent the fact that while their island nation was facing annihilation, America remained neutral. That Britain escaped defeat in late 1940 and 1941 is almost certainly due to Hitler's decision to forego the invasion of Britain and strike at the Soviet Union instead, for if the German army had reached English soil, it would have defeated the British, who had neither the troops nor equipment to stop a full-scale German invasion.

To be sure, America was supplying Britain with war materials more than two years before it entered the war, and long before the attack on Pearl Harbor it had become an undeclared, if reluctant, belligerent. It was American supplies and equipment that permitted Britain to hold out until the United States entered the war, after which time American industries and farms produced a major portion of the supplies for the military forces and civilian population of both Britain and the Soviet Union. America was blessed with bountiful resources, powerful industrial capacity, an economic system that fostered abundant productivity, and a citizenry that was determined to do whatever was necessary for victory.

The dedication of Americans at home to provide the military with the equipment and supplies needed for victory is legend. In addition to war production, civilians contributed in many other ways: they bought war bonds to an extent no one expected, thus fueling the postwar economy and preventing another depression; served in a multitude of civilian defense roles, many of which proved unnecessary but were thought essential at the time; grew Victory Gardens; collected scrap metal, kitchen fats for explosives, paper, and other recyclables; staffed USO centers, entertained servicemen, and wrote billions of letters to keep up morale; rolled bandages and prepared kits for servicemen in hospitals; wrestled with shortages and rationing; and in many other ways worked to bring about victory.

THROUGHOUT THIS BOOK references are made to costs, wages, prices, and expenditures during the war years, all in then current dollars. Translation into current equivalencies is difficult. If the value of the dollar is used, wartime dollars must be multiplied by approximately nine to convert to dollars for the mid–1990s, but that method does not accurately reflect the costs of many items that have grown relatively more expensive or relatively less expensive. For example, a Chevrolet sedan with all accessories that cost less than $1,000 when the war began would cost at least $15,000 in 1995, but the two vehicles are not directly comparable; the latter included many features that were unknown in 1941. And the paperback book that sold for 25 cents in 1939 sold in 1995 for $4.99 or more, at least a 20-fold increase.

On the other hand, because of advances in science and technology, some items cost little more today than they did during World War II. The prices of food and farm products have increased much less than the consumer price index. For instance, as a result of advances in poultry breeding and feeding, the retail price of broiler chickens, which averaged 44.7 cents per pound in 1943, was 87 cents per pound in the early 1990s, but the supply was such that in some stores the price was as low as 69 cents per pound. The average price of large grade A eggs in 1943 was 57.2 cents per dozen; fifty years later they cost about 90 cents a dozen. And the price of wheat, which sold on the Chicago exchange in 1943 for $1.71 a bushel, sold for about $3.30 a bushel in the mid-1990s, less than double the wartime price.

Salaries and wages have increased far more than the consumer price index since World War II, resulting in a much higher standard of living. The average wage of auto workers in Michigan in January 1943 was $1.08 per hour. If that were increased by the consumer price index, the average in 1991 would have been less than $10.00 an hour. In fact, the Bureau of Labor Statistics reported that in 1991 auto workers earned an average of $18.34 per hour. Salaries and wages in most other occupations and professions also increased faster than the consumer price index. Within less than 30 years after the end of World War II, the per capita disposable income—that is, after-tax income adjusted for inflation—had more than doubled, as was reflected in a standard of living for most Americans that could not have been envisioned in the 1930s.

MORE THAN A HALF CENTURY after the end of World War II Americans continue to be keenly interested in the war, as evidenced by the number of books about it published annually. Most of these books deal with strictly military aspects of the war—grand strategy, battles, and combat experiences of individual soldiers. This book examines how the United States got into the war, how it prepared for it, and how it marshalled the energies and spirit of the entire country to achieve victory.

When Hitler ordered the attack on Poland on September 1, 1939, that set off World War II, the German army had more than 3 million men under arms. Although America's armed forces had grown some during the previous year, the army strength totaled only about 200,000. How America's military forces grew from one of the weakest among developed nations in the 1930s to 12 million men and women in uniform when Japan surrendered on August 14, 1945, is a dramatic story, but an incomplete one. Understanding the full story behind America's success in World War II also requires examination of how the American government organized to prosecute the war, the amazing productivity of American industry, and how civilians in every walk of life worked to support the war effort. That is what I have attempted in this book.

It would not be possible to examine exhaustively the involvement of the American people, economy, and institutions before and during the war in a single volume. Many segments of society that a book of this nature could not examine in depth made important contributions to the war effort. For example, colleges and universities participated actively, training hundreds of thousands of servicemen and industrial workers. Public schools trained even larger numbers for a variety of war production jobs. American farms not only provided ample supplies of food for the U.S. armed forces and civilians at home but sent hundreds of shiploads of food to Britain and the Soviet Union. These and many other segments of American society deserve fuller treatment than is possible in a single volume.

In preparation for this book I discussed wartime on the homefront with many individuals who were adults during the war, but they provided primarily impressions and context rather than detailed factual information. In gathering material for the book, I relied almost entirely on documentary sources—books, magazines, newspapers and other printed materials. I have drawn heavily on publications of various agencies of the U.S. government, most of them written shortly after the war when memories of the authors and sources were still fresh but long enough afterwards to allow for better perspective and for sorting out errors in wartime news stories. A major source was the U.S. Army's history of World War II, the so-called "green books" which now number more than 100 volumes, a gold mine of facts and figures about logistics, war production, and related topics in the civilian economy as well as combat activities.

I wish to acknowledge the scholarship of dozens of writers whose works I have relied on in this undertaking, writers who have investigated related topics before, and who are cited by author and or title in the text and listed in the references at the end of the book. I also wish to express appreciation to Dr. Phil Schwartz of the Perry-Castenada Library at the University of Texas at Austin for his assistance; to Gerri Harcarik, U.S. Army Center for Military History in Washington, D.C.; Dr. Thomas A. Manning, command historian, Air Training Command, Randolph Air Force Base, Texas, and his associates Dr. Carl Hoover and Dr. John D. Hunley who were most helpful in making available unpublished materials, including vast amounts of wartime correspondence; Dr. James H. Kitchens, archivist, U.S. Air Force Historical Research Center, Maxwell Air Force Base, Alabama; and Edward J. Reese at the National Archives in Washington, D.C. I am particularly grateful to Henry A. Boudolf for his critical reading of the manuscript.

Chapter I

Stay Out of War!

When Adolf Hitler came to power in Germany on January 30, 1933, no one could have predicted the events of the next decade. World War I had ended only 15 years earlier, and the prospect of another European war seemed remote. There was widespread revulsion throughout the United States about that war, even though American losses were only a fraction of those suffered by Great Britain, France and Germany. Many Americans thought it had been a mistake to participate in World War I and believed the United States should not become involved in another such conflict, or indeed in any kind of war.

It was then widely believed among Americans that maintaining substantial military forces during peacetime was a provocative practice, and that keeping only a small army and a small navy would contribute to peace. This attitude largely shaped American military posture during the interwar years and the background for America's mobilization for World War II. It also accounts for Japan's underestimation of the potential for U.S. success in a war.

This attitude prevailed throughout the 1920s and continued through the 1930s among a large percentage of the population. By 1938, with war clouds growing in Europe, a poll showed that a majority of the population had come to favor a stronger military, but a significant number of opinion leaders and members of Congress still considered a strong military provocative.

It was not that the American public was unaware of what Hitler was doing. The press had reported the chaos in Germany during the 1920s, the growing influence and popularity of the Nazi Party, and the shrewd maneuvering that brought Hitler to the chancellor's office. Hitler's destruction of civil rights and his persecution of Jews, Slavs, gypsies and enemies of the Nazi Party were reported in the American press, albeit incompletely, but few Americans understood Germany's growing military power until near the end of the decade. To be sure, Hitler had repudiated the 100,000-man limit on his army set by the Versailles Treaty on March 16, 1935, and announced that the German army would rearm and reinstate conscription. Actually, the army had been expanding since Hitler took power in 1933. Also in March 1935, Hitler acknowledged the existence of the Luftwaffe. Perhaps the West should have sensed what was ahead from the militancy of Hitler's speeches and the ultranationalist fervor that began to appear throughout Germany under his rule. But the world had never experienced a Hitler and could not imagine what would occur in just a few short years, the atrocities that would be visited on nations and people. Surely he did not intend to do everything he had said he would do in his book *Mein Kampf*, for they were not the actions of national leaders or civilized men!

The world watched his reoccupation on May 7, 1936, of the Rhineland, the area across the Rhine River next to France that in the Locarno Pact of 1925 had been demilitarized. Hitler's generals strongly opposed the action, pointing out that the German army was not yet strong enough to deal with the French army, but Hitler assured them that the French would do nothing. He was proved right. Only a small German force was dispatched, and Hitler admitted later that if the French Army had responded, the German troops would have withdrawn. But the French government feared that opposing the German occupation of the Rhineland would spark war, and did not consider the risk justified.

A few months later, on January 30, 1937, Hitler repudiated the guilt clause in the Versailles Treaty in which Germany had been coerced into admitting that it was responsible for World War I. Hitler told his people that World War I was forced on Germany, and it was free from obligations imposed on her by the treaty. This declaration, too, was unsettling to government leaders outside Germany, but, except for diplomatic responses, nothing was done and world tensions grew.

On March 13, 1938, Hitler's army marched into Austria without a shot being fired. Indeed there was no opposition, since Hitler had intimidated Austria's government by threatening war and its leaders had capitulated. When the German army marched into Vienna, the streets were lined with thousands of Austrians welcoming Hitler and his troops, and the world discovered that Hitler was more popular in Austria than had been reported. To be sure, the militant Austrian Nazi Party had cleared the way by intimidating virtually all opposition to Hitler. After browbeating Chancellor Kurt von Schuschnigg into relinquishing his office to Arthur Seyss-Inquart, the Nazi leader in Austria, Hitler had control of that country. The arrangement was ratified on April 10 by popular vote in which Jews were not permitted to participate.

Throughout 1938, Hitler kept referring in speeches to liberation of the German people in the Sudetenland of Czechoslovakia. Following

World War I, Czechoslovakia had been formed principally from the Czech and Slovak nations plus smaller ethnic sectors. It also included an area, occupied by approximately three million ethnic Germans, which Hitler wanted incorporated into Germany. With the aid of Nazi leadership in the Sudetenland, Hitler moved toward its annexation to Germany, allowing a rumor to spread in May 1938 that German troops were amassed on the Czechoslovak border. Prime Minister Neville Chamberlain of Britain played the peacemaker and in two flying trips to Germany attempted to gain a peaceful settlement of the question. Finally, on the night of September 29, 1938, Hitler reached an agreement with Britain and France to the effect that Germany would be allowed to occupy the Sudetenland, in return for which he signed a peace declaration with Britain and France, thus ending a 15-day international crisis.

Prime Minister Chamberlain returned to London from Munich and as he alighted from his plane made a short speech in which he announced that "peace in our time" was now assured. The ceding of the Sudetenland to Germany occurred without the participation of the government of Czechoslovakia, which, though it had an army of 800,000—large for a country of its size—knew it could not oppose Hitler successfully if France and Britain remained neutral. Hitler moved troops into the Sudetenland from October 1 through October 10, 1938, beginning the destruction of that country as a democratic republic. As many had predicted, Hitler was not satisfied with the annexation of the Sudetenland, and on March 14, 1939, he summoned the President and Foreign Minister of Czechoslovakia to Berlin. There, under threat of destruction of Prague by bombing, he forced them to sign a surrender document giving Germany control over the rest of Czechoslovakia—essentially Bohemia and Moravia—excepting only Ruthenia, which Hungary occupied.

By the time Hitler's army and air force attacked Poland on September 1, 1939, a massive military build-up had been under way in Germany for four years and the country was strong in trained troops, guns, tanks, planes and the instruments of war. German army generals were apprehensive about invading Poland, but Hitler would not be deterred. He very shrewdly neutralized Russia, the one country that posed a direct problem. On August 22, 1939, he dispatched Joachim von Ribbentrop, his foreign minister, to Moscow where he negotiated a non-aggression pact between Germany and the Soviet Union, just nine days before the attack on Poland. It is now known that the price Hitler paid was to acquiesce to Russia's takeover of the eastern part of Poland, Bessarabia (part of Hungary), and the Baltic states of Latvia, Lithuania and Estonia. On September 17, the Soviet Army invaded Poland from the east; by the end of September, Poland was defeated and Germany and the USSR divided the spoils, with Germany assuming control of the larger part of the country.

But Hitler had become too self-confident. He had gambled that France and Great Britain would not come to the aid of Poland, even though they had an agreement to do so. In the past, his generals had warned him that France and Britain would intervene in his expansions; he had assured them they would not and he had been right, but he misjudged in the case of Poland. Britain and France had watched Hitler's expansionist actions and finally decided that with the invasion of Poland, they could no longer tolerate his aggression. In addition, the British Parliament felt strongly that the mutual defense agreement with Poland that Britain and France had signed required them to come to that country's defense. On September 3, 1939, Britain and France declared war on Germany.

For more than seven months, except for minor skirmishes along the Maginot Line and in some aerial scouting, there was little contact between the hostile forces, and this period became known as the sitzkreig or phony war. But Britain began soon to dispatch troops to France and by the end of 1939 had more than 250,000 soldiers on the continent. The delay of military action was a blessing for Britain, allowing her to import supplies and to mobilize industrially and militarily, both in the home islands and in Commonwealth countries.

Britain was seriously underprepared for war in 1939. The people had desperately wanted to avoid another war, remembering the hundreds of thousands of its young men slaughtered in World War I, and refused to spend funds to build a substantial defense force. Due primarily to the efforts of Winston Churchill—even though he was politically out of favor throughout the thirties—some military preparedness did exist before the outbreak of war, but it was far from adequate. Thus, Britain was in no hurry to engage Germany in combat.

In the seven months following the declaration of war, Hitler set several dates for invading France, but each time the plan was canceled, twice due to weather. In the opinion of his general staff, favorable weather was essential for success and Hitler acceded to their request for delaying the campaign. In late 1939 the German military leadership decided that in order for the campaign against Britain to succeed, it was essential to establish German naval and air bases in Norway and Denmark first. Action was precipitated when the Germans learned of a British plan to stop shipments of Swedish iron ore across Norway, cutting off the source of 50 percent of Germany's iron ore supply for its war machine.

On April 9, 1940, the German army, navy and air force invaded Denmark and Norway. Denmark, recognizing the futility of resistance, surrendered in a matter of hours. The Norwegian armed forces fought a delaying action, but in a matter of days, the Germans had occupied Oslo and other major cities, though the Norwegians carried on their struggle in small towns and rural areas. On April 13 the British dispatched a counterinvasion force to Norway to assist the defenders, and it battled the Germans until June 10, when the rout of the Allies in France prompted the British to pull out and Norway surrendered to the Germans.

On May 10, the German army and air force struck Holland, which it conquered in less than a week, and Belgium, which surrendered within three weeks. The German army circled the Maginot Line and crossed the French border on May 12. Although the Allied armies put up stiff resistance, they could not stop the blitzkrieg and the Germans reached Paris on June 14. The city, recognizing the hopelessness of resistance, surrendered without battle, and Germany became the occupier of Paris and much of France—all of it after November 1942—for more than four years. France surrendered on June 22. Meantime, Mussolini saw that Germany was winning and did not want to miss out on the spoils; Italy declared war on France and Britain on June 10.

As the German forces swept into France, the British Expeditionary Forces under General Lord Gort, plus elements of the French, Belgian and Dutch armies, retreated to Dunkirk on the French coast. Hitler's field generals informed him that the annihilation of this force would not be difficult, but Hermann Goering, chief of the Luftwaffe, urged Hitler to allow his divebombers to wipe out the pocket at Dunkirk. He claimed that they could do the job effectively, that his planes would prevent the loss of German lives that would result from ground action and, moreover, that the Luftwaffe was the most loyal of all of the services to the Führer and deserved the honor. Hitler agreed and halted the planned attack by tanks, but three days later changed his mind and allowed them to proceed. A combination of factors—canals and marshes that impeded the progress of the tanks, a fierce defense by the Allies, inclement weather, and others—impeded the advance of the German tanks on Dunkirk. Although German planes did, in fact, inflict severe damage on the refugees and on ships trying to remove them, sinking 226 of the 693 British ships and boats and 17 of the 168 French, Dutch and Belgian craft engaged in the evacuation, the performance of the Luftwaffe was far less successful than predicted by both the Germans and the British, thanks in large measure to British fighter pilots who worked in rotation to protect the troops.

When the evacuation got under way, the British navy put out a call for every boat owner in Britain to go to Dunkirk to evacuate troops. Using naval vessels and civilian craft—yachts, fishing boats, fire-fighting boats, excursion steamers, ferry boats, pleasure boats and seemingly anything else that would float—Norman Gelb reports that they were able to evacuate 364,628, of whom 224,686 were British, although 40,000 troops were killed or captured and virtually all of the equipment had to be abandoned. At the beginning of the evacuation, the British navy predicted that it might be able to rescue 30,000, assuming that the Germans would overwhelm the fleeing troops within two or three days, but the defenders held off the attackers for 10 days, accomplishing a superhuman feat.

Between the wars, France's army was reputed to be the most powerful in the world. On the evening of May 9, 1940, the day before Germany invaded the low countries, at a dinner for President J. B. Conant at Harvard University, the group of notables present all agreed that France had the superior army and would stop Hitler if he invaded. How could a group of individuals so well informed about France and the situation in western Europe have been so wrong? Why did France succumb so quickly to Hitler's invasion forces? There were several reasons. Although France's army numbered 110 divisions, 25 divisions were scattered—in Syria, in her colonies in Africa and Southeast Asia and various islands, and on the Italian and Spanish borders. This left a major force for defense against Germany, but the available arms were largely leftovers from World War I and were not nearly as effective as those of Germany which had been manufactured in the 1930s using the latest designs and technology. Another reason was its Maginot Line, a system of gun fortifications ranging from 25 to 100 miles in depth and stretching from the Swiss border to Belgium, that France had depended on to stop any German invasion. The Germans skirted the Maginot Line, and while this was not entirely unexpected, their strategy was a surprise. The French and British had assumed that the main force, when it came, would be through Holland and Belgium, that the lack of roads and the terrain would prevent an attack through the Ardennes Forest. The German high command predicted this assumption and sent a major force, led by seven tank divisions, through the Ardennes. When it reached the French border, the invasion force faced only two weak divisions at the main crossing, composed largely of reservists and commanded by generals who had never seen combat.

The French lacked communication equipment, and almost every defense effort turned into a debacle. A highly significant factor was the instability of the government and the military. The performance of French army was so poor that during the invasion the head of the government resigned and the chief of the army and 24 other general officers were dismissed; with that and related shuffling of civilian and military leadership, the army lacked direction. Finally, Germany employed a kind of warfare never before seen. It had invented the blitzkrieg, which used large numbers of tanks to move rapidly through the opposition, supported by divebombers. The attack on Poland gave the German army and air force the opportunity to test and refine the strategy, so when the blitzkrieg was employed in Western Europe, it functioned with few errors.

American Response to the War

The specter of war had grown throughout the last years of the 1930s and concerned all Americans. In addition to the invasions of Poland, Denmark, Norway, the low countries, and France, two actions by the American government during 1939-40 further focused Americans' attention on the threat of war. On September 8, 1939, President Franklin D. Roosevelt declared a limited national emergency, the full implications of which were never fully explained. Primarily, it served to alert the nation to the forthcoming danger and to galvanize the country into concerted action toward defense preparation. The second development was the enactment in August 1940 of the Selective Service Act requiring men ages 21 to 36 to register for the draft. Although some motion toward strengthening the army and navy had begun earlier, these two actions date the beginning of America's mobilization for war.

In 1940, the country was overwhelmingly opposed to entering the war in Europe, as evidenced by poll after poll before and after war began in Europe. The popular sentiment has been called isolationist by some, non-interventionist by others. Many saw the war as a manifestation of the endemic inability of European countries to get along with one another, proof that periodically they would inevitably be at war and that the United States should not get involved. Some still believed that the United States had been maneuvered into participating in World War I, and that the same scenario should not be allowed to happen again. For years much of the press had argued that munitions makers were to blame for America's entrance into World War I, and indeed a congressional committee chaired by isolationist Senator Gerald P. Nye of North Dakota held extensive hearings in 1934 trying to prove that the munitions industry had caused the war. A few charged that Britain was more interested in keeping its empire than in saving European democracies. And there was some residue of resentment among the American people because Britain had not repaid the U.S. money it borrowed during World War I; however, there was more sympathy after the Battle of Britain began in August 1940.

A poll on February 14, 1937, asked whether the United States should get involved if war broke out in Europe; 95 percent said no. On April 6, 1939, a poll asked whether the United States should declare war if England and France went to war with Germany, and 95 percent still said no. The day before Germany invaded Poland, a poll asked a different question: "If England and France should go to war with Germany, do you think the U.S. will be drawn into it?" Sixty percent said yes. Even as late as September 17, 1941, however, one poll showed that 87 percent did not think the United States should declare war on Germany.

Responses in polls asking whether the United States should enter the war remained highly negative, but from 1939 onward polls showed that increasing percentages believed the United States would be drawn into the war in Europe; on October 22, 1941, for example, 85 percent thought so. Nonetheless, the antiwar sentiment was so strong that in Washington military officers continued to wear civilian clothes to their offices and when traveling to avoid rude treatment.

The American Institute of Public Opinion (Gallup Poll) asked, over a period of time, whether it was more important that the United States stay out of war, or that Germany be defeated. In May 1940, just after Germany invaded the low countries and France, 64 percent said that it was more important that the United States stay out of war, and 36 percent that it was more important that Germany be defeated. In September, during the Battle of Britain, opinion was almost equally divided, but by the end of 1940, 60 percent said it was more important for Germany to be defeated. In early 1941, 68 percent took that position, with only 32 percent saying it was more important for the United States to stay out of the war.

The Anti-Interventionists

Dozens of groups emerged both before and after the invasion of Poland to lobby for keeping America out of the war, among them the German-American Bund, the Silver Shirts, the Christian Front, America First, the No Foreign Wars Committee, plus several pacifist organizations such as the National Council for Prevention of War, the Keep America Out of the War Congress, the Fellowship of Reconciliation, and the Ministers No War Committee, headed by the Rev. Harry Emerson Fosdick, one of the most respected ministers of the day. The American Communist Party, through its American Peace Mobilization Committee, campaigned against participation in the war, charging the U.S. government with warmongering and imperialism, until Germany attacked Russia in June 1941, at which point it reversed its position to become a strong advocate of U.S. declaration of war on Germany. One or more of the antiwar groups was to be found picketing the White House almost daily from September 1, 1939, until the United States entered the war.

The German-American Bund was the most public of the isolationist groups before the war. It was organized in the mid–1930s, consisting largely of first and second generation German-Americans with strong loyalties to their country of birth or heritage. In public ceremonies they wore brown shirts and ties similar to those worn by Nazi Storm Troopers in Germany, marched in military formation and held public rallies in support of the Nazi Party in Germany. In 1939 a rally in Madison Square

Garden attracted 25,000, although some were probably curious onlookers like journalist Dorothy Thompson, who was thrown out for laughing at their performance. Located mostly in New York City and Chicago, they were anti-Semitic and in other ways aped the stance of the Nazis in Germany. After Pearl Harbor and the U.S. declaration of war the group went underground.

The Silver Shirts, named for their costume and headed by William Dudley Pelly, were militantly anti-Semitic. Pelly preached fascist theology, distributed religious tracts that he composed, campaigned against American entrance into the war, and charged that democracy was a Jewish plot. The Christian Front, whose leader was Father Charles E. Coughlin, was also stridently anti-Semitic. Father Coughlin spoke to a national audience through his weekly radio broadcasts from Royal Oak, Michigan, and his newspaper *Social Justice,* which had a circulation of almost 200,000 at its peak. Coughlin was one of the few who remained vocal after Pearl Harbor, charging the United States was tricked into the war by Jews and Communists, until he was silenced by his church superiors. Generally these and similar organizations were venomous but not overtly traitorous, but in January 1940, 17 young men who were members of the Christian Front were arrested, tried and sent to prison for conspiring to overthrow the government.

The Rev. Gerald L. K. Smith, another radio evangelist, who had been active in the early 1930s in the campaigns of the late Senator Huey Long, formed the Committee of One Million and preached that President Roosevelt wanted to enter the war to promote Marxism in the United States.

Although some of the anti-interventionist organizations were easily dismissed as consisting of misguided extremists, one of them was composed of leading businessmen and intellectuals. The Committee to Defend America First, commonly known as the America First Committee, was established in September 1940 by R. Douglas Stuart, Jr., who served as its executive director. The America First Committee grew out of a similar organization started at Yale University. After the invasion of Poland, a group of students at Yale formed an organization known as College Men for Defense First, which soon had chapters on 59 campuses. The leaders were two Yale law students, Stuart and Kingman Brewster, who became president of Yale in the 1960s. At the end of that term, Stuart left law school to organize America First, and he remained the driving force behind it until it was disbanded in December 1941. Stuart, the son of the first vice president of Quaker Oats Company, was able to recruit a number of leading personalities of the day to its board or other leadership roles: railroad magnate Robert Young; Jay Hormel, president of Hormel Packing Company; William H. Regnery, president of Western

Shade Cloth Company; Alice Roosevelt Longworth, the tart-tongued daughter of former president Theodore Roosevelt; actress Lillian Gish; novelist Kathleen Norris; Philip LaFollette, former governor of Wisconsin; World War I air ace Eddie Rickenbacker; and retired General Robert E. Wood, chairman of the board of Sears, Roebuck and Co., who became the head of the organization. By December 1940, America First had 450 chapters with approximately 800,000 members, although most of them were within 100 miles of Chicago where the organization's headquarters were located. The basic position of America First was that if the United States became involved in the European war, it would bring on collapse of the American free market system and lead to socialism. The group urged a negotiated peace instead.

America First was probably the most effective of the anti-interventionist organizations in its influence on the press, the public and the Congress. Its members included national leaders in business, education and other spheres of activity who were well known in Washington, where many of them had testified before committees of Congress on a wide range of other issues. For the most part, its spokesmen refrained from stridency, avoided some of the extreme positions taken by other antiwar groups and were anticommunist and antifascist. The organization claimed to deny membership to known anti–Semites and returned donations from persons known to be anti–Semitic. Its membership included both liberals and conservatives, although the latter clearly were in the majority.

Despite efforts to appear rational and non-extremist, America First was a lightning rod for attacks by interventionists, who often referred to them as fascists. The positions the group took were opposite to those of the Roosevelt administration and caused the president and his staff a great deal of trouble in their efforts to persuade Congress to support his foreign policy. America First was particularly effective in the Senate where its representatives testified often on matters concerning defense preparation and aid to the Allies, largely because the Senate was more isolationist than the rest of the country at that time.

One of the leading spokesmen for America First was Charles A. Lindbergh, the first person to fly across the Atlantic alone, who was still a national hero and was avidly sought as a speaker. He had begun speaking against the war in September 1939, and when America First was formed he became one of its members and spokesmen. In a speech in Des Moines he argued that the "three most important groups who have been pressing this country toward war are the British, the Jewish, and the Roosevelt administration. Behind these groups, but of lesser importance, are a number of capitalists, Anglophiles, and intellectuals who believe that their future and the future of mankind depends upon the domination of the British Empire. . . ." Lindbergh went on to explain that he could understand why Jewish people, whose families had suffered so much from persecution in Germany, felt strongly about supporting Britain in the war. Nonetheless, the press labeled him anti–Semitic, and even though some leading Jewish spokesmen said they did not consider his remarks anti–Semitic, he lost favor with much of the press, and leaders of America First distanced themselves from him thereafter. When President Roosevelt criticized him for his remarks, Lindbergh resigned his commission as a reserve colonel in the Army Air Corps, which had been awarded to him in 1927 following his solo flight across the Atlantic.

The American Legion vociferously and effectively opposed America First, charging that the organization and its members were simply unrealistic concerning the threat of fascism and the expansionist ambitions of Hitler. By the fall of 1941, with the threat of war becoming increasingly likely, America First had begun to lose its influence. After the attack on Pearl Harbor, America First dissolved and its leadership urged all Americans to support the government in the war. Several members of America First became prominent in the prosecution of the war.

Many Americans regarded the Atlantic Ocean as America's bulwark against Hitler and held that the United States could be prepared to repel any invader. Others doubted whether, if Hitler got control of the British navy, in addition to the ships already under his control in captured countries, the United States could in fact repel an assault by his combined forces. The vulnerability of America's coasts became more apparent after December 7, 1941, when artillery and infantry were strung from Canada to Mexico with the intent to halt a Japanese invasion of the West Coast. There were dozens of points where army presence was so sparse that it could offer little resistance to an invading force. The situation on the East Coast was also serious. As late as February 1942, only 17 fighter planes were based close enough to protect New York City from an invasion, and 11 of them were obsolete.

Anti-intervention sentiment was strong in both houses of Congress, although the Senate got more publicity because of its opposition to rearmament and defense preparation. Among isolationists in Congress there was a strong sense that the movie industry was working to engineer a U.S. declaration of war on Germany. In October 1941, the Senate approved a resolution establishing a subcommittee to investigate "any propaganda disseminated by motion pictures . . . to influence public sentiment in the direction of participation of the United States in the . . . European war." Senator Gerald P. Nye of North Dakota charged that "At least 20 pictures have been produced in the last year all designed to drug the reason of the American people, set aflame their emotions, turn their hatred into a blaze, fill them with fear that Hitler will come over here and capture them...." He added that the movies had become gigantic engines of propaganda with the intended purpose of goading America into entering the European war. He and other members of the committee charged that it was due to Jewish influence in the movie industry. It was true that the owners of most of the major studios were Jewish, including some who had fled Europe ahead of Hitler's forces. Joseph Kennedy, ambassador to Britain and father of the future president, warned the movie studios to stop making pro-war movies, claiming that anti-Semitism was growing in Britain and the Jews were being blamed for the war. No one in the movie industry belonged to America First, a fact used as evidence of pro-interventionist sentiment in Hollywood.

Senators Nye and Bennett Champ Clark, authors of the resolution, began holding hearings in Hollywood to intimidate movie makers against pro-war themes. The committee discovered many movies that were clearly anti-Nazi, but it was difficult to prove that they promoted American entry into the war. The attorney for the studios was Wendell L. Willkie, the Republican candidate for president in the previous year's election, who delivered a spirited defense of the movie industry and its patriotism, then charged that the committee was guilty of anti-Semitism. The accusation so embarrassed the Senate that the committee suspended its hearings. Following the attack on Pearl Harbor a few weeks later, the committee was disbanded.

A sizeable portion of the creative talent in the motion picture industry—writers, directors, producers, musicians—were Jewish refugees from Hitler. The list of such people who migrated from occupied countries to Hollywood during the late 1930s and early 1940s, some of whom were not Jewish but simply incurred Hitler's wrath for their criticism of him and his programs, includes the filmmakers behind a great many of the movies made in that period. The list of emigrés to Hollywood in the 1930s also included a substantial number of non-Jewish Britons, a very influential group whose names were or became legend in the movie industry and who had a considerable impact on the films made during the period.

Some commentators claimed that movies before and after the Pearl Harbor attack were highly patriotic because of Jewish influence; others said that after Germany invaded Russia it was due to the fact that many writers and directors were Communists or Communist sympathizers. Whatever the reason, all agreed that the American movie industry became a major force in building morale and patriotic fervor throughout the war.

The Interventionists

Despite opposition to American involvement, several prominent leaders spoke out early for preparedness and later for intervention in the

European war. On June 10, 1940, in a statement entitled "Summons to Speak Out," 30 prominent Americans called for a declaration of war against Germany. It was widely reported in newspapers but gained little support and received little follow-up attention in the press. More attention was paid to a more moderate group that had been founded a few weeks earlier.

The Committee to Defend America by Aiding the Allies was founded in May 1940 with William Allen White, the renowned editor of the *Emporia Gazette* newspaper, as chairman. The CDA did not support military intervention but strongly supported a policy of providing aid and assistance to Britain short of military intervention. The committee, in effect, spoke for President Roosevelt's policies regarding the war throughout the summer and fall of 1940, and it had little opposition until the American First Committee was founded in early September. The White Committee, as the CDA was sometimes called, had on its board a long list of distinguished personages: Herbert Lehman, governor of New York; Nicholas Murray Butler, president of Columbia University; Mrs. Dwight W. Morrow, mother-in-law of Charles Lindbergh; and Henry Stimson and Frank Knox, both Republicans and soon to be named secretary of war and secretary of the navy. About 750 chapters with some 10,000 members were founded nationwide, though mostly in the New York area. The committee's success was due in part to the credibility of White, who had earlier been pacifist himself, but in January 1941 White resigned as chairman because of pressure from an allied organization—the Century Group—for the American government to become more interventionist, even though such a course was virtually certain to lead to war with Germany.

The Century Group took the position that it was essential for the United States to come to the defense of Britain if democracy was to be saved, that it was better to stop Hitler there than to have to fight him later on American soil. The group began with a meeting of a dozen leading business and professional men in New York City in July 1940. Later, 16 others joined them for the regular weekly dinner meetings at the Century Club, from which the group drew its name. The Century Group was distinctive in that it epitomized the Eastern Establishment, although a few of the group did not live in the greater New York area, in contrast to several other pro-interventionist organizations with a readily identifiable interest in American intervention in the European war. All but three or four were Protestants and most had served in World War I; the group included both Democrats and Republicans. Among the best known were: Dr. Henry P. Van Dusen, professor at Union Theological Seminary; Lewis W. Douglas, president of the Mutual Life Insurance and former congressman and director of the Bureau of the Budget; Joseph

Alsop, newspaper columnist; Elmer Davis, radio newscaster; Dean G. Acheson, lawyer and future secretary of state; Allen Dulles, lawyer and future head of the CIA; and James B. Conant, president of Harvard University, among several other equally prominent personalities.

The Century Group worked diligently throughout the last half of 1940 and early 1941 to counter the anti-interventionist sentiment in the country, particularly in the U.S. Senate. It played a major role in persuading FDR to send destroyers to Britain in September 1940 and in bringing about congressional approval of the Lend-Lease law the following spring. The fact that several members of the group were in the newspaper and radio business helped in communicating, and the prominence of all members of the group meant that they could reach almost any prominent figure on the telephone. The group issued a steady stream of press releases to newspapers all over the country, and its members made hundreds of speeches and radio addresses, initially urging the shipment of food to Britain, the use of American ships to protect Britain, and all out aid short of war. But as the autumn progressed the group became increasingly belligerent, and although it did not yet call for formal declaration of war, it advocated actions that would virtually guarantee that Germany would attack the United States.

In January 1941, the Century Group decided that its small number could not have the effect nationally that it wanted, so it established a national organization called Fight for Freedom which, by April, was well organized with almost 300 chapters across the country. Many local and regional groups merged into FFF, and others allied themselves with the organization. Interestingly, by June 1941, several chapters and individual members of the Committee to Defend America by Aiding the Allies joined the FFF, having decided that a more interventionist stance was required. Although there was little doubt that Fight for Freedom advocated declaration of war, it did not say so overtly (although it did not prevent its members doing so in speeches) until October 1941 when the organization passed a resolution at its national meeting urging declaration of war on Germany. Yet the aggressive campaign by FFF to persuade Americans that it was necessary to declare war on Germany was not very effective; national polls showed that the largest percentage who agreed never exceeded 21 percent.

The interventionist groups represented a cross section of America, not only Jews and ethnic groups from occupied countries but businessmen, lawyers, theologians, persons from communications and entertainment industries, and intellectuals inside and outside universities. They worried about the survival of democracy. If Hitler prevailed in all of Europe, when would he move to invade America? How? Would he strike an alliance with a South American country and establish a base there from which he could maneuver to invade the United States? Was democracy as Americans knew it in real danger? Most refugee intellectuals, many of whom had settled into some of the most prestigious universities, were militantly interventionist.

Many organizations, groups and individuals who were isolationist in 1940 were decidedly in favor of supporting the Allies by 1941, at least with supplies and equipment if not by declaring war. The National Association of Manufacturers was clearly isolationist in 1940; by mid–1941, it had changed its position almost completely. By late 1941, a poll of Episcopal clergymen showed that half of them supported declaring war on Germany, and a national poll on December 1, 1941, found that people believed the odds of the United States entering the war against Germany were ten to one.

Viewed several decades later, the alliances supporting intervention seem strange. Whereas in World War I it was the left that opposed the war, by early 1941 liberals and others of the left were leading the drumbeat for going to war against Germany. Liberal journals of opinion were among the leaders for intervention and refused to accept the work of some of their longtime authors, such as Edmund Wilson, who were less inclined toward American entrance into the war. And in Congress, liberals tended to be interventionist and conservatives were more likely to be isolationist.

The antiwar sentiment should not be misinterpreted; there was an abundance of sympathy for Britain. Dozens of voluntary assistance campaigns were conducted, sending money and supplies to Britain in late 1940 and in 1941. Several organizations were formed to help the British. The British War Relief Society, with offices in New York City, collected money and household goods, and when invasion of England seemed likely, the American Committee for the Defense of British Homes ran advertisements in newspapers asking Americans to contribute pistols, rifles, shotguns, revolvers, and binoculars to be sent to the British so they could protect their homes. The "Bundles for Britain" campaign was not just a slogan; a thousand chapters were founded, with 500,000 members, in communities all over the country. They held fund drives, bingo games, raffles, dances, sales, and concerts to raise funds for aid. There was a steady stream of X-ray machines and other equipment going to Britain, and patriotic women's groups knitted sweaters, scarfs, socks and other woolens to be sent to Britain.

Foreign Policy and Defense Preparation

On the day Germany invaded Poland, Winston Churchill was 64 years of age and had long been out of favor with the Conservative Party in Britain because of his desertion for 20 years to the Liberal Party. He was a thorn in the side of the Chamberlain government. Through his seat in the House of Commons he was constantly challenging Chamberlain and the Party for its failure to prepare for war against Germany. With Germany's invasion of Poland, Churchill's clamor for preparedness got attention and earned growing public support, leading Chamberlain to name him First Sea Lord (head of the navy) which brought him into the cabinet. This gave him an official role in government decisions, but also required that he soften his criticism of Britain's lack of military preparedness. When Germany invaded the low countries on May 10, 1940, the House of Commons demanded that Chamberlain resign. He did, and Churchill was elected prime minister. He formed a coalition government with the Labor Party which lasted throughout the war.

Roosevelt and Churchill did not know one another when the latter assumed the leadership of his government, but they soon began corresponding regularly. Shortly after becoming prime minister, Churchill began to write to Roosevelt, always signing as "A Former Naval Person," an attempt to be ingratiating with Roosevelt who had been assistant secretary of the navy in World War I and was known still to be a strong supporter of the navy. This correspondence, consisting of hundreds of informal communications between the two, continued throughout the war. They first met off the coast of Newfoundland in August 1941, both having traveled secretly by ship. Out of this meeting grew the Atlantic Charter, a document that was essentially a philosophical statement opposing war as a means of accomplishing national goals, upholding the right of self-determination for all peoples and advocating, after the defeat of Nazism, the establishment of world peace. It became the philosophical foundation for the United Nations.

Earlier, in his State of the Union speech to Congress on January 6, 1941, Roosevelt had proclaimed the goal of "four freedoms" for all mankind—freedom of speech and expression, freedom to worship in one's own way, freedom from want, and freedom from fear such that no nation might wage aggression against another country. These four freedoms received widespread publicity and acclaim as an expression of the hopes of the American people in a time of growing world turmoil, and they provided the basic ideas on which the Atlantic Charter and the United Nations were based.

Roosevelt had seen the likelihood and then the inevitability of American involvement in war. As Hitler occupied Austria and then consumed Czechoslovakia, Roosevelt sensed that it was only a matter of time before America would be faced with another European war. When Hitler invaded Poland and France and Britain declared war, the picture became clearer. This led the president to declare a limited national emergency just a week after the invasion of Poland, and to begin a program to strengthen U.S. defense capabilities, a difficult task in view of the country's still lingering isolationist sentiment. Roosevelt knew that the country was ill prepared for defense and that its ability to fight a war had to be improved, but attempts to make the country aware of the problem were met with charges of "warmonger."

America's deep aversion to war had led to the passage of the Neutrality Act of 1935, which made it "unlawful to export arms, ammunition, or implements of war from the United States for the use of countries at war" and forbade U.S. merchant ships to transport other goods to belligerents on the basis that if American vessels were not in hostile areas, the likelihood of the United States' becoming involved in war was diminished. It also forbade Americans to travel on ships of belligerent countries. The act was broadened in 1936 and in 1937 with additional clauses, including a requirement that sales of nonmilitary items to belligerents must be on a cash basis and could not be transported in U.S. merchant ships, and merchant ships could not be armed.

In his State of the Union message in January 1938, Roosevelt had warned of the potential threat to peace in the world, and shortly thereafter recommended to Congress small increases in funding for armaments for the army and navy; the naval appropriations bill, for example, added 20 percent to the navy's strength, large compared to recent history but inadequate in terms of need. The bill generated a long debate and opposition by isolationist members of Congress but was finally approved by 294 to 100 in the House and 56 to 28 in the Senate.

A year later, in his address to Congress, Roosevelt again urged additional appropriations for defense, asking for $525 million as a minimum and reminding Congress that Hitler had violated the Munich Pact, taken over the Sudetenland and assumed control over Austria. In May 1939, the administration attempted to persuade Congress to repeal the arms embargo, but the vote against it in the House was 214 to 173, with the defenders of the embargo arguing that it would help keep the United States out of war.

On September 21, 1939, almost two weeks after declaring a limited national emergency, President Roosevelt called Congress into special session. In those days, it was not unusual for Congress to have completed its work for the year before Labor Day. Again, Roosevelt called for repeal of the arms embargo that prevented the sale of weapons to Britain, France, Poland, India, Australia, and New Zealand. Congress debated the request at length, with strong opposition from non-interventionists who argued that such a move would in effect make the United States a belligerent and invite attack on the U.S. ships.

The fall term had just begun and loud protests against removing or easing the Neutrality Act were heard from college campuses. The Communist Party joined in the protest, having become strongly opposed to intervention following the Soviet-German Non-Aggression Pact of August 22. The repeal of the embargo on sale of arms and ammunition to belligerent countries was approved by Congress and signed by the president on November 4, but Congress inserted several restrictions. Purchases had to be paid for in cash, for example, and could not be transported in American ships, a provision which became known as "cash and carry." The restrictions on arming American merchant ships, travel by Americans on vessels of nations at war, and movement of American ships into combat areas were retained. Congress was reflecting the mood of the country: Stay out of foreign wars! Other legislation forbade credits to any nation in default on its debts from World War I (one such nation was Great Britain). Of all the European countries that had borrowed money or made purchases on credit from the United States during World War I, only Finland had paid its debts.

Congress continued in general to oppose the president's efforts to build up the country's military defenses, but there were exceptions. Shortly after Hitler attacked the low countries and France, Congress responded with applause to Roosevelt's request, in a speech before a joint session, for appropriations to build 50,000 warplanes.

Opposition to the president's foreign policy ideas and to defense buildup were exacerbated by opposition to his domestic program, the New Deal. Not only did Republicans oppose it, but many conservative Democrats were convinced it was a waste of money and a corruption of the role of government.

During the so-called "phony war" period, Britain was frantically struggling to prepare for battle and urging the United States to come to its aid. President Roosevelt realized that Britain did not have the resources to deal with Hitler, and although there was little obvious urgency to aid Britain during this period, the need became more apparent after Germany defeated France in June 1940. Britain had been purchasing war supplies from the United States, but since the Neutrality Act forbade the extension of credit to Britain it had been paying for such purchases with dollar credits which were fast running out.

After the debacle in France in June 1940, Churchill stepped up his requests for U.S. aid, among them a request for 50 overaged destroyers, primarily for use in escort duty. He had first requested "40 or 50 destroyers" five days after Germany invaded the low countries, which was also five days after he assumed leadership of his government. At Dunkirk, 10 of Britain's destroyers had been sunk and 75 were so badly damaged that they had to be sent to dockyards for repairs, thereby giving further urgency to need for the ships.

The United States had an ample reserve of overaged destroyers in its mothballed fleet and could easily spare the number requested. Roosevelt was favorably disposed toward transferring 50 destroyers to Britain but delayed, recognizing that in the antiwar climate that prevailed during the summer of 1940, Congress would not approve such action. In addition to opposition from isolationists, a 1917 law forbade the sale of armed vessels to belligerents and a rider on the navy appropriations bill in June 1940 blocked the sale of surplus vessels. The British request gained widespread publicity and debate in the press, with many prominent leaders issuing public statements either supporting or opposing the transfer. After lengthy delay and discussion, Roosevelt struck upon the idea of exchanging the destroyers for the right to use British naval and air bases since, according to his attorney general, this could be done by executive order and would not require congressional approval. Republican supporters of sending the vessels to Britain persuaded Wendell L. Willkie not to make the destroyer exchange an issue in the presidential campaign then under way, and the exchange was consummated on September 3. The bases were in the Bahamas, St. Lucia, Trinidad, Jamaica, Antigua, and British Guiana. Also included were Bermuda and Newfoundland, but Churchill insisted that the lease of these two be outright gifts in gratitude for American aid, not part of the exchange.

In late December 1941, Churchill made his first visit to Washington to see President Roosevelt, and during the time he stayed at the White House and talked with the president and members of his staff, the two not only got better acquainted but came to an understanding concerning many of the questions that were so essential to their working relationship. At the lighting of the Christmas tree on the White House lawn on Christmas Eve, Churchill pulled the switch to light it and afterwards spoke briefly, to the American people via radio. His short talk marked the beginning of a love affair between Churchill and the Americans that lasted throughout the war.

Lend-Lease

President Roosevelt was occupied during the autumn of 1940 with his re-election campaign, which was especially controversial because it broke the precedent that no president ran for a third term. With the campaign over, Roosevelt could again concentrate his attention on defense. On December 29, 1940, the president delivered one of his many fireside chats on radio, which became known as the Arsenal of Democracy speech. He said that Hitler could not be appeased but that the United States faced less chance of getting into the war if it launched a program to supply Britain with what it needed to do the job: "we must be the great arsenal of democracy," he said. In his State of the Union message to Congress on January 6, 1941, Roosevelt urged that his lend-lease bill be enacted. The president explained to the American people the principle underlying lend-lease: "If I've got a hose which my neighbor needs, I simply connect it up to his hydrant and when the fire is out my neighbor returns my hose or buys me another if it has been damaged." Few expected lend-lease supplies and equipment to be returned or replaced, but the idea of lending them to Britain, and later the Soviet Union, was more politically palatable than proposing to make outright donations of them. When Great Britain declared war on Germany, it had about $4.5 billion in gold and investments in America that could be converted to cash to buy war materials and food. By January 1941, Britain had exhausted not only its government's cash and credits in the United States, but also those of British citizens. If Britain was to continue to receive war materials and other supplies from the United States, some other mechanism had to be found to pay for them.

This was the beginning of Roosevelt's campaign to sell lend-lease to Congress. From this point until the Lend-Lease Act (HR 1776) was passed in the House on March 8 and the Senate on March 11, it was a subject of broad public debate, with many arguing that lend-lease amounted to a declaration of war on Germany. At hearings of the House and Senate Committees, Gerald L. K. Smith of the Committee of One Million testified that lend-lease amounted to the first step in sending one to five million boys across the ocean to die on battlefields, and William J. Grace, chairman of the Citizens to Keep America Out of the War Committee, testified urging that the United States not take sides in the war lest it be drawn into the fight.

The two main organizations testifying before congressional committees were America First on one side and the Committee to Defend America by Aiding the Allies on the other. America First also mounted an aggressive publicity campaign against lend-lease through radio and newspapers. Senator Burton K. Wheeler said lend-lease was the war version of the New Deal AAA policy, forecasting that "it would plow under every fourth American boy" (referring to the administration's first farm program in 1933 in which farmers were paid to plow under a portion of their crops in order to control surplus production and raise farm prices).

As finally approved, the bill did not limit lend-lease to Britain but left to the president the decision as to which countries would qualify. Some members of Congress were willing to vote for lend-lease if it were for Britain only; they did not want to permit it to be used to support the USSR, which they expected to be at war with Germany eventually. But the president had just been re-elected the previous fall by a healthy margin in the popular vote and a landslide in the electoral college, and he knew that members of Congress could not ignore the large number of pro-Roosevelt votes, or the fact that public support for the bill was two to one. He figured he had the votes to get a bill passed in a form that would permit him to use it as needed, and that proved to be true. The final vote in Congress was not close; the bill, as amended, passed the Senate by a vote 60 to 31 and the House by 317 to 71.

The Lend-Lease Program was extended to the Soviet Union in early November 1941, and convoys of ships carrying the products of American factories and farms were soon sailing to Russia, most of them around the northern route to Murmansk. The Soviet Union, because of its alliance with Germany, had been the ally of an enemy for almost two years; now it was an ally of America and Britain. Churchill had no illusions about Stalin and the intent of the Soviet Union, but he took the position that any enemy of Hitler was Britain's ally. Roosevelt took essentially the same position; in addition, according to historians William Langer and Everett Gleason, President Roosevelt had never seen the Soviet Union as a threat to the United States. In their book *The Undeclared War, 1940–1941,* they wrote that "he had more sympathy than most Americans for the Bolshevik experiment, that he regarded the Communist threat as less grave and certainly less immediate than the Nazi menace, and that he fancied that over the years the Soviet and American systems would approximate each other."

With both Britain and Russia to be supplied with arms, equipment, food and other supplies, the United States faced a large task. The Lend-Lease Act gave the president broad powers under which he could send supplies and equipment, defense information and plans to any government, and the only condition was that the terms were "satisfactory" to the president. In the first year alone, Russia received 3,052 planes, 4,084 tanks, 30,031 vehicles of various types, and 831,000 tons of supplies. By the end of the war the United States had shipped 37,000 tanks, 792,000 trucks, 43,000 aircraft and 1.8 million rifles to the Soviet Union, and vast amounts of war materials including magnesium, vanadium, and molybdenum, three gasoline manufacturing plants, a tire manufacturing plant, thousands of tons of steel tubing, and much more. As Francis Walton points out, the Soviet wants were insatiable: on October 1, 1941, for example, Stalin requested 70 different items, including shipments of 400,000 pairs of boots per month. During the two-year period June 30, 1943, to June 30, 1945, the United States shipped to Russia: 28,356 jeeps; 218,888 trucks; 4,177 tanks; 252 heavy artillery pieces, plus locomotives, rails, box cars, flat cars, and aircraft to equip the equivalent of two U.S. air forces. In same period, it shipped to Britain: 76,737 jeeps; 98,207 trucks; 12,431 tanks; 1,031 artillery pieces; and thousands of tons of raw materials to feed

British factories. From 1942 to 1945, most of the equipment and supplies used by the French army, which consisted of 12 divisions, and the French air force was supplied by the United States.

Not only did the United States not receive any payment, then or later, but neither did it receive any expression of gratitude from the Soviet Union. Indeed, the Soviet leadership frequently complained that the United States was not sending enough aid. After Germany declared war on the United States, Stalin took the position that Roosevelt should be glad to supply the Soviet Union with war materials since it was engaged in combat with the Germans, thereby allowing the United States time to prepare for war.

By the end of the war, the United States had provided some $50 billion in aid to foreign countries, of which more than $11 billion went to the Soviet Union and more than $31 billion to Great Britain and its colonies and commonwealth countries. China received $1.5 billion, and the next largest total was to Brazil—$332 million. When compared half a century later to a budget of $1.5 trillion and a gross national product of $6 trillion, the figure of $50 billion does not sound like a large sum, but in view of the fact that the U.S. budget for 1940 was only $9.5 billion and the gross national product about $100 billion, it was clearly a huge outlay. By 1945, 38 countries had received assistance under the Lend-Lease Act, including 19 in the Western Hemisphere, but most of the aid went to Britain and the Soviet Union.

Lend-lease was not entirely a one-way arrangement. Some 436 million pounds of foodstuffs produced in Britain, its colonies and Commonwealth countries helped to feed American troops in Europe. For American forces in the Pacific and Asia, Australia supplied 1,835 million pounds of foodstuffs, New Zealand supplied 800 million pounds, and India 524 million pounds. The United States obtained 259 million gallons of aviation fuel from British refineries in the Middle East. Belgium gave the United States twice as much aid as it received, and Britain built 133 air fields plus other military bases for the United States.

Germany's attack on the Soviet Union on June 22, 1941, took the pressure off Great Britain, which had been expecting and preparing for a German invasion. Most military historians agree that if Hitler had focused his entire might on Britain, he would have prevailed. Although the country had made major strides toward defense, Germany "would have overrun the country" if it had invaded Britain in 1941, according to Sir Michael Howard, Regius Professor of Modern History at Oxford. But Hitler saw Britain as virtually defeated. Further, if he invaded England the chances of the United States coming into the war were increased. Finally, Hitler and the Nazi Party held deep-seated antipathy toward communism and to Slavic peoples, and Hitler seriously underestimated the ability of the Soviet Union to resist.

The German attack on the Soviet Union changed the American situation in several ways. The American Communist Party and its adherents had been strongly anti-interventionist during the period of the Russian-German Pact; now they did a complete reversal and urged an attack on Germany. They also became devoted supporters of Roosevelt, against whom they had railed for two years. At the Fourth American Writers Conference held in New York City just a few days before Hitler attacked the Soviet Union, there were cheers for Russia and the communist ideal and hisses for Roosevelt and America.

Shoot on Sight

In the spring of 1941, tensions between the United States and Germany grew; German submarines were already harassing American ships. On March 30, because of threats to security, President Roosevelt ordered the seizure of all German and Italian merchant ships in American ports, some 66 ships in all, and gave the ships to Britain. On June 14 he froze all assets of Germany and countries controlled by Germany, and two days later he ordered all German consulates in the United States to close by July 10. On May 27 he declared an unlimited national emergency which was just short of putting the nation on a war footing.

On May 21, 1941, a German submarine sank the American merchant ship *Robin Moor* in the South Atlantic, possibly inadvertently. The survivors were adrift in life rafts so long, however, that when they reached land, the political impact of the sinking had dissipated. On September 4, a German submarine fired two torpedoes at the destroyer *U.S.S. Greer* that was escorting ships carrying troops and supplies to Iceland. The attack precipitated an outraged response by the president and the press. (In early July, American troops had replaced British troops occupying Iceland, and American ships were transporting supplies to Iceland for transshipment to Britain.)

On September 11, the *Sessa* and three other merchant vessels were sunk in the Western Atlantic. These actions led Roosevelt, in a radio address, to warn Germany and Italy that U.S. warships would attack Axis warships entering waters vital to U.S. security. He designated the 26th meridian running from the Azores northwards, then zigzagging to the east around Iceland, as the dividing line. Under this new "shoot on sight" policy, American warships no longer had to wait to be fired on first if they were confronted in waters to the west of this line by German submarines or ships that appeared to be hostile.

The policy provoked vigorous debate among non-interventionists throughout the country and in Congress, but such debate in Congress had been under way for a long time. Earlier, on March 31, 1941, Senator Charles W. Tobey of New Hampshire and Congressman Harry Sauthoff of Wisconsin had introduced a resolution into both houses of Congress to ban use of American ships to transport materials to belligerents and the use of navy ships to escort them. That measure had been defeated, inspiring the administration to hope, albeit unsuccessfully, for an interpretation of the bill's failure as a mandate for immediate naval escort.

The president did authorize American naval vessels to look for German submarines and other warships and, upon spotting any, to inform the British of their whereabouts, and continue to provide surveillance over the enemy ships. Anti-interventionists issued tirades of criticism of the administration, alleging that this policy would inevitably lead to American naval ships being fired on by German submarines. Stymied in his hope to provide naval escort to merchant ships of other countries, the president decided that American merchant ships could transport materials intended for Britain, and later Russia, to Iceland, where they were turned over to British and other ships. Roosevelt asserted that this practice did not violate the Neutrality Act.

By October 1941, American merchant ships were being threatened and attacked frequently. President Roosevelt asked Congress to revise the Neutrality Act to permit merchant ships to be armed, but anti-interventionist senators and others outside Congress argued that it would lead the nation into war. This was a continuation of the position that any action by the United States to prepare for war was tantamount to provoking war. While the amendment was being debated, two American destroyers were attacked by German submarines. On October 15, the destroyer *U.S.S. Kearny* was torpedoed about 350 miles southwest of Iceland and badly damaged, killing 11 of its crew. The American press was enraged, but the attack should not have been a surprise in view of the fact that the *Kearny* had been sent to aid a westbound British convoy which was under attack by German submarines. Amid the dropping of depth charges on the German submarines, it is little wonder that they were not selective in choosing targets. On October 30, the *U.S.S. Reuben James,* also a destroyer, was sunk with loss of 115 crewmen, including all officers.

There is little doubt that these two events influenced Congress to approve Roosevelt's proposed amendment to the Neutrality Act, on November 7 in the Senate and November 13 in the House. The sentiment in the country had also changed. A poll conducted the previous April found that only about 30 percent thought the Neutrality Act should be changed to permit American ships with American crews to carry war materials to Britain; by November, when the amendment was approved,

61 percent agreed and 81 percent supported the change. The vote to permit the entry of American cargo vessels into war zones and the arming of American merchant ships was 50 to 37 in the Senate and 212 to 194 in the House, close considering the changing mood of the country.

Following the shelling of the *Kearny,* General Robert E. Wood, chairman of American First, urged President Roosevelt to ask Congress for a vote on whether the United States should enter the war, arguing that the time had come for the representatives of the American people to decide one way or the other. With such a suggestion from the leading spokesman for isolationists, Roosevelt felt that the country was moving toward accepting the necessity of entering the war and that if the country were attacked, the people were ready to respond. It was fairly clear to most people that America was on a collision course with Germany, that sooner or later the two would be at war.

From the beginning of Britain's entrance into the war, British ships had transported war materials, as well as food and supplies for the civilian population, across the Atlantic regularly, losing a sizeable percentage to German submarine attacks. Shipments increased when lend-lease was approved, and after Germany declared war on the United States, American ships carried most of the cargo. Most of the sinkings never received publicity, due to voluntary censorship by the news media. In early 1942, after the United States entered the war, German submarines were sinking American merchant vessels faster than they could be built. In the two-month period beginning January 15, 1942, German submarines sank 132 American merchant ships in the Western Atlantic. Although the merchant ships were running without lights, they were silhouetted at night against the glow of lights from New York City, Miami and metropolitan areas in between, which had not yet been blacked out; this led to the sinking of many of the ships within a few miles of American coastlines. Most of the sinkings occurred at night, but the submarines became bold. Vacationers sunbathing one afternoon at Virginia Beach watched as two merchant ships were torpedoed and sunk by submarines.

As the autumn of 1941 approached, the United States was providing growing amounts of war materials, food, and other supplies to Great Britain and, later, the Soviet Union; this action brought increasingly hostile action by German submarines. It was becoming clear to some observers that the United States and Germany were moving inexorably toward open conflict.

Chapter II

Pearl Harbor

The years of wondering and worrying about whether the United States would be drawn into war ended on December 7, 1941, when Japanese bombers attacked Pearl Harbor on the island of Oahu in Hawaii, wreaking extensive damage to ships, planes, and gun installations and leaving 2,638 dead and 946 wounded. The devastation of the attack coupled with the complete surprise achieved by the Japanese shocked and enraged the American people.

The attack began at 7:50 A.M. Divebombers struck neatly parked army and navy planes on the ground and together with torpedo bombers hit the large ships, especially battleships, in the harbor. The first wave lasted almost half an hour. About 30 minutes after it ended, a second wave of 167 planes arrived and struck ships, planes, the navy yard, Ford Island in the middle of the harbor, and assorted targets. Thanks to Japanese intelligence information, the attackers had known where ships would be parked and were prepared for precision bombing. Finally, almost two hours after the attack began, the last planes, with their load of bombs emptied, roamed around strafing airplanes, hangars and other facilities.

When the attacks ended, four of the eight battleships in the harbor had been sunk or capsized and four others were damaged. A ninth, the target battleship *Utah,* was also sunk. The *Nevada,* badly damaged, managed to get under steam, but the harbor commander ordered it grounded lest it be sunk in the channel where it would block the entrance to the harbor. Several smaller ships were able to get out of the harbor, but the cruiser *St. Louis* was the only large ship to make it to sea. Three destroyers, three cruisers and four service ships were badly damaged and set afire, along with several smaller vessels. Luckily no aircraft carriers were damaged. One of the three in the Pacific command—the *Saratoga*—had earlier been dispatched to the West Coast for repairs, and the other two were away from Pearl Harbor that day; the *Enterprise,* however, was close enough to launch eighteen divebombers, four of which were shot down by nervous and confused American anti-aircraft artillery gunners.

The navy had 301 planes on Oahu, of which 202 were operative; when the raid was over only 52 navy planes were capable of flight, including none of those at the Naval Air installation at Kaneohe. The Army Air Corps had 231 aircraft parked at Hickam, Bellows and Wheeler airfields, most of which were destroyed along with hangars and other facilities. When the attack ended, only 79 planes were still flyable. The damage was exacerbated by the fact that the planes had been moved from scattered locations and placed wing to wing in rows in the open so guards could protect them against sabotage, which military commanders had concluded was the real threat. At the Ewa Marine Air Station all but two planes were destroyed. The Army Air Corps had managed to get 25 fighter planes in the air, but none of the Navy and Marine Corps planes parked on the ground got airborne.

The Japanese had shrewdly chosen early Sunday to attack. As they had learned through espionage, most American ships at sea returned to Pearl Harbor for weekends and most of the sailors and soldiers were away from their posts, leaving the ships vulnerable to surprise attack. The 8 battleships, 29 destroyers, 5 submarines, and 50 or so service vessels lay tied in pairs in Pearl Harbor, neatly arranged for the attackers. The Japanese also knew that if they attacked just at dawn, most military personnel would either be at home or, if aboard ships, still asleep from Saturday night partying. There were widespread rumors in the American press within days that many of the sailors and soldiers had been hung over from excessive drinking the night before, but there was no evidence for this and no reason to believe that their partying the night before had been anything more than usual.

How did the attack happen without warning and find the military so unprepared for it? There were so many signals that were fumbled or that fell prey to "Murphy's Law" that it was uncanny. For example, at 7:02 A.M., Army Signal Corps Privates Joseph L. Lockard and George A. Elliott, monitoring a long-range radar detector on Oahu, saw an unexplained blip on the screen. Lockard at first thought it might be an error since radar was still new and at that time still somewhat experimental, so he tested his equipment; again the blip appeared. They estimated it to be about 130 miles due north, and after tracking it for several minutes, Elliott called Hickam Field to report it, but Lt. Kermit Tyler, the Air Corps officer on duty, told him to ignore it, that the signal was undoubtedly caused by the twelve B-17 bombers due to arrive at 8 A.M. for a refueling stop, on their way from California to their new station in the Philippines. The fact that the blip was from planes coming from due north while the B-17s were coming from the east should have caused the lieutenant to be suspicious, but he was new, having been assigned as duty officer to provide him some experience.

Earlier that morning, before daylight, a minesweeper on patrol a short distance from the entrance to Pearl Harbor spotted the periscope of a submarine where no American submarine was supposed to be. The minesweeper signaled the destroyer *Ward* some two miles away and reported what it had seen; the *Ward* began looking and shortly before 6 A.M. spotted the periscope of a baby submarine, not an American type, and sank the vessel. This was reported to the naval headquarters in Hawaii at 6:54 A.M., almost an hour before the attack, but by the time the message passed through various hands and reached the navy commander, Admiral Husband E. Kimmel, Japanese bombs were falling.

Those were not the only signals fumbled. Navy intelligence had broken the Japanese diplomatic code with its MAGIC codebreaking machine in the summer of 1941 and had been monitoring communications from Japan to the Japanese Embassy in Washington, which meant that the U.S. State Department often had translations of messages received by Japanese diplomats before their emissaries visited the Secretary of State. Over a period of months it had become increasingly clear from messages intercepted by naval intelligence that the Japanese expected to launch a war, but where, when and against whom was not clear. On November 26, the United States had sent a 10-point plan for peace to the Japanese, but a response did not come to the Japanese Embassy until December 6 when the navy's codebreaking machine intercepted what was identified as the first 13 parts of a 14-part message. When President Roosevelt was shown the message at about 10 P.M. on Saturday, December 6, he said, "This means war."

Early Sunday morning, December 7, navy intelligence in Washington intercepted a message to the Japanese ambassador—the fourteenth part. It was an ultimatum, directed to be presented to the American State Department at precisely 1:00 P.M. Washington time (7:30 A.M. Hawaii time). It also called for the embassy to destroy codes, code machines and all secret documents. This information reached General George C. Marshall, chief of staff of the army, and Admiral Harold R. Stark, chief of naval operations, shortly before noon. They grasped the implications of the intercept and immediately directed their communications staffs to send a message containing the essence of the Japanese intercept to all commands in the Pacific, telling them that its meaning was unknown but that commanders should be on alert for something to happen. General Marshall assumed responsibility for notifying Hawaii since the army was responsible for the security of ships in port there. But atmospheric disturbances around San Francisco and Hawaii made the army's radio communication system to Hawaii inoperable, so the message was sent commercially via Western Union to San Francisco and from there by RCA radio communication system to Hawaii, arriving at 7:33 A.M., Hawaii time. Western Union dispatched a man on a motorcycle to deliver the message to Lieutenant General Walter C. Short, the army commander in Hawaii, but the message was interrupted by Japanese bombers; the attack was under way.

Other signals had begun to appear months earlier. On July 2, 1941, the Japanese called two million reservists and draftees to active duty, instituted censorship of mail, and called merchant ships from the Atlantic. Clearly, something unusual was being planned. Only a few days before the attack, Rear Admiral Richmond Kelly Turner, chief of naval war plans, told his superior that there was a 50–50 chance that Japan would attack Pearl Harbor, a prediction he had made months earlier when he was in Pearl Harbor but, as noted by A. A. Hoehling, an officer on duty in the Navy Department in the days leading up to the attack, Turner was not a popular man in the peacetime navy and his warnings were discounted. In Hawaii the FBI had had the Japanese consulate under observation for some time and for several reasons had concluded that war was imminent. It was fairly clear that the 217 assistant consuls scattered over the island were there to spy, not solely to assist Japanese nationals in Hawaii.

On December 6, the Office of Naval Intelligence intercepted a message to Tokyo from the Japanese commander in Peiping which read as if Japan were already at war with the United States and Britain, but because of the heavy radio traffic and lack of cryptographers on duty—they were civil servants and there were no funds with which to pay them for overtime work—it went onto a pile that did not get deciphered until December 11. In 1991, Frederick Parker, senior historian with the National Security Agency, analyzed 2,600 messages intercepted in 1941 but not decoded at the time; 188 contained clues that could have alerted the United States to the attack. He acknowledged, however, that there was nothing in the messages that would have caused military intelligence to identify Pearl Harbor as the target.

Not only did Japan win a decisive military victory at Pearl Harbor, but the psychological impact on the American people was devastating. The Japanese military leadership had hoped to so incapacitate the U.S. Navy that Japan would have at least six months to occupy Southeast Asia and establish its hegemony over the whole area without interference. Except for the battle of Midway in early June 1942, where the Japanese navy suffered a serious military defeat and great psychological damage, and the naval battle of the Coral Sea in May, which was essentially a draw, this objective was achieved. In less than six months, Japan occupied the

Philippines, Malaya, Singapore, Hong Kong, the Dutch East Indies, most of Burma, Thailand, the Solomon Islands, New Guinea, and other major island groups in the Southwest Pacific, in addition to Indo-China, Manchuria and North China, which had been occupied earlier. It had occupied the Marshall Islands, the Marianas, and the Carolines since the end of 1919 when the World War I treaty placed them under Japanese trusteeship, and had held Korea and Formosa (Taiwan) since their military conquest a half century earlier.

The American forces in the Philippines learned immediately of the attack on Pearl Harbor, but again bad luck prevailed. The Army Air Forces in the Philippines consisted of 35 B-17 bombers, 30 medium and light bombers, 223 fighter planes and 23 other assorted aircraft, most of them stationed at Clark Field, 60 miles north of Manila, and at Nichols Field near Manila. Not more than half of the more than 300 planes were suitable for combat, however. The Pearl Harbor attack occurred at 3 A.M. Manila time, December 8. Although the message sent by General Marshall to Hawaii was also sent to the Philippines, before it arrived a navy radio operator in Manila picked up a message from the navy in Hawaii and a commercial radio station also heard about it; commanding officers were notified almost immediately.

Just after daylight the heavy bombers at Clark Field were dispatched to patrol the waters off the coast of northern Luzon, but shortly thereafter they were recalled to load bombs for an attack on the Japanese on Formosa. They had just landed and begun to refuel when at 12:15 P.M. 54 Japanese bombers and 30 Zero fighters attacked Clark Field, destroying most of the 15 B-17s and most of the fighter planes. Only four American fighters were in the air when the attack came. At Iba Army Air Field, 40 miles west of Clark Field, a Japanese formation caught a squadron of American P-40 fighters returning from patrol and shot down all but two of them and destroyed the air base. Of the 35 B-17s, 17 had been removed to the southern Philippines island of Mindanao for safety, where they remained for about three weeks, assisting the remaining flyable planes on Luzon in striking at the Japanese. But the AAF presence in the Philippines was inadequate for the task, and except for the 14 remaining B-17s on Mindanao, which escaped to Australia, all planes on Luzon were eventually destroyed by the Japanese.

Why there was no warning of the approach of the Japanese planes is not clear and was peculiar in view of the fact that other flights headed toward other targets were detected earlier. The Signal Corps had a half dozen radar detectors in the Philippines, but only one—on the northwest coast, an ideal location for detecting attacks—was up and working. It reported sighting enemy planes on several occasions until it was attacked and destroyed that day, but not before it had notified the Signal Corps center at Neilson Field near Manila of planes headed for Clark Field. The Signal Corps Center immediately notified Clark Field and was satisfied the message had been received, but afterwards the communications staff at Clark Field claimed not to have received it. Even discounting the message, Clark Field should have been prepared for an attack, since it knew of the attack on Pearl Harbor. Several investigations have been undertaken since, but none has explained satisfactorily why Clark Field was not prepared. Thus the debacle at Clark Field remains something of a mystery.

On Monday, December 8, just after noon, President Roosevelt spoke to a joint session of Congress and read a speech that was less than 10 minutes long but was the most historic and far-reaching he had given. It began, "Yesterday, December 7, 1941—a date which will live in infamy—the United States of America was suddenly and deliberately attacked by naval and air forces of the Empire of Japan." He added that on that morning and the previous evening, the Japanese had also attacked Hong Kong, Guam, the Philippine Islands, Wake Island, Midway Island and Malaya. He closed with a request that Congress declare war on Japan, which it did by a vote of 88 to 0 in the Senate and 388 to 1 in the House, the one negative vote being cast by Jeanette Rankin, representative from Montana and a devoted pacifist who had voted against war with Germany in 1917. Among the public, there was very little disagreement with the president. Senator Dewey Short of Kansas, a leading isolationist, immediately became strongly pro-war, as did most of those who had worked to avoid war and even many members of the peace movement. A national poll conducted on December 10 revealed that 96 percent of those polled supported the declaration of war; only 2 percent opposed it.

Yet the isolationists and peace activists had labored to the end to keep America out of war. On Friday evening, December 5, Professor George W. Hartman of Teachers College, Columbia University, a leading pacifist, took a strong stand against American entrance into war in a speech to a Conference of Progressive Educators at the New Yorker Hotel. And on December 6, Peace House ran an ad in the *New York Times* imploring readers to write to their congressmen urging that the United States not enter the war, but by that time most Americans assumed that war was inevitable. Vincent Sheean, the celebrated journalist, in a speech on the evening of December 6, predicted war with Japan would occur soon. A short time earlier, *Time* magazine had written that the odds of war with Japan were nine to one.

On December 11, Germany and Italy declared war on the United States, in keeping with the Tripartite agreement they had signed with

Japan on September 27, 1940. The U.S. Congress passed legislation declaring war on Germany and Italy that same afternoon and President Roosevelt signed it later in the day. The president had been urged to ask Congress to declare war on Germany and Italy at the same time it declared war on Japan, but he chose not to do so. On November 29 the British had intercepted a message from Germany to Japan that it was able to read because it had broken Germany's code; in it, Germany promised again to join in if Japan became involved in war with the United States. Knowing this, Roosevelt felt that the American people would be more strongly committed to the war if Germany and Italy declared war on the United States than if the United States declared war first. The shock of Pearl Harbor had so consumed the emotions of most Americans that when Germany and Italy declared war on the United States, most took it in stride, but they recognized that it meant total war.

Immediately after the Pearl Harbor attack, President Roosevelt sent Secretary of the Navy Frank Knox to Hawaii to make preliminary inquiries into what happened. When Knox returned, the president appointed a commission headed by Supreme Court Justice Owen J. Roberts to make an official investigation. After interviewing 127 witnesses, the commission reported to the president just five weeks later. Admiral Kimmel and General Short, the commanders on Hawaii, had already been relieved of command. The commission concluded that the president; the secretaries of state, war and the navy; the chief of staff of the army; and the chief of naval operations were without blame. The commission reported that there had been a serious air of complacency in Hawaii and that the main problem lay in the failure of the army and navy chiefs there to communicate. If the two had made it a regular practice to talk with one another, reported the Commission, defense would have been improved. (This finding is curious because Short and Kimmel played golf regularly on Sundays and had a game planned for the morning of December 7.) Further, the report said, neither service had done a satisfactory job of patrolling far out to sea, and there was excessive focus on preservation of resources instead of being prepared for war. For example, anti-aircraft artillery could not fire initially because the shells were locked away and gun crews did not have access to the storage areas.

The commission charged Kimmel and Short with dereliction of duty, and they were retired from active duty. This satisfied the country's need for scapegoats, although Roosevelt's opponents in Congress demanded a more thorough investigation, which was delayed because of the need to prosecute the war. Immediately after V-J Day, in 1945, Congress initiated an investigation of the Pearl Harbor debacle and was able to reveal some evidence that had not emerged in the Roberts Report because of the need for wartime secrecy, but the congressional investigation revealed little that was not already known. A minority report charged President Roosevelt with negligence, but since the war was over and Roosevelt was dead, the country was not much interested. Although Kimmel and Short were not court-martialed, both felt that they had been unfairly made scapegoats and that the congressional investigation should have absolved them of failure of command.

Historians who have since investigated the responsibility for the lack of preparation at Pearl Harbor distribute the blame more broadly. The army and navy commanders in Hawaii apparently deserved a large share of the blame, as stated by the Roberts Commission, but they had in fact taken steps to prepare; they were not guilty of total inaction. Further, they had relied on Washington for intelligence and advice—and the conclusion of the military leaders in Washington, as well as intelligence officers in Hawaii, was that an attack on Hawaii was not even remotely likely, that it was too far from Japan to be a viable target. The American ambassador to Japan, Joseph C. Grew, had reported in January 1941 that he had picked up a rumor that if trouble with the United States developed, the Japanese planned a surprise attack on Hawaii, but this warning was apparently filed away and forgotten or not considered in the fall of 1941. In 1925 a novelist named Hector Bywater had published a book, entitled *The Great Pacific War,* describing an attack on Pearl Harbor by the naval and air forces of Japan with a degree of accuracy that uncannily predicted the real attack. Since it was fiction, U.S. Navy planners had never taken the book seriously. Its prophetic description led Houghton-Mifflin, the publisher, to reissue it again in 1942.

While intelligence officers and military commanders were convinced Japan would attack, they thought it more likely that it would be in the Philippines or somewhere else in Southeast Asia. The chief of naval operations had sent a message to Admiral Kimmel in Hawaii on November 27 warning that the secret intercepts indicated war was likely, but added that it seemed more likely to begin in the Philippines, Thailand, Borneo, or the Kra Peninsula (Malaya). On December 6, the British reported that a flotilla of 46 Japanese ships, including a battleship, 7 cruisers and several destroyers, had been spotted passing Indo-China headed south, evidently en route to Thailand or Malaya, thus confirming to Admiral Kimmel the speculation that the first strike would come in Southeast Asia. American and British intelligence agreed that Japan would likely attack Malaya or Siam (Thailand) within hours. Early Sunday morning scouting planes from the Philippines reported seeing the flotilla again, still headed south. There was good reason for those who read the report to conclude that war was indeed about to begin but that the armada headed to southeast Asia constituted the attack force.

Why did the Japanese choose December 1941 to attack? There were three primary reasons. When the United States cut off oil shipments to Japan in the summer of 1941, Japan tried unsuccessfully to negotiate with the Dutch East Indies (now Indonesia) for additional supplies. Unless alternative sources of oil could be found, Japan's navy and economy would come to a virtual halt. Second, support for the war was not unanimous at home, and the military feared that if they delayed too long, antiwar sentiment might increase. Finally, in the autumn of 1941, Japan's fleet was larger than the U.S. Pacific fleet. Although the American fleet had more battleships, destroyers and submarines, eight of its battleships, four aircraft carriers, and many smaller craft had been dispatched to the Atlantic. Japan was aware of the crash program of shipbuilding that had begun in the United States in the summer of 1940 and knew that if it waited, its navy would have an increasing number of American ships to contend with. The planners felt they must move while the Japanese navy had a chance to destroy the United States Pacific fleet, and December 1941 was the earliest they could strike Pearl Harbor.

Prelude to Japanese Aggression

The war in Europe had been under way for more than two years when Japan attacked Pearl Harbor, and most American attention had been directed toward the possibility of going to war with Germany. True, the American government had been engaged in diplomatic maneuvering with Japan for many months and this had been reported in the press, but the main focus was on Europe.

How did the United States come to war with Japan? Could it have been prevented? What might have been is always difficult to determine, but examination of the decades prior to Pearl Harbor provides some clues. Until past the mid-nineteenth century, Japan had been an insular and xenophobic country. In 1853 Commodore Matthew C. Perry sailed into Tokyo Bay with a strong U.S. naval squadron and presented a demand from the American government that Japan sign a treaty to open trade with the United States and allow foreigners to live there. Japan's military government, a dictatorship, felt it was too weak to resist and in 1854, when Perry returned, signed the treaty, which led not only to trade with the West but to participation in international affairs.

In 1867, Emperor Mutsuhito, known as Meiji Tenno, became the ruler of Japan and brought an extended period of progressive rule. He sent emissaries to Prussia, from which Japan drew its constitution, and in the late nineteenth century established several universities based on the German model. Delegations visited England and brought back ideas that shaped Japan's industrial development.

In the 1890s events began which arguably laid the foundation for the eventual attack on America. The military began to gain increased authority under the emperor, although he was a strong ruler and maintained control of the military and the government until his death. When Japan defeated China in their war of 1894–1895 and occupied Korea—as it would continue to do until 1945—the military felt its power growing. It was at this time that the seed of military control that completely dominated the government during World War II was planted. By tradition (and by law after 1936) only admirals and generals on the active list were eligible to serve as ministers of navy and war. In both cases, they served at the pleasure of their respective military establishments, which, if the army or navy leadership chose, could require the minister of war or navy to resign, thereby bringing down the government. And by refusing to approve a particular general or admiral as minister, the army or navy could prevent the formation of a government. From about 1901 onward, a government could be formed only if it was acceptable to the army and navy. As late as July 1940, the leadership of the army felt that Prime Minister Yonai was practicing appeasement of the West and withdrew its support of the army minister, and his government fell. This practice also explains the appointment of General Hideki Tojo as prime minister immediately preceding World War II.

Prior to the turn of the century, Japanese people began to immigrate to America but encountered racism, an experience new to them. Alarm about the invasion of the "yellow peril" appeared openly in American newspapers and magazines, and West Coast politicians fanned the flames of anti-Japanese sentiment. Japanese immigrants and visitors were denied service in restaurants and other public accommodations and were subjected to insults. When this treatment was reported in Japan, the upper classes and especially the military became infuriated. Not only did they consider themselves not inferior to Americans, but the warrior classes, with their Samurai heritage, considered themselves definitely superior to Americans, whom they saw as a crude people lacking in culture and noble values. The Immigration Act of 1924 barred Japanese immigration to the United States and limited Japanese visitors to two years of temporary residency. The Japanese military was enraged by this action, and anti-American sentiment in Japan swept not only the military but the entire country.

When Emperor Mutsuhito died in 1912, he was succeeded as emperor by his son, Yoshihito, who was not only a weak ruler but eventually was judged mentally unfit. Mutsuhito, a strong emperor, had been able to handle the growing power of the military, but when he died and Yoshihito became emperor, the military expanded its control over the government. When Yoshihito died in 1926, he was succeeded by his

25-year-old son, Hirohito, who was never able to re-establish the control over the military that had been exercised by his grandfather. For a period beginning about 1924 until 1931, civilian premiers exercised considerable power contrary to the military but never became completely free of its control. In 1932 the newly seated premier was assassinated and a group of young ultranationalist army officers attempted to overthrow the government. Though the coup attempt failed, the power of civilian political parties in the government increasingly flowed to the military from then onward.

In September 1931, the military occupied Manchuria under the pretense of protecting the Japanese-owned South Manchurian Railway. From that time on the power of the military grew, intimidating the emperor's advisers and other moderate leaders. In the mid–1930s Japan extended its occupation into China; its actions caused a number of international incidents, about which the United States protested to the Japanese government, always without avail. Japanese forces engaged the Chinese army in a gun battle at the Marco Polo Bridge just outside Peking in July 1937, marking the beginning of all-out war between Japan and China. In a speech in Chicago in October 1937, President Roosevelt strongly condemned Japan's action and advocated a quarantine of aggressor nations, but accusations of "warmonger" from the isolationists were so shrill that he had to tone down his criticisms. The League of Nations issued a critical communiqué, but it was irrelevant because Japan had withdrawn from the league when it criticized Japan's invasion of Manchuria.

On December 29, 1935, Japan announced that it would abrogate its treaty with the United States and Britain limiting the number of capital ships (battleships and battle cruisers) that it could build when the treaty expired at the end of 1936. In 1922, representatives of Britain, the United States and Japan had met in Washington and agreed upon a ratio of 5-5-3 capital ships. Japan's smaller number was based on the proposition that its navy was concentrated in the Far East while the United States had two oceans to patrol and the British had seven. The treaty had been extended in the London conference of 1930, but efforts by the United States and Britain at a second London conference in 1935 to renew the treaty failed, and when the treaty expired at the end of 1936, Japan rapidly embarked on a large scale shipbuilding program. Meantime, Japan had been expanding its fleet of destroyers, cruisers, and other smaller ships not covered by the treaty and, as noted earlier, had very likely been at work surreptitiously building ships that violated the treaty.

Meantime, relations between the United States and Japan deteriorated. In July 1939, the United States gave Japan a required six-month notice that it would not renew the trade treaty which had been in effect since 1911, signaling that it expected to cut off shipment of war materials, a decidedly threatening move. In 1939 Japan depended on the United States for 45 percent of its imports, including 50 percent of its petroleum, and for years had been buying large amounts of scrap iron and other metals. As late as 1938, Japan was buying airplanes and parts from American manufacturers, though such shipments were halted in the summer of that year when the secretary of state invoked a "moral embargo" on shipments of planes to countries engaged in bombing civilian populations. In February 1940, a poll found that 75 percent of Americans favored an embargo on all exports to Japan.

Under the authority of the Export Control Act, President Roosevelt cut off the export of steel and scrap iron to Japan on October 16, 1940, having already ended shipments of aviation gasoline in July. However, he stopped short of cutting off all shipments of oil, recognizing that to do so might provoke "unfriendly acts" by Japan, including immediate attack on the Dutch East Indies, a major source of its oil. In fact, during the spring of 1941, the United States shipped more oil to Japan than to Great Britain, and it was not until June 20, 1941, that President Roosevelt cut off all exports of oil to Japan. Secretary of State Hull stated at the time that the cutoff of oil virtually assured that Japan would be at war with the United States soon. Japan had an agreement with the Dutch East Indies for oil, but the agreement did not satisfy nearly the real needs of the country. This meant that steps would have to be taken to secure additional supplies of oil, which almost certainly meant war unless an agreement could be reached with the United States that would allow Japan to proceed with its expansion.

During 1940 and 1941, the United States expected Japan to declare war on the Soviet Union, and although for a time the Japanese seriously considered doing so, it was decided that expansion throughout Southeast Asia was more central to Japan's objectives in its Greater East Asia Co-Prosperity Sphere. Following the decision not to attack Russia, the Japanese leadership began to seek an arrangement with the Soviet Union to assure nonintervention with Japanese expansion elsewhere. The Japanese foreign minister signed a Neutrality Pact with the Soviet Union on April 13, 1941, and while the two countries were not allies, this was a way of assuring that each could pursue its objectives without fear of the other. After Germany attacked the Soviet Union on June 22, 1941, Hitler or his foreign minister Ribbentrop attempted on several occasions to persuade the Japanese to attack Russia from the east, but since Japan had focused on expansion to the south, it did not want to get involved in a war with Russia.

Immediately after the Germans defeated the French in June 1940, the Japanese approached the French governor general of Indo-China with several proposals for establishing a Japanese presence there. Following considerable haggling and negotiations between the Japanese and the Vichy government, with efforts by the Americans to dissuade Japan from its ambitions, an agreement was reached between Japan and the governor general, not because France was sympathetic to Japan's aims but because it was in no position to resist Japan's wishes. Japan was particularly interested in establishing a base in northern Indo-China from which it could cut off the supply route into the south of China and conduct its campaign against China. The agreement allowed Japan to station a limited number of troops in the north and made available three airfields in Tonkin.

Several times during 1941 the United States attempted through diplomatic channels to persuade Japan to give up occupied areas, specifically China and Indo-China. Failing that, Secretary of State Hull repeatedly proposed to the Japanese that Indo-China be neutralized and troops withdrawn. On July 24, 1941, the United States learned that Japan was in the process of expanding its occupation of Indo-China, occupying not only the north but the south as well. In an undiplomatic note to the Vichy government on July 14, 1941, Japan demanded that it be allowed to occupy eight airfields in southern Indo-China, plus the naval bases at Saigon and Camranh Bay; that it be allowed freedom of movement of Japanese troops in the south; and that French troops be evacuated from military bases that Japan proposed to occupy. The Vichy government, again in no position to resist Japanese demands, signed the accord on July 21. Japan immediately moved 50,000 troops into the south of Indo-China, placing Japanese planes and naval forces in a position to threaten the Philippines, the Dutch East Indies, and Malaya as well as the southern supply route into China.

On July 26, 1941, President Roosevelt froze Japanese assets in the United States and essentially stopped all trade between the two countries; some have characterized his actions as a declaration of "economic war." On August 28, Japanese Prime Minister Prince Fumimaro Konoye suggested a meeting between himself and President Roosevelt, to which Roosevelt responded favorably but with the suggestion of certain conditions. The Japanese ambassador in Washington hinted that failure to move quickly to a conference between Roosevelt and Konoye might lead to the replacement of Konoye, a relative moderate among the hotbed of militarists in the Japanese government, by someone less devoted to peace. He was prophetic. On October 18, Konoye was indeed replaced by the head of the army, Lt. General Hideki Tojo, who served as premier until he resigned in mid-1944. There has been some speculation that Emperor Hirohito's advisers wanted to name a moderate civilian as premier, but because of the veto power of the military in the formation of the government, the emperor was forced to accept Tojo, who filled his cabinet with military officers and ultranationalist civilians.

In early November the Japanese government named Saburo Kurusu, who spoke excellent English and whose wife was American, as special representative to assist the ambassador to America, Admiral Kichisaburo Nomura, in negotiations with the U.S. government. Nomura had tendered his resignation as ambassador, but the Japanese government rejected it. Nomura remained nominally the lead negotiator, but in fact Kurusu was in charge, and from his arrival onward, the two of them met almost daily with the U.S. secretary of state. It became clear that Japan was not prepared to end its aggression.

On November 20, the Japanese offered a proposal for peace, provided the United States continued to supply Japan with oil, released Japan's assets, resumed trade, and stopped giving aid to China and Indo-China. The American secretary of state responded on November 26, in effect rejecting the Japanese conditions and stating that the American conditions for peace and resumption of normal trade relations would require a nonaggression pact among the Pacific powers and Japan's return of the territories it had won by conquest in Asia.

The stiff terms of Japan's diplomatic negotiations and the wording of communications from Japan to its ambassador in Washington led Roosevelt and most of his advisers to conclude that Japan would definitely initiate an attack. The so-called War Council, consisting of the secretaries of state, war and the navy, recognized that Japan would strike soon but thought that it would be from Indo-China against Thailand, Malaya, or the Dutch East Indies. The British Joint Intelligence Committee had reached the same conclusion.

Notwithstanding the tense negotiations between Japan and the United States in the fall of 1941, which were fully reported in the press, a substantial minority of Americans still thought that war could be averted. In fact, a poll on the eve of the attack found that 27 percent thought the United States would not go to war with Japan and 22 percent were undecided. At the same time, there was a rising tide of sentiment among the American people, fed by truculent newspaper editorials, against any appeasement of Japan. It was clear then to the secretary of state and those who were involved in the negotiations with Japan that the only basis on which peace could have continued would have been on Japan's terms, which were unacceptable to the United States.

On December 6, President Roosevelt sent a cable message to Hirohito saying that the expansion of Japanese power in Indo-China was a threat to peace between the two countries and urging that Japan and the United States refrain from any hostilities. The message failed to reach Hirohito before the attack on Pearl Harbor, however. The die was already cast, for the Japanese fleet had been at sea bound for Hawaii since November 25. Admiral Isoroku Yamamoto and his staff had been at work since January 1941 planning the Pearl Harbor attack, which was brilliant in planning and execution.

Japan's response to the secretary of state's offer of peace was the aforementioned 14-point memorandum, 13 points of which arrived at its Washington embassy on the evening of December 6 and the fourteenth the next morning. Kurusu and Nomura were instructed to deliver the memorandum to Secretary of State Hull at precisely 1:00 P.M. Washington time, just minutes before the scheduled attack on Pearl Harbor, but they were tardy for their appointment. Hull had already learned of the attack on Pearl Harbor when they arrived. Reportedly, Kurusu and Nomura had not. The memorandum issued a number of false charges against the United States, including preventing peace between China and Japan, fomenting war, and several corollary charges, and indicated that Japan was ending negotiations. Hull, outraged over the falsehoods in the memorandum and the duplicity of the Japanese government, proceeded to give the two diplomats a blistering tonguelashing.

The Japanese refer to the attack on Pearl Harbor as a "surprise" attack. President Roosevelt called it a "sneak" attack, because the Japanese diplomats in Washington had been pretending to negotiate while the Japanese fleet was headed for Pearl Harbor. After December 7, 1941, "Pearl Harbor" denoted not only a geographical location but an event.

There are conflicting opinions concerning Emperor Hirohito's role in the war. Various historians have speculated that he tried to prevent war but was unable to change the expansionist fervor of the army. Others find no evidence to support that theory; in fact, material emerged in 1993 that led military historians to conclude that Hirohito made no effort to deter the Japanese army's aggression and may have supported it. Unfortunately, Hirohito died in January 7, 1989, without clarifying his role in the prosecution of the war.

CHURCHILL HAD ASSURED Roosevelt that if Japan attacked the United States, Great Britain would declare war on Japan. The news of the attack on Pearl Harbor reached England on the 9 P.M. newscast, and the British breathed a sigh of relief. Finally, their beleaguered island would have overt assistance from America. Although the House of Commons did not normally meet on Mondays, it assembled at 2:45 P.M. on December 8 to hear Churchill's speech in which he announced that the Japanese were landing in Malaya and asked for a declaration of war on Japan. Doubtless Britain would have entered the war against Japan as promised even if Japan had not invaded its colonies in the Far East, but the attack on Malaya cinched it.

In view of the seriousness of its situation at home, Britain could provide only limited support in the Far East, yet it did have troops stationed in its colonies—India, Burma, Malaya, and smaller colonies—and limited naval forces there. The first encounter the British had with the Japanese was a disaster. Its newest and most prized battleship, the *Prince of Wales*, and the heavy battle cruiser *Repulse* were attacked off the coast of Singapore by Japanese torpedo planes on December 9 and both were sunk. Hong Kong fell on Christmas Day. Then, on February 15, 1942, the British forces at Singapore, out of food, water, ammunition and gasoline, were forced to surrender their 32,000 Indian, 15,000 British, and 13,000 Australian troops to a force of 30,000 Japanese. The surrender of Singapore doomed the East Indies and most of Southeast Asia. On February 19, the Japanese landed on Timor in the Dutch East Indies, within easy striking distance of Australia. On March 12 the Dutch East Indies fell to the Japanese and soon Japan had occupied portions of most of the countries in Southeast Asia—including the Solomon Islands, which were even closer to Australia.

Chapter III

Internal Security

In World War I, there were gross violations of civil liberties and mistreatment of persons of German ancestry in the United States. The mistreatment was not so much by the federal government as by local governments and by individuals and groups. Immigrants from Germany and the Austro-Hungarian empire were subjected to rude treatment and persecuted. Many of those teaching in colleges and schools were harassed and dismissed, regardless of their loyalty. The teaching of the German language was abolished in many schools and colleges. Professors of German suspected of disloyalty were dismissed at the universities of Illinois, Nebraska, Oregon, Virginia, and Michigan (where six members of the German faculty were discharged, virtually wiping out the department), and several other schools. Anti-German hysteria swept the country. At July 4 celebrations German books, especially books by German authors, were burned in massive bonfires.

Non-Germans opposed to American entry into the war were also persecuted, and pro–German speech of any kind was censured or punished, if not by the government, by society generally. A famous professor of psychology at Columbia University was dismissed for writing a letter in which he advised young men not to volunteer for military service.

The Enemy Alien Act of 1798 authorizes the president to incarcerate enemy aliens in time of war. When the United States entered World War I the government arrested about 6,000 aliens but eventually released all but 2,300, with the remainder placed on parole or simply turned loose. Of those released, less than 1 percent were later involved in espionage or other acts of disloyalty.

With the exception of the evacuation and internment of the Japanese, the extremes of World War I were not repeated in World War II. Although efforts were made to avoid the excesses of World War I, internal security was still taken seriously. Even so, it is the nature of an open society such as the United States that the enemy could and did obtain much information of military value not only through lack of proper security but through normal channels of communication. Persons suspected of espionage were prosecuted, but there were few prosecutions for speaking in opposition to the war. As of June 1944 the American Civil Liberties Union reported that about 130 persons had been prosecuted for allegedly speaking or publishing about matters that obstructed the conduct of the war, compared with 1,500 in World War I. In its annual report, the ACLU stated that there was an "almost complete absence of repressive tendencies," in contrast to World War I.

Response to Pearl Harbor

The attack on Pearl Harbor was an event that remained permanently etched in the memory of every adult living in the United States at that time. For hours after the attack, people stayed glued to the radio trying to find out what had happened and what might happen next. At first, most reacted with disbelief. Some cried. A few went into a rage. Anti-Japanese sentiment soared. There was a public clamor to chop down the Japanese cherry trees around the Tidal Basin in Washington, D.C., and indeed a few were cut down. Japanese and other Asians underwent considerable harassment in cities and towns throughout the country, leading many Chinese-Americans to wear signs on their chests that said "Chinese." In a small town in Wyoming, a merchant burned all of the novelties in his shop that were marked "Made in Japan." In Boston, former governor James Curley mailed back a decoration Japan had awarded to him in 1917.

Within hours newspapers had issued extra editions, reporting the Pearl Harbor attack (in pretelevision days, newspapers frequently issued special editions to report unusual developments). In New Orleans, the *Times-Picayune* had an extra edition on the street by 3:25 P.M. The *Chicago Sun* was on the street by 7 P.M., beating all other Chicago papers. In Dallas, the *Journal* issued extra editions at 3:50, 5:09 and 8:07 P.M. and delivered a free copy to all subscribers; the *Dallas Morning News* was on the street with its first extra edition at 5:50 P.M. and sold 20,000 copies in 50 minutes.

Without exception they decried the attack in most forceful terms; most editorials expressed the rage felt by everyone. The Portland, Maine, *Press Herald* editorialized as follows in its Monday edition:

> No better proof of fundamental Japanese treachery, of which the country has been hearing for many decades, could be found than the foulness of conduct that launched attack upon this nation while it was earnestly trying to seek a peaceful settlement of the Far Eastern situation. ... Secretary Hull said he had

> never known a document so filled with infamous falsehoods as that delivered on Sunday to him by the Japanese emissaries in this country. . . . The issue is between democracy and despotism . . . democratic powers against world slavery . . . the U.S. against Hitler, his satellites and stooges. If Congress has the guts . . . it will declare war upon every enemy of peace and decency.

The *Chicago Tribune*, the leading isolationist paper in the country, had its first Monday edition on the street Sunday evening at 7:00. It editorialized:

> Thus the thing that we all feared, that so many of us have worked with all our hearts to avert, has happened. . . . America faces war through no volition of any American. Recriminations are useless, and we doubt that they will be indulged in, certainly not by us. . . . All of us, from this day forth, have but one task. That is to strike with all our might to protect and preserve the American freedom that we all hold dear.

Correspondents for *Time*, *Life*, and *Fortune* magazines monitored the responses of the media and the public during the first 30 hours after the attack on Pearl Harbor, which were published in their book *December 7: The First Thirty Hours*. They reported that newspapers all over the country were swamped Sunday evening and Monday with calls from anxious and hysterical relatives of soldiers and sailors involved in the Pearl Harbor attack. By 5 P.M. Sunday, 2,000 people had assembled around the Japanese consulate in New Orleans, requiring police protection for the consulate. About all that happened was the burning of consular papers in the back yard of the consulate, prompting someone to call the fire department.

On Sunday afternoon, the FBI, local police and other law enforcement agencies began to take Japanese nationals into custody. Within two hours after the attack was announced in Norfolk, Virginia, site of a major naval installation, the local police had jailed 14 Japanese. In Omaha, the FBI removed K. Hayashi, a member of the Japanese consul staff in San Francisco, from a United Airlines plane. On the West Coast, many Japanese were apprehended; early radio broadcasts in Los Angeles reported that 3,000 Japanese nationals had been taken into custody. Terminal Island, near Los Angeles, held huge refinery tanks that officials considered a prime target for saboteurs; at the ferry landing police and soldiers searched automobiles for Japanese and took more than 300 into custody. In San Francisco, the FBI arrested hundreds of Japanese.

At 12:38 P.M. radio station KNX in Los Angeles interrupted its broadcast to announce that all army and navy furloughs and leaves had been canceled, and that all soldiers and sailors were to report to their posts immediately. In New Orleans, the Orpheum Theater interrupted the movie under way at 9 P.M. to announce from the stage that all servicemen were to report to their duty stations immediately; about 25 men left the theater. Similar announcements were made all over the country where there were army, navy or marine bases.

All over the country military and civilian police were stationed at militarily sensitive installations and other facilities that were thought to be in danger. The mayor of San Francisco declared a state of emergency, immediately setting aside funds for civilian defense directors and calling on all parties then involved in a strike to settle it in the interest of the country. The governor of Oregon proclaimed a state of emergency, and the city of Portland stationed guards on its reservoirs, pipelines and city bridges. The Bonneville Power Administration in Oregon doubled the guard around the dam, power plant and substations, and in Seattle police and army and navy patrols posted guards on bridges, water purification plants, and gas and electric facilities. In San Diego all special police were called to duty Sunday afternoon at the Consolidated Aircraft factory, and the officer in charge of the army's West Coast Procurement Office ordered the public to stay away from defense plants unless they had official business there.

In Washington, D.C., soldiers with fixed bayonets were stationed around the White House, the Memorial Bridge over the Potomac, and other installations. On Monday morning, 200 marines were placed around the Capitol and 200 secret servicemen and 400 Capitol police were scattered throughout the Capitol, adding to the chaos and confusion that permeated Congress that day. In Wyoming, the state superintendent of highways stationed 24 hour-a-day guards at bridges and highway maintenance shops, and in Richmond, Virginia, city police placed a 24 hour-a-day guard at the city water supply.

On December 8 the government placed guards on all airfields in the country and monitored departures of airplanes. Airplanes owned by aliens were seized. Soon after Pearl Harbor the Federal Communications Commission ordered ham radio operators to cease transmitting, lest there be a few among them who might communicate defense information to the enemy. Later about 2,000 ham operators were permitted to continue to transmit to ham operators in other countries information that had been approved by the government.

Hawaii expected an invasion immediately after the bombing. As soon as the attacking planes left, rumors swept through the islands that more attacks were to come, that paratroopers would be landing shortly and that Japanese fifth columnists would be sabotaging military facilities. None of these happened. It is very likely that if Japanese forces had attempted to invade Hawaii following the attack on Pearl Harbor, a large force could have landed successfully, but a landing was not a part of the attack plan. In addition, the commander, Admiral Chuichi Nagumo, was a cautious officer who departed without exploiting significant bombing opportunities, particularly the oil tanks which, had they been destroyed, would have required many months, perhaps up to two years, to reconstruct and refill with oil. Nonetheless, for several months the American government thought an invasion of the islands was likely and prepared for it, even printing special currency for Hawaii in case the islands were overtaken.

The Hawaiian Red Cross and civilian defense workers were in action almost immediately, providing food and shelter and transporting people from military bases to schools, churches and homes for safety and treatment. They proceeded on the assumption that the worst was yet to come. A curfew was imposed, everyone was required to carry an identification card, and between January and March 1942, every civilian was issued a gas mask. Military judges replaced civilian judges in all courts in Hawaii, a measure which was ruled unconstitutional by the Supreme Court in 1946.

Curiously, hysteria was even greater on the West Coast than in Hawaii. Lt. General J. W. DeWitt, commander of the Western Defense Command with headquarters at the Presidio in San Francisco, realizing the implications of the attack on Pearl Harbor, proceeded to try to do everything possible to prepare for a possible landing in California. There were many military installations and defense plants in California and some in Oregon and Washington—including aircraft plants in Santa Monica, Long Beach and Seattle, shipbuilding yards in Portland, large Navy installations in San Diego, and the large petroleum industry in Southern California.

The fact that Japanese submarines had sunk a tanker, a freighter and some smaller ships off the California coast between December 18 and 24 added credibility to the perceived threat of invasion. General DeWitt made it clear that if there was an invasion of the West Coast he did not plan to be caught in the same position as the army commander in Hawaii. He prevailed on Governor Olson to ban all public festivities in California, including the Rose Bowl game on January 1, 1942, between Oregon State and Duke, which was played instead on the Duke campus, in Durham, North Carolina.

Clearly excessive precautions were taken, including measures that were not only unnecessary but harmful. At the time, however, the threat of an invasion seemed real. An editorial in the *Seattle Times* on December 8 expressed the feelings of many: "It is not altogether impossible that a Jap aircraft carrier could slip through close enough to our coast to conduct a foray upon our airplane and shipbuilding plants." Over much of the country there were black-out lights or dim-out lights to protect against bombing raids, and air raid drills were held in many locations in anticipation of bombing raids. At the urging of Civilian Defense officials, boxes of sand and pails of water were placed at strategic locations throughout buildings in preparation for fires to be expected from bombing. Other steps were taken which in retrospect seem unnecessary and even foolish, yet there was genuine fear that a Japanese attack on the West Coast was imminent. The main actual benefit of the hypercaution was to give the civilian populace a feeling that they were playing a role in the war, but at the time that was not its purpose.

The army believed that invasion of the West Coast was a real possibility and immediately set about building up its defenses. Several antiaircraft batteries were set up, and immediately squadrons of airplanes and two army divisions were moved to the coast. On the night of February 24, 1942, a report that enemy planes were over Los Angeles set off antiaircraft firing in which almost 1,500 shells were fired at what many later called "phantom planes," although subsequent investigations reached mixed conclusions. Secretary of War Henry L. Stimson said the planes were real; Secretary of the Navy Frank Knox said there were no Japanese planes.

On February 23, 1942, a Japanese submarine surfaced off the coast of Santa Barbara, California, and lobbed a few shells into an area filled with oil tanks, doing little damage but managing to frighten people and convince many that the anticipated invasion was about to begin. On the evening of June 21, another submarine fired several shells onto the beaches of Oregon, but again no one was injured. This was enough, however, to frighten residents on both the East and West coasts, where dim-out lights now became the norm and windows were curtained and drawn at night. The whole country was caught up in hysteria. There was widespread fear that the Japanese would invade the mainland. Rumors of invasion and bombings abounded, not only on the West Coast but inland as well. The Japanese did not attempt an invasion, but the hysteria did not subside soon.

Trains were tied up for weeks transporting military units from all over the country, a major logistical undertaking, eventually moving a total of 600,000 troops to the West Coast, Panama, and Alaska. Hundreds of fighter planes were sent immediately from Long Island and other East Coast airfields. After the artillery and other ground forces were in place it became apparent that they were scattered so thinly along the West Coast from Canada to Mexico that it would have been impossible to deny a Japanese landing at any of several locations had one been attempted.

In northern California air raid warnings continued through January 1942, but the shelling of Santa Barbara was the only major attack on the American mainland until November 1942, when a plane launched from a submarine flew over Oregon and dropped incendiary bombs. The pilot, Flying Officer Nobuo Fujita of the Japanese navy, actually flew over the area twice, once in the daytime and the second at night, with the intention of setting fire to the forests, which were then very dry, but his mission accomplished little. The towns were blacked out but he had no trouble navigating, thanks to the lighthouse off the coast; in many cases a town would be blacked out but the lighthouse off the coast would be shining brightly.

The final Japanese attack on the U.S. mainland took place more than two years later in an act allegedly aimed at revenge for the Doolittle Raid on Tokyo in which Lt. Col. (later Lt. General) James H. Doolittle, commanding a group of specially trained B-25 bomber crews, launched a raid from an aircraft carrier that bombed Tokyo in April 1942. While it did not do extensive damage, it provided a morale boost in the United States and a warning to the Japanese that they were vulnerable. In November 1944, the Japanese launched 9,000 balloons carrying incendiary bombs across the Pacific Ocean with the prevailing winds, with the intention that they would land in the forests of the northwest and cause widespread property and psychological damage. The bombs were designed to work in two stages: the first was an explosive and the second was incendiary. Only a few of them reached the United States, although one drifted as far as Maryland. At least one that landed in Oregon killed some curious people who stopped to investigate it, but most did no serious damage.

The reluctance of the vast majority of Americans to enter the war disappeared. Their country's reaction to the attack on Pearl Harbor ensured solidarity in support of the war and cemented their dedication to the cause—a commitment that suffered only minor cracks throughout the war. Opposition to mobilization disappeared.

Aliens and Security Risk

Long before the war began, there was growing concern throughout the country about espionage and subversion, exacerbated by the prominence of the German-American Bund and other groups whose members were largely immigrants from Germany and Italy and were openly and noisily pro-fascist or pro–German or pro–Italian. Their agitation led to the June 1940 passage in Congress of the Alien Registration Act, known as the Smith Act, which provided the authorization under which the FBI subsequently registered almost five million aliens, including Germans, Italians and Japanese.

Although virtually the entire American population was composed of immigrants and their descendants, there was widespread fear of persons of foreign extraction. It was widely believed that there were large numbers of Fifth Columnists located in strategic sites about the country to spy and commit sabotage. The press had dwelled on this theme for many months and it had become accepted as fact. The army, including Secretary of War Stimson, was fully convinced that the country was honeycombed with Fifth Columnists, and Secretary of the Navy Knox stated that the success of the Pearl Harbor attack was due in large measure to the work of Fifth Columnists. Fear of Fifth Columnists was so strong in 1940 that officials and staff of the federal Works Progress Administration, a major New Deal program to put the unemployed to work, were required to sign an oath swearing that they were neither pro-communist nor pro-Nazi. The fear of and antipathy toward persons believed to be disloyal was so intense that pacifists, if their views were known, were assaulted and harassed. When Jehovah's Witnesses refused to salute the flag, the court ruled that they were required to do so.

The Fifth Column fear was excessive but was not altogether without foundation. J. Edgar Hoover, director of the Federal Bureau of Investigation, which had been busy looking for Fifth Columnists for some time, stepped up his investigations after Pearl Harbor and reported that the numbers of such persons were far smaller than presumed. He undertook a thorough investigation of the situation on the West Coast and concluded that fears that the huge war manufacturing plants there were in danger from Fifth Columnists were overstated, a conclusion that was highly unpopular with the press and the public. Frequent reports by persons on the West Coast that they had seen signal lights from what they presumed to be Japanese submarines and ships fed the fears of the public.

Prior to American entrance into the war, the FBI, in cooperation with the Office of Naval Intelligence and army intelligence, had prepared a list of persons suspected of potential disloyalty to the United States. Immediately following the attack on Pearl Harbor, the FBI began to round up both aliens and citizens whose names appeared on its security lists. In the first 18 months after the Pearl Harbor attack, a total of about 3,500 Italians, 6,000 Germans, and 5,300 Japanese had been apprehended. Those arrested as potentially dangerous had made public statements supporting Mussolini, Italian fascism, Hitler, Nazism, or Japanese expansionism, or else belonged to such organizations as the German-American Bund, Fasci Abroad, or the Hokubei Japanese society. All received a hearing and most were released without being detained. Those who were detained were transported to one of 17 Justice Department internment camps such as Fort Lincoln, North Dakota; Lordsburg, New Mexico; and Missoula, Montana. They were permitted to appeal, and if there was judged to be no reason to detain them further, they were released.

Although the 600,000 Italians constituted the largest number of aliens in the United States, the attorney general determined that they showed little evidence of disloyalty, and on October 12, 1942, President Roosevelt issued an executive order removing Italians from the enemy alien category. All of the Italian internees who were not considered dangerous were then released. In its 1942-43 annual report, the ACLU reported that as of March 1943 the Justice Department still held 4,083 aliens—1,715 Germans, 242 Italians, 2,119 Japanese and 7 others.

Although there was only limited Fifth Column activity on the West Coast, the public and much of the press believed it to be potentially much more serious, and there was considerable agitation for the internment of all aliens. For a time it appeared that Italians and Germans living in California, as well as Japanese, might be interned.

It is often assumed that the Japanese were in the majority of the foreign born living in California at the outbreak of war. On the contrary, the 1940 census found that the foreign born in California included 100,911 Italians, 71,727 Germans, and 33,569 Japanese. About half of the Italians and more than two-thirds of the Germans, but none of the Japanese, had been naturalized by December 1941. When war was declared almost 70,000 alien Italians and Germans were living in California, more than twice the number of alien Japanese.

Presidential Executive Order 9066 authorized the army to remove anyone considered dangerous from restricted areas on the West Coast. Many in the army assumed that the order included not only Japanese but Italian and German aliens. In February 1942, the army commander in charge of West Coast security ordered all Italian and German aliens who lived in restricted areas along the California coast to move inland. As historian Stephen Fox has noted, most of them moved just a few miles to get outside the restricted zone, usually within the same county, and in San Francisco, their trek was often just across town. They were also subjected to curfew and travel restrictions. Italian fishermen were forbidden to go to sea, and the army and navy confiscated about 750 of their boats for war service. The army and FBI visited homes of Italians and Germans and confiscated firearms, explosives, maps, codes, selected documents, cameras, and shortwave radios.

In early 1942, General DeWitt gave the impression that evacuation and internment of Italian and German aliens would begin as soon as the Japanese had been evacuated. In March, however, the army announced that only Japanese and dangerous enemy aliens would be removed from the western half of the Pacific states. Several factors influenced the decision not to include Italians and Germans in the mass evacuation and internment program. The congressional committee that held hearings in California on internal security opposed the inclusion of Italians and Germans, as did John J. McCloy, the assistant secretary of war who had been put in charge of the supervision of Executive Order 9066. Attorney

General Francis Biddle had carried on a running battle with the War Department against moving persons of any nationality from their homes. Further, while the Japanese were employed largely in fishing, farming and their own small businesses, many of the Italians and Germans were employed in critical sectors of the economy, including some that were important to the war effort, which would be impaired if they left. A major reason, however, was the sheer numbers, for the number of alien Italians and Germans, including children, would have made internment unmanageable. Finally, if Italian and German aliens on the West Coast were interned, would those living elsewhere also be rounded up? If so, the task was beyond comprehension.

On March 20 the president signed Executive Order 9106, which exempted certain categories of Italians and Germans from the earlier decree. In June the army apparently realized it had made a mistake in ordering Italian and German aliens to move out of restricted areas and rescinded the order. Most of the fishermen got their boats back and resumed their prewar lives, although as Stephen Fox has commented, it was not without some bitterness. As noted earlier, Italians were removed from the enemy alien category in October 1945, but some restrictions remained on Germans living on the West Coast until the end of the war, including requirement of a permit to travel.

Although there was some espionage on the West Coast, German espionage had made considerably more progress in the eastern part of the country well before America entered the war. In the summer of 1941, the FBI arrested members of a German espionage ring that it had been observing for some time; 33 members of the ring were convicted and sentenced to prison. In March 1942, members of another German spy ring were arrested and sentenced to prison, bringing an end to large-scale, organized German espionage in the United States.

But that did not end Germany's attempt to set up spies in the United States. On June 13, 1942, a German submarine landed four saboteurs on Long Island. After burying their gear in the sand, they had the misfortune to encounter a Coast Guardsman whom they paid for his promise to keep quiet about seeing them. The Coast Guardsman quickly reported to his superior, who informed the FBI. The leader of the group, George Dasch, had once lived in the United States for 15 years and had married an American woman before returning to Germany in 1939. As originally planned, he and Peter Burger, one of the other spies, traveled to Washington and checked into a hotel. After settling into the hotel, he reassessed the situation and, reflecting on the mistreatment he had suffered in Germany, decided to contact the FBI voluntarily (not knowing the agency already knew of the mission) and become a hero. Burger, who had been mistreated by the Gestapo, agreed to the plan. Dasch revealed to the FBI that another team of four spies had been landed from a submarine off the coast of Florida. The FBI arrested all eight, and they were tried, found guilty and sentenced to death. Because Dasch and Burger had testified for the government, President Roosevelt commuted their sentences to 30 years' imprisonment, and President Truman pardoned both in 1948 and ordered them deported to Germany.

But the greatest danger to U.S. military secrets was due not to espionage but to carelessness and lack of secrecy among ordinary Americans. For that reason, a great deal of effort was devoted to ensuring secrecy regarding military and war production activities. Almost all military installations were off limits to civilians, except those with official business. Access to most manufacturing plants serving the war industry was limited. The most complete security surrounded the Manhattan Project. The army was able to operate the Los Alamos Laboratory and the facilities at Oak Ridge, Tennessee, and other sites without revealing the purpose of research conducted there, although it was learned after the war that at least one scientist and one technician, and possibly others, were reporting progress on the development of the atomic bomb to the Soviet Union. Merchant ships and tankers did not reveal their sailing times, their destinations or routes, and sailors were constantly cautioned not to reveal such information. Bars near ports posted signs: "Loose Lips Sink Ships." Soldiers and sailors were rarely told their destination when going overseas until they were at sea. All mail from combat zones was read by military censors, and any portion that might provide useful information to the enemy was cut out.

Soldiers and sailors were also cautioned about revealing troop strength, equipment they were using, or information about the military capacity of their units. Much of it was probably excessive caution, but the military services took the position that it was better to be overly cautious than to take a chance on vital information leaking to the enemy.

The Smith Act directed the government to prohibit certain subversive activities but was vague. The army and the FBI were charged with monitoring war production plants for evidence of subversive activity, and there were many cases in which the army was convinced that workers in those plants, particularly including some labor leaders, were fomenting labor unrest in order to slow down production. Prior to the German invasion of Russia, much of the problem was caused by Communists who loudly opposed America's entry into the war, charged that war production was evidence that America was a warmonger, and led walkouts and slowdowns rather than sabotage. In 1941 the War Department identified 550 cases of suspected sabotage in defense plants, but it took the position that in peacetime it had to be careful not to violate workers' civil liberties, and no action was taken. After Germany invaded Russia, Communist leaders in the labor movement stopped hampering production and, in fact, became dedicated to maximum production, especially after the Soviet Union was included in the Lend-Lease program.

After war was declared, the FBI and War Department stepped up the screening of suspected sabotage in war plants, and by April 1942 the army had established a plan for screening workers suspected of subversion. In early 1943, the system was improved to provide greater protection of civil rights, including provisions for a hearing and an appeal process. Thereafter, more than 100 were dismissed from war plant employment for sabotage almost every month. Altogether during the war years some 2,400 were dismissed; almost all of them appealed, and 458 were reinstated in their jobs.

Japanese Evacuation

Immediately following the attack on Pearl Harbor there was little concern about persons of Japanese lineage living in the United States, but in time many Americans became fearful that among them were individuals who were spying for Japan, reporting on military preparedness and the location and condition of military installations, or who were potential spies or would commit acts of sabotage.

Most of the Japanese-Americans in the United States lived on the West Coast, more than three-fourths of them in California. As an ethnic group they had not integrated into American society; they remained to themselves, and few Caucasians knew them well. Few if any had intermarried with Caucasians (California law forbade intermarriage), and few had joined clubs and other organizations that were not composed entirely of persons of Japanese ancestry. They said their preference not to associate with people other than Japanese was due to racism among Caucasians. Japanese in California were openly discriminated against in employment, admission to social organizations, and access to public services. Many restaurants and other establishments posted signs saying "No Japs." Generally, no distinction was made between Japanese aliens and persons of Japanese ancestry who were American citizens. Persons of Japanese lineage consisted of Issei, the Japanese immigrants who were not eligible for citizenship; Nisei, their sons and daughters born in America; and Sansei, the third generation. The Nisei and Sansei were U.S. citizens by birth.

Rumors of spying grew, and gradually there developed a sense among a growing number of people that the "Japs" were a security risk. With increasing debate about the matter in the press, discrimination and harassment spread, including damage to their businesses and more overt mistreatment of them personally. Issei who were employed on the railroads and in other industries that might be subject to sabotage were dismissed from their jobs as a precautionary measure.

A campaign to remove the Japanese-Americans from war sensitive areas on the West Coast was heard not only in California but from throughout the country. A radio commentator in Los Angeles propounded that 90 percent of the Japanese in California were loyal to Japan. Henry McLemore, a nationally syndicated newspaper columnist, was virulently anti–Japanese, and agitated for their internment. So did Westbrook Pegler, arguably the most caustic syndicated newspaper columnist of the twentieth century (in his column he always referred to the president's wife as *la boca grande*), and indeed there were leading opinion makers of many different political stripes who supported evacuation. Several commentators of the time believed that a series of three columns by Walter Lippmann that appeared in several hundred newspapers triggered the decision to seek their evacuation. Lippmann, a liberal and the most respected columnist of the day, argued in his nationally syndicated column on February 5, 12, and 14, 1942, that the security of the country had to overrule the rights of the Japanese on the West Coast and that they should be interned. On February 12 he wrote: "The Pacific Coast is officially a combat zone; some part of it may at any moment be a battlefield.... Nobody's constitutional rights include the right to reside and do business on a battlefield." He was supported by some of the leading spokesmen for the political left, including the noted writer Dwight McDonald, Congressman Vito Marcantonio, and the American Communist Party.

Even the ACLU agreed that the people of Japanese ancestry should be moved from sensitive zones on the West Coast to other parts of the country, although it did not approve of interning them. Earl Warren, then attorney general of California and later chief justice of the U.S. Supreme Court, testified to a congressional committee that he feared the Japanese in California would bide their time until Japan invaded the West Coast and at that time become active spies. He thought the Nisei were a greater threat to national security than their parents, because of their youth, and argued that internment was necessary to ensure the safety of military and industrial installations. The *Los Angeles Times* editorialized repeatedly for internment of all Japanese in California.

The matter was debated heatedly in the administration. Attorney General Francis Biddle, with the support of FBI Director J. Edgar Hoover, argued that the Japanese-Americans could not be interned without due process, especially in the case of the Nisei and Sansei, who were American citizens, and Republican Robert Taft protested the action on the floor of the Senate, but Secretary of War Stimson argued strongly that the security of the country should take precedence over the rights of the Japanese-Americans. On February 19, 1942, President Roosevelt signed the aforementioned Executive Order 9066 authorizing the Secretary of War and military commanders whom he might designate to prescribe military areas from which "any and all persons may be excluded." The commander of the Western Defense Command, to whom the secretary delegated the task, identified all of California, Oregon, and Washington extending about 200 miles inland plus a portion of Arizona. While the exclusion order did not specify any race or ethnic group, and initially many thought it was intended to include persons of Italian and German ancestry, it was well understood that it referred primarily to persons of Japanese ancestry.

The first step was to encourage residents of Japanese ancestry living in those areas to leave voluntarily. On March 2 the commanding general of the West Coast announced that all persons of Japanese lineage should leave voluntarily from the western half of the 200-mile strip, and some 5,000 moved inland. But, as anthropologist Edward H. Spicer explains, the response from some of the communities to which they moved, not only from Caucasians but from Japanese-Americans as well, was such as to lead the commanding general to halt voluntary departures. For example, greater Denver had about 800 residents of Japanese ancestry before Pearl Harbor, but when another 800 moved there between Pearl Harbor and the evacuation, local Japanese-Americans resented their arrival lest it upset good relations with local Caucasians.

One of the major barriers to voluntary relocation was opposition from governors in the mountain states who did not want persons of Japanese ancestry coming through their states for fear they would stop there. Another major barrier was cultural: Many Issei did not know anyone outside California and were not yet sufficiently integrated culturally to know how to proceed to move to the Midwest or where to go.

On March 18, 1942, President Roosevelt signed Executive Order No. 9102 establishing the War Relocation Authority and defining its task. The War Department soon announced that it would move West Coast Japanese to relocation centers. By the end of May all but a few thousand of the 112,000 who were to be evacuated had been assembled in fairgrounds, racetracks, and athletic stadiums (thirteen in California and three in Oregon and Washington) until they could be sent to relocation centers. Ten centers were eventually established: Manzanar and Tule Lake in California, Poston and Gila in Arizona, Rohwer and Jerome in Arkansas, Minidoka in Idaho, Topaz in Utah, Granada in Colorado, and Heart Mountain in Wyoming. The largest was located at Tule Lake; later, most of the evacuees there were moved to other centers and Tule Lake served as the center for those who refused to swear allegiance to the United States.

Many of the Japanese-Americans sold their farms and businesses at a fraction of their market value. For many, ownership of land was nominal. The Issei held their farms in the names of their children who were citizens, with themselves designated as guardians, in order to circumvent the California Alien Land Act of 1913 which forbade ownership of land by persons ineligible for citizenship. Japanese and other Asian immigrants had been ineligible for citizenship since 1790 when Congress enacted legislation limiting naturalization to "free whites," a law which was tested in the courts and ruled constitutional by the U.S. Supreme Court in 1922. (Exceptions were made to the law several times, and it was repealed in 1952.) As noted earlier, after Congress passed the Immigration Act of 1924, which prohibited the immigration of aliens ineligible for citizenship, Japanese immigration ended, with the exception that it was legal to visit the United States for up to two years.

A few were unable to sell their property before being evacuated, and it was sold later for taxes, sometimes at a total loss. Some placed their property in the hands of surrogates, a few of whom cheated the owners or misused their authority. Not everyone agreed with the evacuation, but most people who disagreed remained quiet lest they be tagged Communist, fascist, or fifth columnist.

The relocation centers were like Army camps, with temporary Army type barracks, 20 by 100 feet, covered with tar paper and partitioned into apartments, usually housing 20 persons. Food was served in large—40 by 100 feet—mess halls. The camps included recreation halls, hospitals, schools, welfare counseling and evacuee-owned shops. The centers were surrounded by wire fences guarded by soldiers. While life in the camps was not punitive—indeed, by some evacuee accounts the administration of the camps could be benevolent—it was by its very existence repressive. The evacuees resented the lack of privacy; the women were especially offended by the community toilets. The food furnished by the army was not what the evacuees were accustomed to. For some of the poorest, life in the camps was no worse than conditions to which they were accustomed, but the fact of internment was in itself demeaning.

The evacuees, as they were usually called at that time, established self-governing councils, generally with limited direction from camp authorities. They performed all of the work required to operate the camps, except guard duty. The men were allowed to accept outside employment as farm workers, and were much in demand. Because of the farm labor shortage that developed during the war, their labor in food production was an important contribution to the war effort. "Seasonal leave" to work was common; in fact, when offered the opportunity to leave the camps, some preferred not to do so since their families were cared for at the camps while they were away engaged in farm work.

Many of the evacuees were experienced in vegetable growing and grew large quantities of vegetables in the camp areas. At Heart Mountain the evacuees grew more than 2,700 areas of vegetables in 1943 and 1944. The standard pay for evacuees who worked in the camps was $16 a month, with an additional $3 for physicians, block managers, farm foremen, mess chiefs, and others in critical jobs. Those who worked outside the camps were paid the going wage.

When the draft began in 1940, Nisei were inducted into the army like everyone else, but in the spring of 1942 the Selective Service refused enlistment of the Nisei; of those already in the military service, some were released and others were assigned to non-sensitive positions. In January 1943, the army was persuaded to accept enlistment of Nisei, and many young men in relocation centers volunteered, most of them going to the 442nd Regimental Combat Team (all Japanese) which fought in Italy and France and became the most decorated unit in the American army. Dillon S. Myer has pointed out that 9,000 Nisei served in the 442nd, which suffered 9,480 casualties, including 600 killed. In addition to 9,500 purple hearts (many in the 442nd received two or three each), combat decorations included one Medal of Honor, 52 Distinguished Service Crosses, 360 Silver Stars with 28 Oak Leaf Clusters, 4,000 Bronze Stars with 1,200 Oak Leaf Clusters, 22 Legions of Merit, plus several awards by the French and Italian governments, and the Presidential Distinguished Unit Citation, presented by President Harry S Truman. (The Oak Leaf Cluster was awarded in lieu of a duplicate second medal; for example, a soldier who won the bronze star twice would receive an Oak Leaf Cluster the second time which would be mounted on his first ribbon.) A few ended up in the 100th Infantry Battalion, an all–Nisei unit from Hawaii which later became a part of the 442nd. A number were recruited by universities that were offering Japanese language training for the army and the navy, and some became interpreters for various elements of the army and navy, including service in the Pacific and Burma. Altogether some 21,000 Nisei served in World War II.

In January 1944, the army reconsidered and began to draft the Nisei again. In June 1944, 63 Nisei who were interned at the Heart Mountain Relocation Center in Wyoming were tried, convicted and given three-year sentences in federal prison for refusing military service. Most had refused military service on the grounds that their First Amendment rights had been denied, but they did not represent the majority view for at the time they were convicted, 384 former evacuees from Heart Mountain were serving in uniform.

One of the objectives of the War Relocation Authority (WRA) was to help relocate evacuees to jobs outside the West Coast. In fact, the WRA staff initially considered the camps as primarily way stations until the evacuees could be relocated to other parts of the country, and to that end the agency set up relocation offices in Cleveland, Chicago, Des Moines, Denver, Salt Lake City, New Orleans, Spokane, Minneapolis, New York City, Boston, Kansas City and various other places—42 cities altogether. By the end of 1942 some, mostly Nisei, were finding jobs, primarily in the mountain states, but significant numbers settled in the Midwest and the East—Cleveland, New York and especially Chicago. In fact, requests from employers in the Chicago area in 1943 for evacuees to meet the manpower shortage exceeded the number willing to relocate. About 2,000 evacuees accepted jobs with Seabrook Farms in New Jersey. In most cities, churches set up hostels, providing temporary lodging, assistance in securing employment, and a sense of security.

By the end of 1943, about 30,000 had relocated to jobs all over the country, except the West Coast, and almost 18,000 more did so in 1944, but many, especially older Issei, were reluctant to leave for fear they would encounter discrimination and harassment, a likely prospect. Some of those who accepted jobs in the mountain states encountered insults and humiliation, but those who moved to Chicago, the Midwest, and the East Coast reported few unpleasant incidents.

In July 1943, the WRA decided to segregate all of the evacuees suspected of disloyalty in one camp and chose Tule Lake. In September, individuals who indicated that they wanted to go to Japan after the war—about 8 percent of those at Heart Mountain, for example, and those of like mind at other centers—were sent to the Tule Lake Center. The center also included troublemakers transferred from other camps, as well as those considered disloyal.

In late 1943, the administration of the relocation program distributed forms to all evacuees with two critical questions: first, would they swear loyalty to the government of the United States, and second, would they foreswear allegiance to the emperor of Japan? Most were willing to answer positively to the first question, but many refused to answer the second. If they said no, they were refuting their positive answer to the first question. Most of the Issei found it impossible to denounce Japan. And in addition to the emotional feelings they held for Japan, there was a very practical problem. Since the Issei did not hold American citizenship, they feared that if they swore allegiance to the United States and denounced the emperor, Japan might cancel their citizenship and leave them without a country. Four days later, the government recognized the dilemma and withdrew the second question, but the damage was done. It had exacerbated the Issei's bitterness and further alienated them from the U.S. government.

In addition to those transferred to Tule Lake because they refused to sign the loyalty oath, there were some who went there to avoid the draft, which had been reinstituted for the Nisei by that time, justifying their position on the basis that because of the government's treatment of persons of Japanese ancestry they did not owe military service to the United States. The transfer of several thousand evacuees from the other nine camps to Tule Lake and the movement of a like number from Tule to the other camps was upsetting to the evacuees and resulted in a great deal of resentment. About 6,000 evacuees who had been at Tule Lake before the exchange began objected to moving and were allowed to remain there.

The Reverend Daisuke Kitagawa, a Protestant minister at Tule Lake, though not a dissident himself, reported that whenever radio news announced a Japanese victory in the Pacific there was high jubilation in the camp among the Issei and some Nisei, particularly the Kibei. The Kibei, who were born in the United States, had been sent to Japan for elementary and secondary education and like all children in Japanese schools had received military training and indoctrination and were militantly pro-Japan. Of the total of 112,000 interned, about 72,000 were Nisei and Sansei, of whom 9,000 were Kibei, a large enough number to create considerable trouble in some of the camps. In fact, the National Student Relocation Council, which was formed to assist Japanese-American college students who had been removed from the West Coast to enter colleges elsewhere in the country, refused to intervene for Kibei.

The pro-Japan group demanded that those at Tule Lake who were loyal to the United States be sent to other camps or segregated, and the WRA did so, in part to ensure their safety. Even so, gangs of young men at Tule Lake began to physically abuse evacuees whom they suspected of informing or who did not show proper fealty to Japan. The disorder created by those loyal to Japan forced the WRA to call in the army in late 1943 to operate Tule Lake under martial law for a couple of months, further inciting the evacuees to militant behavior.

The evacuees at Tule Lake formed two organizations, the "Organization to Return Immediately to the Homeland to Serve," which was composed largely of Issei, and the "Young Men's Organization to Serve Our Mother Country," which consisted of Nisei. Historian John Culley writes the following of them: "They practiced nationalistic activities with military overtones, including marching and drilling, bugle calls, playing the Japanese national anthem, celebrating the eighth of each month in commemoration of the attack on Pearl Harbor, wearing short military-style haircuts, and wearing rising-sun emblems on their coats and shirts. They were also implicated in acts of intimidation, coercion, and physical violence against their opponents."

In December 1944, 5,589 at Tule Lake renounced their U.S. citizenship, and their militancy and violence grew. Finally, in early 1945 several hundred of the most militant were transferred to Santa Fe, New Mexico, where the Immigration and Naturalization Service (INS) of the Justice Department maintained a detention center. It had been established early in the war to detain Issei and others suspected of disloyalty; most of the Issei, after a hearing, had been released or allowed to join their families in relocation centers. But it was essentially a prison, in contrast to the WRA relocation centers. The Kibei continued to be troublemakers at Santa Fe, and after the war some 1,300 of them chose to be repatriated to Japan. There were several other INS detention centers in addition to the one in Santa Fe: for example, Seagoville and Crystal City, Texas, where families were allowed to live together; Ft. Sill, Oklahoma; Camp Livingston, Louisiana; Lordsburg, New Mexico; and Bismarck, North Dakota.

Pro-Japan sentiment among evacuees was not confined to Tule Lake and the Kibei. At some of the camps, Greater East Asia Co-Prosperity clubs were founded; since that was the slogan of Japan's attempt at hegemony in the Far East, the implication was clear. However, the pro–Japan groups encountered opposition. In all of the camps there were Nisei who, in spite of the treatment they had received, remained militantly pro–American and often engaged in gang fights with Kibei and other pro–Japan gangs.

Until the end of the war, many Issei continued to believe that Japan would be victorious, based in part on shortwave newscasts from Japan, plus rumors and hope. American newscasts of victories in the Philippines, Guam, Okinawa, and Iwo Jima were discounted as propaganda.

The order excluding persons of Japanese ancestry from the West Coast was lifted in December 1944, freeing evacuees to leave, and in April 1945 they were told that all camps would be closed within one year. In fact, all closed by the end of November 1945, except Tule Lake, which closed in late March 1946. Initially many of the evacuees did not want to leave their camps. Some feared discrimination in the communities where they had lived; others felt the government had an obligation to continue the camps as long as the evacuees chose to remain, that by having been interned involuntarily the evacuees were owed that consideration. To some, the camps had become homes of sorts, or as one young woman put it, the camp had become "a town, and you can't close a town." By the late summer and fall of 1945, however, they were leaving in large numbers.

The exact number repatriated or expatriated to Japan during and immediately following the war is not known, although it is estimated to be about 8,000. The WRA reported that 4,727 who had been in relocation camps were sent to Japan, almost all of them by choice. Most of those sent from Tule Lake to detention camps of the Immigration and Naturalization Service were presumed to have been deported or chose to go to Japan. Earlier, several hundred had been repatriated in an exchange of diplomats, businessmen, tourists and other civilians including, for example, more than 1,000 American civilian construction workers captured by the Japanese at Wake and other Pacific islands; in the exchange, about 1,200 Japanese from Latin America who had been interned at Crystal City, Texas, were sent to Japan. The number repatriated or expatriated would have been much larger, except that most of those who earlier had renounced their American citizenship at Tule Lake and expressed a desire to go to Japan after the war reconsidered and remained in the United States.

By most accounts, the management of the relocation camps was about as humane and considerate as could be expected, given the circumstances. Milton Eisenhower, the first director of the WRA, resigned after three months to become deputy director of the Office of War Information. He was succeeded by Dillon S. Myer, a longtime government official, who served as director until the program ended almost four years later. Myer, much to the displeasure of racists in California and Congress, opposed punitive action toward the evacuees. He wrote in March 1943 that the relocation centers "are undesirable institutions and should be removed from the American scene as soon as possible. Life in a relocation center is an unnatural and un-American sort of life. Keep in mind that the evacuees were charged with nothing except having Japanese ancestors. . . ." And in 1971 in his book *Uprooted Americans* he wrote, "As director of WRA, I believed, and still believe, that selective evacuation of persons of Japanese descent from the West Coast military area may have been justified and feasible in early 1943, but I do not believe that a mass evacuation was ever justified; furthermore I believe that there was no valid argument for the continuation of the exclusion orders beyond the spring of 1943, as indicated in our letter to Secretary [of War] Stimson in March 1943."

After the war, the Japanese American Citizens League, almost all of whom had lived in the relocation centers for some period of time, presented a citation to Myer which read in part, "Who so capably and ably administered the War Relocation Authority under the most difficult of circumstances and against the most vicious opposition in a manner which commended him to the American people and to the evacuee population at large, this testimonial scroll is gratefully presented by the Japanese-American Citizens League and their friends at this banquet in his honor at the Roosevelt Hotel, New York City, May 22, 1946."

Redress

Shortly after the war ended, Congress appropriated $38 million to compensate the evacuees for losses incurred in sales of property when they were evacuated, which the evacuees said repaid them only a fraction of their actual losses. For several decades, evacuees and their supporters lobbied for Congress to pay each person evacuated $25,000.

In the early 1980s a special commission was appointed by Congress to review the internment. It concluded that military necessity did not justify the evacuation and internment and made several recommendations which were enacted into law in 1988. Most Americans agreed with the recommendations. While it has been charged that all members of the commission were on record condemning the evacuation prior to being named to the commission, it is unlikely that an unbiased commission would have reached a substantially different conclusion. The two key elements of the 1988 law were that the United States government formally apologized for the internment of the Japanese-Americans, and that each internee was to be paid $20,000.

Reasons for Internment

Why were persons of Japanese ancestry evacuated from the West Coast and moved to relocation centers? Few would deny that it is a permanent blight on the American conscience. Viewed a half century later, it is difficult to understand, particularly for those who were not adults in the United States at the time.

Milton Eisenhower, brother of General (later President) Dwight D. Eisenhower and himself later president of Kansas State University, Johns Hopkins University and Pennsylvania State University, in resigning three months after the program began, said that the moral aspect of the program caused him sleepless nights. He said at the time that he feared the American people would live to regret the internment of the persons of Japanese ancestry in relocation camps.

Most Americans would agree that no ethnic group in the United States has surpassed the Japanese as model Americans. Their parents brought with them from Japan values most admired among Americans—literacy, education, industry, thrift, self-discipline, and a desire for self-improvement. These values have characterized Japanese-Americans in the post–World War II era. They are law abiding, among the least likely of ethnic groups to engage in crime. As a demographic group, their educational level is high, and they are major contributors to the American economy. If they chose not to integrate into the Caucasian culture before the war, they have become typical Americans in that respect since

1945. Japanese-American children are among the highest achievers and best behaved in school and among the lowest in juvenile delinquency, further reflection of values inherent in their culture.

While it is perhaps impossible to justify the internment policy, it can be understood in the context of the time. It is important to remember the national hysteria in the weeks following the attack on Pearl Harbor. As noted already, many people were persuaded that Japan's military forces would invade the West Coast, which influenced their views regarding the Japanese in this country.

Further, since the Issei generally did not speak English and did not mix with non–Japanese, they were suspect. In any country, an ethnic group that does not mix with other members of the society becomes suspect to the dominant society, especially in times of crisis. Many have attributed the internment of the Japanese-Americans solely to racism, since mass internment of first and second generation Germans and Italians did not occur.

To be sure, racism was virulent in the tabloid press, among many politicians, and among many Westerners, but it is too simple to say that it was all due to prejudice, for a great many people who had suffered from bigotry themselves thought internment was necessary, as did a large number of prominent civil libertarians. The matter reached the U.S. Supreme Court in late 1944, and on December 18 its ruling supported the government's action. Justice Hugo Black, a leading voice of civil liberties on the court, wrote the opinion and Justice William O. Douglas, another prominent civil libertarian, avoided the question of constitutionality.

Why did so many people whom one would not accuse of bigotry have approved of the internment of the West Coast Japanese? When the Japanese army invaded Manchuria in early 1931, many Issei were open about their pro–Japan sentiments and sent money to Japan and kits to Japanese soldiers. Their war relief to Japan continued for several years, notwithstanding American condemnation of the Japanese invasion of Manchuria and later China proper, and President Roosevelt's strong statements against it. The organization through which relief was sent was initially called the Military Virtue Society, but because of the warlike sound of the name, it was later changed to the Cherry Blossom Society. The attitudes of West Coast Japanese toward Japan's invasion of China caused even liberals and some friends of the Japanese to criticize them for what was perceived as disloyalty, and their actions and attitudes influenced the thinking of many Americans.

In the roundup of German, Italian, and Japanese aliens suspected of disloyalty in the days immediately following the Pearl Harbor attack, the first Japanese to be picked up by the FBI were those who had supported Japan when it invaded China. Alfonso Zirpoli, then an assistant U.S.

attorney in the Bay Area of California who conducted hearings of Germans, Italians, and Japanese who had been rounded up, stated in an interview with Stephen Fox that one of the questions he asked all of them was, "Who do you want to win the war?" Of all the Japanese questioned, none said "the United States." They answered "Japan" or "neither." To the same question, all of the Germans and Italians answered "the United States." Zirpoli said that the Japanese understood the implications of their answer, but explained, "You have to understand that I was born in Japan."

The Japanese Association, with chapters throughout the West Coast and Hawaii, functioned much as what we would today call a support system. It was in response to the anti-Japanese treatment they encountered, but more a result of the assumption that they would encounter discrimination in Caucasian society. The interpretation among Caucasians was that the Japanese did not want to integrate into American society, and that their loyalty remained with Japan. But the desire for self-isolation was confined largely to the Issei and Kibei. The Nisei did not agree and in 1928 founded the Japanese American Citizens League (JACL), whose purpose was to counter the image of the Japanese reflected by the Issei, and especially to establish the fact that JACL members were loyal Americans. This caused serious rifts between the Nisei and their parents, who were not allowed to become members of the JACL. By the time of Pearl Harbor the JACL had 20,000 members, but the image projected by the Cherry Blossom Society and the Japanese Association was prominent in the minds of Americans, particularly on the West Coast where almost all of those of Japanese ancestry lived. After Pearl Harbor the Japanese Association offices closed, but the "all Japanese together" sentiment that had united the Japanese remained, fortified by the growing anti-Japanese attitudes of the majority population.

One explanation for the responses of the Issei was provided by the Reverend Daisuke Kitagawa, the aforementioned Protestant minister, who was himself an Issei, in his book *Issei and Nisei: The Internment Years*, Rev. Kitagawa explained that to the Issei, regardless of where they lived, they were never divorced from their roots: "To be a Japanese is to be loyal to Japan, and not to be loyal to Japan means one has never been a Japanese." The fact that they lived in America or any other country did not sever their ties to their native land, nor terminate their feelings for Japan. Kitagawa emphasized that a non-Japanese could not understand the deep reverence an Issei held for the emperor of Japan, that it could not be explained in terms familiar to others. Perhaps not, but intellectuals such as Walter Lippmann were aware of the Issei's devotion to the emperor which led them to wonder whether, in case of an invasion, the Issei, perhaps Nisei, and especially the Kibei, could *all* be depended on to be loyal to the United States. Might not some feel obligated to respond to a request from the emperor for information or even sabotage?

The loyalty and devotion of the Issei to the emperor and to Japan was manifested in several ways in the WRA camps. For example, when army and navy representatives went to the WRA camps to recruit Japanese linguists to become translators or teachers in language schools, many of the Nisei responded favorably. It gave them the opportunity to demonstrate their loyalty to the United States and to do something useful in the war. But the Issei were enraged, first at the recruiters for their audacity, then at their sons, whom they attempted to persuade not to accept the invitation. It led to serious intrafamily tensions. The Issei could not understand how their sons would willingly take a step that might lead them into combat against Japan.

The foregoing may account for the attitudes of some of the general population, but what convinced President Roosevelt to sign the executive order for internment? John J. McCloy, wartime assistant secretary of war, who was assigned the task of supervising the establishment of the relocation program, said in a letter to Jane B. Kaihatsu in 1984 that through MAGIC, the codebreaking machine that made it possible to intercept and read diplomatic messages from Japan, the American government had learned of plans by the government of Japan to use West Coast Japanese to sabotage defense plants. Further, McCloy added, "The President had ample and, indeed, striking evidence of the existence of subversive Japanese and Japanese/American agencies on the West Coast, poised to frustrate any defense against Japanese acts of aggression." Forty years later McCloy said he was still convinced that the internment program should be credited for the lack of serious acts of sabotage on the West Coast.

In his study of the internment, Professor Eric Sundquist, University of California-Berkeley, concluded that there is no question that prior to the Pearl Harbor attack the Japanese were engaged in espionage on the West Coast. Through its MAGIC machine, ONI had learned that significant Japanese spying was occurring in defense plants in Seattle, Portland and several California cities, including the use of Nisei who worked in aircraft plants to provide information. A State Department report completed in November 1941 concluded that in case of war with Japan few Japanese in the United States were likely to be disloyal but that a small number of Kibei might very well engage in sabotage of "dams, railroads and power stations."

As it turned out, the army of Japan did not invade the West Coast, and the hysteria was based on unjustified fear, but invasion seemed not only possible but likely at the time. Had the Japanese army invaded the West Coast, how would the Issei and Nisei, and especially the Kibei, have responded? No amount of speculation can answer that question satisfactorily.

A half century later, most Americans believed that the mass evacuation and internment of the Japanese-Americans was not justified. The obvious question remains: If it was true that the FBI, with the assistance of navy and army intelligence, had developed a file on every person of Japanese ancestry in the United States suspected of possible disloyalty, why was it necessary to intern those not suspected of potential disloyalty? On the other hand, some Americans who were adults during World War II continue to argue that based on the situation at the time, they believe internment was a prudent and justifiable action.

Internment and Relocation Beyond the U.S. West Coast

The 1940 U.S. census found 157,905 persons of Japanese ancestry living in the Hawaiian islands, at least two-thirds of whom were native born. Some 10,000 were investigated, and 1,441 were apprehended, of whom 980 were interned in Hawaii throughout the war, along with about 50 Germans and Italians, because of questionable loyalty, but there was no general roundup as on the West Coast, possibly because their labor was needed. There is some indication, however, that the army, specifically Chief of Staff Marshall, thought their incarceration was unnecessary. They were kept under surveillance throughout the war and their travel was regulated, but otherwise they were left alone. About 1,000 moved to the mainland and voluntarily chose internment in order to be with relatives. Nor were Japanese living elsewhere in the country subjected to internment, although many of them suffered harassment. Some Japanese-owned businesses were not only boycotted but were damaged or destroyed by vandalism or arson.

Evacuation of persons of Japanese ancestry was not limited to the United States. Canada also relocated its Japanese from its west coast, although it did not intern them. After the war the Canadian government undertook to deport its Japanese, including Canadian citizens, to Japan, of which about 4,000, or approximately 25 percent of the total, were deported before the program was halted. In 1988, shortly after the American Congress voted redress, the Canadian government took similar actions, with payments of $21,000 Canadian to each of its evacuees.

The Japanese in Mexico were required to move to either Mexico City or Guadalajara, and in all Latin American countries that touched the Pacific Ocean the Japanese were moved. Approximately 1,800 of the Japanese population in Peru were moved to the United States where they were interned; in 1942 almost 500 were sent to Japan in exchange for American civilians interned by the Japanese, and another 750, whom

Peru refused to permit to re-enter, were sent to Japan after the war. Most of the Japanese exchanged during the war were transported on the Swedish ship *Gripsholm* to the then Portuguese East Africa colony of Mozambique where it met Japanese ships bringing Americans from Japan and Shanghai. Cuba interned all adult Japanese males in Havana. Brazil, with the largest Japanese population in Latin America, was the only country in the Western Hemisphere that took no action toward its Japanese, probably because Brazil does not touch the Pacific Ocean.

The British also interned non-citizens from countries with which it was at war. Following the declaration of war on September 3, 1939, Britain took a lenient view toward enemy aliens living in the United Kingdom, interning only 439 for suspicion of disloyalty by March 1940. But after the invasion of the low countries and France in May 1940, Britain rounded up Germans, Austrians, and Italians living in Britain and interned them on the Isle of Man. The British made no distinction between German Jews and other Germans; as a consequence, many of those interned were Jews, some of whom had escaped from Nazi concentration camps. In July 1940 the British government established tribunals to hear each case, and most were released. As of November 1941, only 2,411 of 19,127 Italians and 6,152 of 73,353 Germans and Austrians were still interned.

Chapter IV

Military Mobilization

Although the United States was definitely underprepared for war in December 1941, it was not altogether unprepared. Military and industrial preparation had been accelerating steadily since the fall of 1939, and indeed some buildup in military preparedness had begun earlier after reaching an alltime low. As a practical matter, President Roosevelt's declaration of a limited national emergency on September 8, 1939, following Germany's attack on Poland and the declaration of war on Germany by Great Britain and France, signaled the beginning of America's preparation for that which most people hoped would never occur—American involvement in another war.

Congress had increased military appropriations, and major improvements had been made in the defense posture of the country, though it was still far from adequate. Significant industrial defense production was under way, and the nation could boast a civilian defense program that, if not yet entirely sufficient, had made vast strides from its inception. It is important to remember that in 1939 defense expenditures were less than 1.5 percent of gross national product.

The citizenry as a whole, or at least those who read newspapers and listened to radio, had become much better informed about the world situation and the possibilities of war. National opinion polls showed that while Americans still hoped fervently to avoid getting into war, they were realistic and a growing majority thought war was inevitable. American journalists, official observers, and tourists returning from Germany in the mid-1930s began to report on that country's military expansion and Hitler's belligerence. Although few would have predicted events that ensued, Congress became increasingly aware of the puny state of the American defense posture and some members of Congress pushed diligently for improving it. To be sure, the isolationist sentiment was strong, especially in the Senate, but Congress did begin to make modest improvements.

Army

In May 1940, when the Germans invaded Belgium, the Netherlands, and France, the American Army was nineteenth in size in the world. In the interwar years, the American military establishment had declined to historically low levels, first because of the negative popular reaction to America's involvement in World War I and the antiwar sentiment following that war, and later because of the Great Depression.

The National Defense Act of 1920 had authorized an army of 280,000 men, but funding for the army during the interwar years never approached that figure. For most of the interwar years, the army was funded for approximately 125,000 enlisted personnel and 12,000 commissioned officers; by June 30, 1932, the actual enlisted strength had dropped to 119,913 on active duty, including about 6,000 Philippine Scouts, making it smaller than the armies of many Third World countries today. In 1933, the monthly pay of a private in the army dropped from $21.00 to $17.85, compared to $30 a month paid members of the Civilian Conservation Corps.

In 1937, Congress authorized expansion of the army to 158,000 enlisted personnel. Its strength had grown to 188,565 (174,079 enlisted men and 14,486 officers) by July 1, 1939, when an increase to 210,000 was authorized. On September 8, 1939, when President Roosevelt declared a limited national emergency, he authorized an increase in army enlisted personnel to 227,000. The German invasion of Poland and the declaration of war on Germany by Great Britain and France led the American government to become more serious about building its defense forces, but the American army's active duty strength on September 1, 1939, amounted to little more than 10 percent of the 1.5 million German troops that marched on Poland that morning.

In March 1940, the War Department (changed to Department of the Army after the war) requested additional funding for expansion of personnel, facilities and equipment; Congress denied the request, but in early May 1940 the invasion of the low countries and France frightened Congress and changed its views. On May 16, President Roosevelt requested more than $1 billion to begin to build defense installations, purchase equipment and increase the Army by 28,000 personnel, of which 13,000 would be allocated to the Air Corps. The German invasion of western Europe shocked the American people, and the still generally isolationist Congress not only approved the president's request but appropriated funds to increase the army's strength to 255,000.

When on May 31 President Roosevelt again presented a request for improving the nation's defenses, Congress exceeded his recommendation and on June 26 authorized an army of 375,000. But it took time to convert authorization into reality. On June 30, 1940, the army's actual strength consisted of 267,767 enlisted men and 18,326 officers, plus the National Guard, comprising 241,612 officers and enlisted men who had not yet been called to active duty.

The administration had sent to Congress in the summer of 1940 a bill to mobilize the National Guard, but because there were not enough military camps to provide housing, President Roosevelt allocated $29.5 million from his emergency fund on August 2, 1940, for the construction of 12 army camps. Within days, Congress approved the law authorizing the president to mobilize the National Guard and the reserves, then approved the Selective Service Act, and on September 9 voted $128 million for the construction of military bases. Defense preparations were now under way seriously, but there was much progress needed to establish a viable defense against military attack. The Japanese had been well aware of the weak defense posture of the United States, which led them to believe that the United States not only could not amass sufficient military strength but lacked the will to do so. Japan saw the United States as morally weak, lacking the strength of character and courage to defend itself against a committed opponent.

During fiscal year 1940-41 the army constructed 45 military camps, half of which were on entirely new sites, including 21 replacement training centers. The mobilization of the National Guard and the reserves and the drafting of young men under the Selective Service Act had to be staged to coincide with the completion of housing and facilities. The burgeoning army so swamped military facilities that some of the draftees had to use tents and makeshift facilities during their first months in training, leading many to write to their congressmen to complain about living in mud and snow. By November 1944, the army had built housing for six million soldiers; however, all but 270,000 of them were housed in temporary buildings. In 1985 some 24,000 of the World War II "temporary" buildings were still standing.

Mobilization in the fall of 1940 moved faster than would have otherwise been possible because of the availability of army reserve officers who could be called to active duty and were utilized to staff training units, new divisions, and to fill vacancies in regular army and National Guard units. The National Guard was mobilized as complete units—battalions, regiments and divisions—although all of them had vacancies which were later filled by draftees and reserve officers. There were then over 100,000 army reserve officers available, most of them products of college Reserve Officer Training Corps programs.

Legislation passed by Congress and signed by the president on August 27, 1940, authorized the president to call the National Guard and reserves to active duty for 12 months for the purpose of training. On

September 16 the first elements of the National Guard were activated; thereafter, at intervals, National Guard units were called to active duty until the last reported on June 23, 1941. Most of the units were severely understrength when activated, but with the addition of draftees and reserve officers following mobilization, National Guard units grew toward authorized strength.

National Guard units continued to recruit after the Selective Service law was approved, with the ad: "Join the Guard and go with boys you know." And several thousand young men who could see that they would be drafted shortly joined the guard so they could be mobilized with friends. Upon mobilization, however, several thousand others were exempted from active duty and released: almost 5,000 were underage; about 4,000 were released for physical disabilities; and 51,501 in the lowest three ranks were released either before or after mobilization because they had dependents and at that time the army had no provision for supporting dependents. In October 1941, another 19,703 in the lowest ranks were released because they were over 28 years of age, although they later became subject to recall when the draft age was raised.

When fully mobilized, there were 18 National Guard divisions on active duty, plus dozens of units of less than division size such as coast artillery battalions and regiments, Air Corps observer squadrons, engineer battalions, Signal Corps companies and other units not assigned to or integral components of divisions. The number of National Guard personnel mobilized totaled 20,519 officers and 278,526 enlisted men, but by October 1941, after large numbers were allowed to resign, 19,542 officers and 213,449 enlisted men remained of those mobilized in the past year. Enlisted strength in guard units then totaled 397,272, of which about 46 percent consisted of draftees and volunteers.

The National Guard was critical to the mobilization of the army in 1940-41, although by standards of the regular army it was poorly prepared and led. One of its problems was the lack of training of its officers; only about one-third had attended a school to train for their job, such as schools for company commanders, executive officers, intelligence officers, and others that all regular army officers had attended after commissioning to prepare them for their specific duties.

The National Guard was to a considerable degree a social organization. Many of the officers owed their appointments more to social connections than to merit, and the guard, which was and is under the command of state governors, was headed in each state by an adjutant general appointed by the governor. Typically this officer was a major general in states where he headed a division; the same was true in the 1990s. Thus it is no surprise that when the National Guard was mobilized it included 21 major generals and about the same number of brigadier generals who had been appointed by governors. Lt. Gen. Leslie J. McNair said that none of the National Guard generals was qualified to perform the job for which a general was responsible, though his claim was perhaps an overstatement by the officer responsible for training a fighting army. Only one National Guard general was promoted to lieutenant general during the war—Raymond S. McLain, the commander of the mobilized 45th Division, which consisted of units from Oklahoma, New Mexico and Arizona.

In part because of the social nature of the guard, many of the officers were at least 10 years overage for their rank and the positions they held. In June 1941, 22 percent of the first lieutenants in the National Guard were over 40 years of age, 919 captains were over 45 years of age and 100 lieutenant colonels were over 55. The army was faced with a large number of officers who were unskilled for their duties or who lacked appropriate training, in addition to those who were simply overage. The army was forced to keep some of them during the growth period until younger officers arrived from officer candidate schools to replace them. Later, those over the maximum age for their rank and the most incompetent were discharged and others were posted to administrative and service duties not involving command of troops. In many cases, they were well qualified for these positions because of civilian experience. Historian John K. Mahon points out, however, that of 273 full colonels called to active duty with the National Guard during 1940-41, only 148 were still in service at the end of the war.

The army had requested authority to mobilize the National Guard in May 1940 with a view to using the summer for training while the climate permitted the use of tents, and meanwhile preparing permanent facilities. A delay in securing congressional approval of the mobilization request, along with the passage of the Selective Service Act at the end of the summer, found the army with inadequate facilities for housing the National Guard troops. Construction of the 21 replacement training centers was progressing, but most of them were not ready for occupancy until March and April of 1941 and were not ready for full capacity until June. It became necessary to delay induction of draftees and mobilization of reserve officers and National Guard units; some who expected to be called to duty in late 1940 did not receive induction orders until well into 1941.

Although the National Guard was fully mobilized by June 30, 1941, many reserve officers had not yet been called to active duty. In mid-1940, there were 104,228 members of the Officers Reserve Corps eligible for active duty, but many of them were overage for their rank, had not trained regularly, and were therefore unfit for active duty command though technically eligible. Since National Guardsmen were mobilized as units, the army could not choose which guard officers to activate but reserve officers were called as individuals. This gave the army the opportunity to be selective and avoid some of the problems experienced with National Guard officers. By July 1, 1941, only 56,700 army reserve officers had been called to active duty.

Reserve officers whose civilian employment was considered critical to the war effort were often not called to active duty immediately, and indeed some were never mobilized. For example, Senator Harry S Truman, a colonel in the reserves, volunteered for active duty, but Chief of Staff Marshall told him that his service in the U.S. Senate was more important to the nation and that, at age 56, Truman was too old. Some, like Congressman Lyndon Johnson and state district judge Joseph McCarthy, foresaw that a record of military service would be useful to their future careers in politics and volunteered for active duty, some for only a few months of service, following which they returned to their political or judicial posts.

Although many of the reserve officers had little active duty experience in the army, several thousand had served in the Civilian Conservation Corps during the 1930s. The CCC had been created by the New Deal administration in the spring of 1933 to provide work for unemployed young men—building parks, roads and bridges; planting trees; controlling soil erosion; and performing other conservation work. With only a few days' notice, the army was handed the task of building and managing the camps, a job it resisted—unsuccessfully—since it would detract from training. In the first few months, regular army officers assumed most of the responsibility; in fact, about one third of the army officers were detailed to the CCC, along with a smaller number of reserve officers. General H. H. Arnold, wartime commander of the Army Air Forces, relates how he, then a major commanding an Army Air Corps unit in California, got orders to drop everything and assign all of his officers to establishing CCC camps. For several months, Arnold worked full-time supervising 30 CCC camps. Eventually, 4,500 camps were established, though not all were in operation at one time.

By February 1934, all but about 500 of the regulars had returned to the army; reserve army officers, along with a few navy and marine officers, volunteered for active duty and took over the task of directing the CCC camps. There was no dearth of volunteers for there were many reserve officers among the vast number then unemployed. Since the CCC was not a military organization, the officers did not have the same degree of control over the men they would have had over soldiers. As a result, the officers were required to rely on leadership, persuasion, and diplomacy, skills which proved valuable later for both regular and reserve officers. General George C. Marshall, one of the regulars initially assigned to the CCC, stated after the United States entered the war that the CCC experience was of particular value in preparing officers to manage the civilian army created for the war.

Approximately 6,000 reserve officers were on duty with the CCC at any one time, initially serving 18 months though in 1937 the army limited reservists' tours to six months in order to give leadership experience to as many reserve officers as possible. In 1939, in response to growing protest from the antiwar movement against the army being used to direct the CCC, plus other political considerations, the president ended the practice of calling reserve officers to active duty to direct the CCC. The change was mostly cosmetic, for most of the officers simply removed their uniforms and remained in charge as civilians. The CCC was terminated on June 30, 1942.

When mobilization began, the military services not only lacked housing but were severely deficient in training facilities and equipment. Many draftees in training in 1940 and 1941 had to use wooden rifles due to the lack of standard rifles, and the horse artillery was still in the process of converting to motorized transport. The Army had only a small supply of the newer 105 mm. howitzers, making it necessary for artillery units to train with 37 mm. and World War I–vintage French 75 mm. guns. Much of the 37 mm. ammunition was more than 20 years old and some of it dangerous. Part of the reason for shortages was that at that time half of the war production of American industry was being shipped to Great Britain.

It is axiomatic that most armies prepare to fight the last war. There was some progress in the 1930s in preparation for tank warfare, goaded by Major George Patton, but in the spring of 1940 the army had no heavy tanks and only 144 medium and 648 light tanks on hand or on order. Much of the military leadership still thought in World War I terms. The outdated thinking of the military and Congress concerning modern warfare was demonstrated in early 1941 when Congress authorized another cavalry division, including the purchase of 20,000 horses; in only a few months the army realized that there would be little need for horse cavalry in this war. (The division—the Second Cavalry—was shipped to North Africa in late 1942, but was soon disbanded to provide troops for service units.)

When Congress authorized an army of 375,000 in June 1940, recruitment did not fill the quota immediately but was not as difficult as might have been expected, considering the antiwar sentiment in the country. It should be remembered that the antiwar sentiment and the antimilitary demonstrations occurred mostly on college campuses and involved a minority of the student population, but these were not the men who would volunteer for the army. There were millions of unemployed, uneducated young men looking for something to do. Granted, not all of them were eager to join the army, but many who had served in the Civilian Conservation Corps and were still unemployed found the army attractive, as did other unemployed men and still others who saw in the army a chance to see something of the country—many of them had never traveled outside the county where they lived. And during the 1930s the army had become a refuge for criminals. It was common practice at that time for the courts to give petty criminals the option of going to prison or joining the army, and in fact some had been charged with more serious crimes, including murder.

Later in the war, when Selective Service was failing to meet the demands of the military, men in penal institutions were allowed to join the army. They volunteered for military service by the thousands and many were inducted into the army. The army was selective in admitting those who volunteered and managed to keep the percentage of bad choices to a level considered acceptable. Wyoming historian T. A. Larson cites the head of corrections in that state who said that four out of five who left the penitentiary for the army served creditably. Approximately 3,000 prisoners and former prisoners from Illinois entered military service; of 785 sampled by psychologist J. D. Lohman after the war, 87 percent had received honorable discharges and 13 percent had received either dishonorable or other-than-honorable discharges.

In the year since laws were enacted authorizing selective service and calling the National Guard and reserves to active duty, the army had expanded rapidly. On July 1, 1941, a total of 1,460,998 officers and enlisted men were on active duty, and one year later the number had risen to 3,074,184. The following year, ending June 30, 1943, brought the total to 6,993,102, an increase of almost 4 million in one year. Another million were added in 1943-44, then the numbers remained fairly stable until the end of the war. All of these figures encompass all components of the army, including the Army Air Forces.

In 1940, when Congress authorized the activation or construction of dozens of army camps, many small, placid towns became beehives of activity. The small town of Starke, Florida, was a good example. In 1940 it had a population of 1,500; when Camp Blanding was built in 1941, Starke became the fourth largest city in Florida with a payroll of $3 million a month, labor shortages, and people living in tents. The sleepy town of Alexandria, Louisiana, whose only prewar military installation was Camp Beauregard, which served principally as a National Guard and reserve training center, was overwhelmed within just a few months following construction of three nearby army camps—Camp Livingston, Camp Claiborne, and Camp Polk—and later Esler Army Air Field.

Although there were far more servicemen converging on Washington, D.C., Chicago, Los Angeles and other major cities on weekends than on smaller towns, the large cities could handle the numbers more easily. The problems were magnified in small towns like Starke and Alexandria and others that suddenly found themselves swamped with people because of the establishment of military bases or industrial war plants.

Army Air Forces

As World War II approached, the Air Corps was so young that its commander, General H. H. Arnold, had been one of only three flying personnel in its earliest days when it was known as the Air Service. The Air Service was a part of the Signal Corps until 1926 when Congress enacted legislation establishing the Army Air Corps as a separate branch. In 1941, the Army Air Forces was created, subsuming the Air Corps. The change occurred through a change in Army regulations (AR 95-5, 20 June 1941) issued by the secretary of war, not through legislation.

On March 9, 1942, the army underwent major reorganization in which it was restructured into the Army Ground Forces, the Services of Supply (later named Army Service Forces), and the Army Air Forces. This change, which was ordered by President Roosevelt in Executive Order 9082, had the effect of making the Army Air Forces a semi-autonomous component of the army, and as a result the Air Corps remained as a component of the Army Air Forces until the National Security Act of 1947 established the Department of the Air Force.

The distinction between the Air Corps and the AAF was clarified by Air Force historian John C. Warren in *A History of the U.S. Air Force, 1907–1957:*

> In March 1944 . . . the AAF reached a personnel peak of 2,411,294. . . . Of these, eighty-two percent of the officers and seventy-seven percent of the enlisted men belonged to the Air Corps. The rest were members of the Signal Corps, the Engineers, the Quartermaster, and other arms and services with the AAF. . . . Because it had been established by law, the Air Corps remained in existence as the chief component of the AAF, and officers continued to be commissioned in the Air Corps.

After the Army Air Forces was created, almost everyone—members of Congress, other civilians, and military personnel alike—continued to call it the "Air Corps." To be sure, there were exceptions; a magazine named *Air Force* emerged, as did a movie by the same name, and individuals would occasionally refer to it in the singular. In an interview in May 1994, Herman Wolk, senior historian, Department of the Air Force, stated that throughout the war, General Arnold always referred to the AAF as the "air forces," as did some of the senior officers on his staff; however, below that level, the AAF was called the "Air Corps" in ordinary conversation. The term "air force" was used to refer to components of the AAF, such as the 8th Air Force, the 15th Air Force, and the 20th Air Force.

A measure of autonomy was granted the Air Corps in 1935 when it was reorganized and placed under single command; prior to that time, individual Air Corps units had been under the command of corps commanders who were not airmen. The Air Corps had rankled under the command of ground commanders and from time to time flirted with attempts to split off into a separate arm, equal to the army and navy. In the March 1942 reorganization, the AAF came solely under the command of General H. H. Arnold, who also served as deputy chief of staff of the army, responsible only to General Marshall. In practice, the AAF was treated almost as a separate arm—similar to the Marine Corps under the navy. General Arnold occupied an equal place at meetings of the chiefs of the army and navy, a privilege not usually accorded the heads of the Army Ground Forces and Army Service Forces.

Under the 1920 National Defense Act, when the army was authorized 280,000 personnel, the Air Service was authorized 1,516 officers and 16,000 enlisted men, including 2,500 flying cadets. Like the rest of the army, the Air Service was not funded for these numbers for almost two decades. In 1926, when the Air Service was renamed the Army Air Corps, it had 919 officers and 8,725 enlisted men, including 142 flying cadets. By 1932 personnel strength had grown to 1,305 officers and 13,400 men, but, like the rest of the services, the Air Corps was starved for funds during most of the Depression years. In 1938, the Army Air Corps had a total of 18,000 enlisted men and 1,600 officers plus 3,200 reserves—2,800 officers and 400 enlisted men—and had 1,700 planes, ranking seventh in the world.

In January 1939, President Roosevelt sought $300 million from Congress to increase the Air Corps to 6,000 planes, to build and strengthen air fields in Hawaii, Puerto Rico, Alaska, and Panama, and to provide pilot training for 1,200 men. Congress approved the request, including expansion of the Air Corps to 3,203 officers and 45,000 enlisted men, its largest increase ever. But the money appropriated was sufficient to purchase only 3,251 additional planes, bringing the Air Corps total to 5,500.

The Air Corps did not have facilities for training that many pilots, so it contracted with civilian flying schools, initially seven of them, to provide primary flight training. The private flying schools, 23 of which were approved by the Civil Aeronautics Administration, blossomed. Most had been existing on meager revenues from civilians who wanted to learn to fly, but now suddenly they were in business in a major way, and despite the primitive facilities at some of them, they made a significant contribution to the training of Air Corps flyers. Primary training cost less in private schools than in military facilities, and best of all the private schools could go to work immediately. After graduation from primary training, the cadets entered basic, then advanced flight programs at Air Corps bases such as Randolph and Kelly. For most of the war, the AAF continued to contract with private flying schools—41 were eventually in use—to provide primary training for pilots. It also contracted with commercial airlines, trade schools, and other agencies for training mechanics and other technicians, and for repair and maintenance of aircraft.

When Germany invaded Poland in 1939, the Air Corp's total strength had grown to only 26,000 officers and men, compared to 100,000 in the RAF and 500,000 in the German Luftwaffe. Equipment was still lacking, as well. The B-17 bomber had been designed in 1935, but at this time the Air Corps had only 23 of them.

In May 1940 President Roosevelt startled the country when he asked Congress to provide funding for 50,000 planes—36,500 for the Air Corps and 13,500 for the Navy. After June 1940, following the fall of France, appropriations for expansion of the Air Corps grew rapidly, with Congress piling appropriations upon appropriations. Within days the Air Corps was furiously drafting specifications and contracts for hundreds of different items, in addition to aircraft. By the fall of 1940, more than 1,000 manufacturing contracts were let in a single day. In the next 18 months, Congress authorized the purchase of approximately 37,500 airplanes, but it would take time to bring them off the production lines. In fact, the new airplane manufacturing plants constructed as a result of the May–July 1940 appropriations had not produced their first plane by December 7, 1941.

Between July 1940 and December 1941, American aircraft manufacturers turned out 22,077 planes, but the Air Corps got only 9,932 of them and the navy 4,034, with the remainder going to Britain. As of October 1941, the president directed the AAF to allocate two-thirds of the tactical aircraft coming off production lines to Britain and other anti–Axis countries. This plan, of course, changed in a matter of weeks when the United States entered the war.

Air Corps strength expanded with the induction of the National Guard; among the first Guard units to be mobilized in September 1940 were four squadrons of Air National Guard, and by the end of 1940-41 more than 15 other squadrons had been mobilized. By January 1941, the Air Corps had grown to 6,180 officers, 7,000 flying cadets and 88,000 enlisted men. At the time of the Pearl Harbor attack, the Air Corps numbered 354,000 officers and men, including 9,000 pilots and 59,000 mechanics and other technicians; the problem was lack of aircraft, which, in spite of growing production, had not yet begun to be produced in adequate numbers. The Air Corps had at that time only 2,846 combat planes of which 1,157 were operative; of this number, only 154 were four-engine bombers.

As the newest of the services, the Air Corps had been lacking in manpower, equipment and facilities, but it performed a phenomenal feat in building a vast air armada. Fortunately, aircraft design had made signal progress during the 1930s, thanks in large measure to the fact that the lion's share of research and development money appropriated for the army went to the Air Corps. Thus, with the exception of the B-29, the P-51 and P-61, all of the combat planes flown in World War II had been designed by 1940, and were in production not later than the following year.

At the beginning of 1939, the Air Corps was aiming for 300 pilots to complete flight school annually. This number was soon raised to 1,200, as noted above, then in 1940 to 7,000, later that year to 12,000 and by February 1941 to 30,000 annually. In July 1940, the Air Corps was authorized to recruit flying cadets essentially without limit. To train so many pilots so rapidly, the Air Corps set about building airfields all over the country, particularly in the South and Southwest—eventually more than 40 in Texas alone—where weather permitted more days of flying per year. In many cases, the Air Corps leased an existing air field, often a municipal airport, and with minor modifications began training pilots, navigators, or bombardiers.

When war came, the AAF was in the process of establishing an Aircraft Warning Service, with 13 stations along the East Coast and 10 on the West Coast. Later in the war these were staffed mainly by members of the Women's Army Corps, supplemented by the Ground Observer Corps, which was composed of volunteer civilians.

In August 1940, the Air War Plans Division of the AAF had predicted that if the United States became engaged in a war with both Japan and Germany, the Air Corps would need 63,467 aircraft and 2,164,916 officers and men. The prediction was amazingly accurate; at its peak the AAF strength totaled approximately 2.4 million officers and enlisted personnel and about 80,000 aircraft. By the end of the war the AAF had trained 200,000 pilots, more than 50,000 navigators and bombardiers, and 265,000 aerial gunners plus thousands of glider pilots, flight engineers, radar observers and other flight and ground specialists. This achievement involved rapid expansion of training programs without adequate time for planning. After the Pearl Harbor attack the need to expand rapidly presented space problems of major proportions, but it was not possible to construct facilities with the time and money constraints the AAF faced. The solution was to lease more than 500 hotels, garages, warehouses, resorts, athletic fields, parking lots and other facilities—including more than 100 hotels and resort facilities in Miami Beach, several hotels in Chicago including the Stevens (now the Michigan Hilton) and most of the major resort hotels in Atlantic City. This made it possible for the AAF to move ahead with training much sooner than if it had waited to construct its own training facilities, and it saved a great deal of money.

The training of pilots was aided by the Civilian Pilot Training Program, begun in 1939. The Civil Aeronautics Board contracted with more than 1,000 colleges and other educational institutions to provide the ground training and with nearby flight schools to teach flying. The program was renamed the War Training Service in December 1942 and taken over by the AAF and the navy. By the time it ended, the CPT/WTS had given flight training to more than 400,000 persons, many of whom became pilots in the AAF or navy.

Navy

The reduction in the navy's manpower and ships in the years between the wars was the result of the general de-emphasis of the military services following World War I, but especially a result of the arms reduction treaty of 1922. The navy was authorized funding for approximately 100,000 enlisted personnel and about 9,000 officers during most of the interwar years, although the number on active duty did not reach the authorization due to lack of funds. In 1922, the number of enlisted men fell from 121,632 to 90,975, and by 1933 to 80,925, but in 1937 was back up to 95,398. While the army tended to measure its preparedness primarily by the number of soldiers on active duty, the navy focused primarily on the number and types of ships in its fleet and their level of modernization.

The navy had begun a large shipbuilding program in 1916, and construction continued for three or four years after World War I ended. Except for a shortage of heavy cruisers, the American fleet was impressive, partly due to having begun construction of the first of 16 battleships in 1916. But Congress began soon to agitate for downsizing the navy. By 1921 the United States had made major steps toward reducing its fleet by decommissioning 376 vessels.

The U.S. Congress began to raise the question of disarmament beginning with the 1919 peace conference. Britain was reluctant to downsize its navy, but within three years a feeling of increased security and heavy indebtedness prompted it to scrap unilaterally many of its older ships—38 battleships, 89 cruisers, 300 destroyers and torpedo boats and 106 submarines. Thus, when the United States called for a naval disarmament conference in Washington for late 1921, Britain was fully in accord. Japan, France, and Italy joined in, although less enthusiastically.

In the arms reduction treaty of 1922, Japan, Britain, the United States, France and Italy agreed to destroy part of their fleets and to limit their battleships and aircraft in both number and size—battleships to a maximum of 35,000 tons each and 16-inch guns, and carriers to 27,000 tons each, for a total of 135,000 tons. The United States had no carriers at that time, although that year it converted an old coal carrier into the aircraft carrier *Langley*.

As a result of the treaty the United States was required to destroy 28 capital ships. Under the treaty, none of the powers could begin construction of battleships for ten years, the life of the treaty, nor replace battleships with less than 20 years of service, cruisers with less than 17 years or destroyers with less than 12 years, in each case the presumed life of the vessel. In 1924, Congress authorized the navy to add eight cruisers and six river gunboats, but only two cruisers were begun that year; the others were started in 1927. Then, in 1927, Congress authorized one aircraft carrier and 15 heavy cruisers, later reduced to 10 because of the 1931 arms reduction treaty. Construction was begun in 1929 and completed between 1935 and 1939.

Whether it was due to his Quaker pacifism, the Depression, his antimilitary secretary of the treasury, or other reasons, Herbert Hoover's presidency saw no new ships authorized, although several destroyers and two submarines begun earlier were completed and the conversion of the aircraft carriers *Lexington* and *Saratoga* from battle cruisers was completed. When President Hoover recommended in 1932, over protests of the navy and its friends in Congress, that no funds be appropriated for ship construction, newspaper support for his position was five to one. Hoover was reflecting the mood of the country and of the majority in Congress. With the Depression at its worst and feelings of pacifism and isolationism growing in the country, the public was not in favor of spending for navy construction.

The second arms reduction conference, held in London in 1930, resulted in limits on heavy cruisers and changed the replacement age for battleships and aircraft carriers to 26 years, 20 years for cruisers, 16 years for destroyers and 13 years for submarines. Several other conditions were set, most of which presented no serious problems for the United States.

The limit on ships by the arms reduction treaties was not a major factor in the navy's preparedness, since throughout the 1920s and 1930s the United States did not rebuild its navy to the level approved in the arms treaties. The problem for the American navy was modernization. If it was to be a viable fighting force it needed ships of modern design.

At the beginning of 1932, the American fleet consisted of 148 combat vessels, compared to Britain's 187 and Japan's 219. When Franklin D. Roosevelt became president in 1933, he found a weak navy. Most of the destroyers and submarines were overage, and the number of aircraft carriers was still far short of that allowed under the treaties. A shortage of manpower forced the decommissioning of several vessels, and active ships were operating with 81 percent of authorized crews. The thinness of personnel was due to lack of money, not difficulty in recruitment of personnel, which in the depths of the Depression was no problem; 90 percent of the enlisted personnel were re-enlisting.

Carl Vinson, chairman of the House Committee on Naval Affairs and champion of the navy, informed Roosevelt after the 1932 election that in the decade since the 1922 arms reduction treaty the United States had lagged far behind other countries in ship construction. According to historian Stephen E. Pelz, in the previous decade the number of ships begun was as follows, with total tonnage in parentheses; United States, 40 ships (197,640 tons); Japan, 164 ships (410,467); France, 196 ships (507,737); Italy, 144 ships (297,072); Great Britain, 148 ships (471,311). The good news was that the navy's air arm had made progress through the 1920s, reaching its goal of 1,000 planes one year ahead of its 1931 target.

Roosevelt had served for eight years as assistant secretary of the navy (1913–1920) and had a special affinity for the navy (General Marshall once chided him for referring to the army as "they" and the navy as "us"), so the navy was delighted when FDR moved into the White House. Roosevelt did, in fact, institute what has been called a navy renaissance, but he did not undertake a crash navy building program. He had to deal with an isolationist Senate, a country in which many of its people felt a strong military was an invitation to war, and the Depression which demanded that the civilian sector have first call on available funds.

In 1933 the Roosevelt administration managed to allocate a limited amount of funds for construction of military projects, albeit without specific prior approval of Congress. In the 100 days following his taking office in 1933, President Roosevelt got a large amount of legislation approved by Congress to ease unemployment and to fight the Depression. One of those bills created the Public Works Administration to provide jobs and to rebuild roads, bridges, and other public facilities, though the legislation gave the president considerable latitude concerning projects for which the money could be spent. Of the $3.3 billion appropriated, Roosevelt allotted $238 million by executive order to build up the navy, including the construction of two aircraft carriers (*Enterprise* and *Yorktown*), four cruisers, twenty destroyers, four submarines, two gunboats, 130 combat planes and harbor facilities at Pearl Harbor, Guam, and Wake Island. The army received more than $100 million of PWA funds, of which $68 million went for construction, including 50 civilian and military airfields and improvement of 32 army posts, $10 million for vehicles, $7.5 million for aircraft and equipment, and $6 million for ammunition. And the Coast Guard received $37 million of the PWA funds. Interior Secretary Harold Ickes, who was responsible for administering the PWA, later recalled that the isolationists in the Senate were incensed over the fact that part of the funds had been spent in ways not intended by Congress, and in the 1934-35 appropriations act, expenditure of PWA funds for military purposes was prohibited. Even so, by 1938 the army had received $250 million of federal relief funds of various kinds for rebuilding the military, most of it for construction of armories, camps, posts and stations, and for the Corps of Engineers.

In 1934 Congress authorized the navy to bring its fleet up to the level set under the 1930 arms limitations treaty. The bill authorized 70 warships and 730 airplanes to be built between 1935 and 1939 but provided funding for only a small number of cruisers, destroyers, and submarines. However, Congress provided funds every year throughout the remainder of the decade for the navy to increase or replace combat vessels, as well as support vessels and other support resources.

On December 12, 1937, Japanese planes sank the *U.S.S. Panay,* which was guarding American merchant ships in the Yangtze River in China. This incident goaded Congress to approve by a vote of 294 to 100 in the House and 56 to 18 in the Senate funding for a bill introduced in January 1938 by Rep. Vinson authorizing a 20 percent increase in funding for the Navy, including an 11 percent increase in combat vessels and more than 1,000 additional airplanes. But it was an authorization bill, not appropriations; the construction was to be completed over a period of 10 years.

Altogether, between 1933 and 1939, Congress authorized construction of 41 submarines, 65 destroyers, 17 cruisers, 8 battleships, and 5 aircraft carriers. This program would bring the American navy to a 10:8 ratio of battleships with Japan, still short of the 10:5 ratio that had been approved in arms limitations treaties of 1922 and 1930, and the 10:7 ratio for cruisers and smaller ships approved in 1930.

The 1930 London naval arms treaty was set to expire in 1936. The signatories met again in London in 1935-36 to negotiate continuation of the treaty, but the conference did not go well. On December 30, 1934, Japan gave the two-year required notice that after 1936 it would not be bound by the treaty, and although its representatives attended the 1935-36 conference, they did not sign the treaty. The treaty was signed by Britain, the United States and France, but the absence of the Soviet Union and Germany, the latter of which had begun developing its navy, left the treaty incomplete.

Although it was difficult to prove, U.S. naval intelligence was convinced that Japan had violated the treaty limits on shipbuilding and sizes of ships and guns throughout the early 1930s. After 1936 Japan began a crash program of naval expansion, although the rest of the world was not able to determine the extent of its shipbuilding because of the secrecy surrounding it. The United States was aware that Japan was building a large number of ships but chose not to try to match the increase. President Roosevelt continued to face the opposition to military expansion that he encountered when he entered office, but as noted already, some increases in naval strength were permitted by Congress annually.

In his proclamation of a limited national emergency on September 8, 1939, Roosevelt authorized an increase in the number of enlisted navy men to 191,000 and the call of some retired and reserve officers, who volunteered, to active duty. Within days after the German invasion of France and the low countries, Roosevelt asked Congress to create a "Two Ocean" navy and to provide $4 billion to fund it. On June 14, 1940, Congress appropriated full funding for the 1938 Vinson-authorized expansion, then turned immediately to further consideration of the president's remaining request. On July 19, 1940, the president signed legislation creating a "Two-Ocean" navy, which authorized an increase of approximately 70 percent in total tonnage of naval vessels, the largest increase in naval tonnage ever. Appropriations in June and July together resulted in funds for construction of 13 battleships, 6 aircraft carriers, 32 cruisers, 101 destroyers, 39 submarines, and assorted other vessels, totaling 257 ships. The legislation also funded the expansion of navy yards, the conversion of merchant ships to escort carriers, and significant expansion of other naval facilities.

When legislation was passed in August 1940 authorizing the call to active duty of reservists and retirees, the navy's reserve units and retired officers and noncommissioned officers were recalled to active duty and the rebuilding of the navy began. On the East Coast, 40 destroyers were taken out of mothballs and put into active service, and then shortly, as officers and crew became available, all of the remaining mothballed destroyers and submarines were put into service.

In December 1941, the navy had 17 battleships, 113 submarines, 208 cruisers and destroyers and 7 aircraft carriers, plus other assorted vessels for support and service. In response to pleas from the British, slightly more than half of the vessels were in the Atlantic, including 8 battleships, 4 aircraft carriers, 13 cruisers and approximately 90 destroyers. As a result the Japanese had a superior fleet, both in number and quality of vessels, in the Pacific.

Although the navy was lacking in ships at the time of Pearl Harbor, a massive construction program was already in progress. As shown in Chapter VI, the production of ships during the war was nothing short of astonishing.

Like the army and Air Corps, the navy moved rapidly in its mobilization after congress authorized funds. When the president declared a limited national emergency on September 8, 1939, 126,418 officers and enlisted men were on active duty in the navy. The number had grown to 161,000 by July 1940 and to 325,095 by December 7, 1941. On June 30, 1945, navy personnel totaled 3.4 million.

Marine Corps

On July 1, 1939, the Marine Corps consisted of 19,432 officers and enlisted men on active duty, only moderately above its 20-year low of 16,361 which it reached in 1934. Except during World War I the Marine Corps had always been relatively small in size. But in 1939 it had an active reserve force of 16,025, due in part to the marine reserve bill of 1938, which was guided through Congress by Minnesota Congressman Melvin J. Maas, a reserve marine colonel and later a World War II hero.

When general mobilization orders were issued on October 15, 1940, calling the National Guard and reserves to active duty, the Marine Corps ordered all of its reserve units, which consisted of 23 organized battalions and 13 aviation squadrons, to report for duty in November. Unlike the Army National Guard, which was mobilized as units and remained so throughout the war, the marine reservists were integrated into regular marine units. Volunteer reservists—that is, those who did not belong to a unit—were mobilized individually in two stages, the first on December 14, 1940, and the second on May 12, 1941. By December 7, 1941, the Marine Corps had almost 64,000 officers and men on active duty.

When war was declared, applications for the Marine Corps rose rapidly; 22,686 volunteers were inducted in January 1942, compared to 1,978 in November 1941, bringing the total to almost 104,000 by February 1, 1942. On V-J Day, 1945, the Marine Corps strength totaled 484,631 officers and men, including 118,086 in aviation.

Coast Guard

On June 30, 1939, the Coast Guard consisted of 10,064 officers and men, 34 cutters, 125 patrol boats, 50 aircraft and 200 lifesaving stations. In September 1939, an increase in the number of personnel began and in November 1941 it had 24,000 personnel on active duty. It expanded rapidly, reaching its authorized strength of 171,939—not including the Temporary Reserve—by the end of 1943 and remaining at that level until the end of the war. The final figure included almost 9,000 in the Coast Guard Women's Reserve (SPARS).

In June 1939, Congress authorized the Coast Guard Auxiliary, a civilian organization composed of individuals who owned small boats and were willing to serve in patrol work at their own expense. In February 1941, Congress created the Coast Guard Temporary Reserve whose members served without pay, on either a full-time or part-time basis. The Temporary Reserve consisted largely of members of the auxiliary who were mobilized as complete units, along with their boats. They received enlisted or officer rank and enjoyed the same privileges as regular Coast Guardsmen. However, as noted by Marvin Schlegel, the historian of World War II Virginia, not all Coast Guard Auxiliary units were mobilized immediately; some continued to function in auxiliary status well into the war period. For example, Flotilla Division V at Newport News, Virginia, was not activated until early 1944, when as Unit 3 of the U.S. Coast Guard Temporary Reserve it was assigned to patrol port installations in the Newport News area. By March 1, 1944, the Coast Guard Temporary Reserve had grown to 70,000.

Between July 1, 1940, and the end of the war, the Coast Guard added more than 6,000 vessels of various types, including not only those constructed in shipyards, but many that were purchased, leased or otherwise acquired from private individuals. Many patriotic citizens loaned their yachts and other pleasure craft to the Coast Guard for the duration of the war. In the fall of 1942, the Coast Guard acquired some 2,000 pleasure craft from civilians, either through purchase or charter, in the latter case some of them in the off season only. Most of these craft were used on Coastal Picket Patrol.

On November 1, 1941, the Coast Guard was transferred from the Treasury Department and put under the command of the navy where it remained until January 1, 1946. While under the navy it participated in a variety of activities, including escorting convoys of cargo ships to Europe, manning landing boats for invasions in both Europe and the Pacific, rescue operations, submarine search and destroy activities, manning army cargo craft for inter-island shipping in the Pacific, weather service, and many more.

Merchant Marine

The Merchant Marine Act of 1936, establishing the U.S. Maritime Commission, laid the foundation for expansion of American shipping. By 1938 the Maritime Commission had 37 cargo ships under construction, in addition to those being constructed by private companies with subsidies provided under the 1936 act. In 1939 the construction program was stepped up again.

Since the merchant marine was not a military organization, it floundered early in the war due to lack of coordination. Most of the cargo ships were in the hands of private corporations, along with a smaller number owned by the Maritime Commission, the navy and the army; many of the latter two were for inland waterways transportation. On February 7, 1942, President Roosevelt signed an executive order creating the War Shipping Administration with authority over all U.S. merchant shipping, making it possible to coordinate shipping and allocate it in accord with national needs. The WSA also had control over recruitment and training of personnel. The Maritime Commission retained control over ship construction.

In 1941, the U.S. merchant marine consisted of 55,000 officers and seamen; in 1945 it consisted of 270,000 personnel. Enlisting in the merchant marine was viewed by some draft-age young men as a good way to avoid the draft, and as a result merchant seamen were suspected of trying to avoid military service. They were also the object of no little envy because merchant marine personnel drew civilian salaries, which were substantially higher than in the military. Yet the merchant marine was not a safe haven; approximately 700 American merchant ships were sunk and some 5,600 seamen lost their lives during the war. Most of the merchant ships sunk were in the North Atlantic where, if the explosion did not kill the crew, the icy water would soon freeze them. Occasionally, rescue ships had to leave merchant men whose ships had been sunk in the water lest the rescue ship itself be sunk by a U-boat. In addition, merchant mariners were not military and hence did not receive veterans' benefits after the war.

Wartime Troop Strength

The U.S. Army had planned to create 105 divisions, but as the war progressed this was trimmed to 100, then to 90, and finally to 89 divisions when the 2nd Cavalry division, then in North Africa, was deactivated to provide personnel for urgently needed service units. This total seems small compared to the peak numbers of divisions other countries had during the war: Germany, 313; Japan, 120; Soviet Union, 550; and China, 300. Both Germany and the USSR created many more divisions during the course of the war than their peak numbers represent, but many of the divisions were either destroyed or so nearly destroyed on the eastern front that they were abandoned. Further, different nations' divisions were of different sizes and fighting strengths; a Chinese division, for example, was often not much larger than an American regiment. German divisions were misleading, too, because Hitler developed the practice later in the war of creating new divisions when some of those in combat consisted of fewer than 5,000 troops due to losses of personnel who had not been replaced. And although Russian divisions were authorized 12,000 to 14,000 troops, depending on type of division, Marshall Zukov told General Eisenhower after the war that he tried to maintain a troop strength of 8,000 in combat, but that due to battle losses, divisions often had not more than 3,000 or 4,000 men.

The total numbers of military personnel mobilized during the war, not at one time but *in toto,* were estimated as follows: Soviet Union, 22 million; Germany, 17 million (although an uncounted number of soldiers in the German Army were conscripts or volunteers from France, Belgium, Denmark, the Ukraine and other occupied countries); Britain, its colonies and the Commonwealth countries, 12 million. At peak strength, in May 1945, there were 12,124,418 men and women serving in the U.S. armed forces. A total of 15,145,115 men and women served in the U.S. armed forces in World War II—in round numbers, 10.4 million in the army, including the AAF; 3.9 million in the navy; 600,000 in the Marine Corps; and 250,000 in the Coast Guard.

Although the United States was not prepared to fight a war in December 1941, it was dramatically better off than two years earlier. Had the war come to America even one year earlier, the consequences would have been even more disastrous, for the country's armed forces were pitifully lacking. Those who foresaw the inevitable, including the president, had served the country well by pressing to increase its defense capability. Many anti-interventionists charged that the president had manipulated events to make war inevitable, that he in fact led the country into war. This charge began long before Pearl Harbor and, though it abated during the war, it continues to be a part of the debate concerning the period immediately preceding the war and has not been satisfactorily answered. There is some evidence to support the charge. During the president's meeting with the British prime minister near Newfoundland in August 1941, Churchill pressed him to bring the United States into the European war, but Roosevelt reportedly responded that the country would not support such action, that in order for the United States to enter the war an incident was necessary. Further, the former executive secretary of Fight for Freedom stated in an interview with historian Mark Lincoln Chadwin in the 1960s that his office spoke by phone with two of President Roosevelt's closest assistants "at least once or twice a day" at the time FFF was advocating declaration of war. While Roosevelt did not publicly identify with the interventionist group, he clearly opposed the anti-interventionists.

In November 1941, members of the War Department staff urged the president to make concessions to the Japanese that would delay any attack until the army and navy were better prepared to defend the country, but Roosevelt decided against such a move on the basis that it would not mollify the Japanese and might cause them to conclude that the United States was weak and that they should attack it earlier.

Clearly, the president took actions that led the Japanese to declare war, but there is evidence that the Japanese attack was virtually inevitable. After the war, historian Stephen Pelz discovered records in the files of the Japanese Navy from the early 1930s documenting Japanese plans for expansion into Southeast Asia, including the Philippines. It is clear from the records that the Japanese military felt certain that the United States would come to the defense of the Philippines and, thus, war with the United States was inevitable.

Building the Officer Corps

Following passage of the Selective Service law, hundreds of thousands of draftees entered the army to fill out undermanned regular army and National Guard units and to fill new divisions, but the building of an officer corps was more difficult, since there was not time to train them as rapidly as they would be needed. The Officers Reserve Corps of just over 100,000 was a godsend. The majority were graduates of college Reserve Officer Training Corps, but the ORC also included about 10,000 World War I officers who had kept up their commissions, medical and dental officers and certain other specialists who had received direct commissions, plus graduates of CMTC.

In 1921, the army created the Citizens Military Training Camps through which civilians could qualify for appointment as reserve officers or noncommissioned officers. Young men ages 17 to 24 who completed four summers of training of one month each could apply and, if they met other qualifications, were awarded reserve commissions in the army. The CMT camps were popular; in 1931, 82,642 young men applied, of which 37,500 were accepted and received training at 51 army reservations. During the 1930s when federal appropriations declined sharply, smaller numbers could be accommodated in CMTC summer camps. This program ended in the summer of 1941 having supplied fewer than 6,000 reserve officers. One of those receiving reserve commissions through CMTC was future President Ronald Reagan, in spite of bad eyesight which disqualified him for combat when war came.

In the summer of 1941, before the first class of second lieutenants graduated from officer candidate schools, reserve officers accounted for 75 to 90 percent of officers in the regular army divisions and almost half of those in National Guard divisions. Chief of Staff Marshall stated that the availability of reserve officers following enactment of the Selective Service law when there was not time to train a cadre of officers was critical to the mobilization of the nation's defenses.

Following passage of the Selective Service Act, General Marshall asked the chiefs of infantry, field artillery and the other branches whether officer candidate schools should be established. All of them responded in the negative since, at that time, an army of only 1.4 million was planned and they believed that National Guard and reserve officers, plus those who would graduate from ROTC in the future, would meet the need. By the summer of 1941, Marshall had decided to establish officer candidate schools anyway for two reasons: first, the prospect of American entrance in the war was growing, and second, he felt that for morale purposes, outstanding enlisted men in the civilian army should have the opportunity to earn commissions. Initially OCS was a three-month course and its graduates were known pejoratively as "90-day wonders." In the summer of 1943, the training period of army OCS courses was increased from 13 to 17 weeks, except in the AAF administrative school which was increased from 11 weeks to 16 weeks.

In 1942, the army faced a serious shortage of officers and was unable to fill the need by sending enlisted men from the ranks to officer candidate school. In addition, the AAF and the navy were siphoning off the best talent from enlistees, and until March 1944 enlisted men in the ground forces could volunteer for the AAF, a further drain on talented candidates for Army Ground Forces officer training. In an attempt to increase the number of more capable candidates, the army came up with a plan to enlist civilians who had been deferred for dependency reasons. These individuals were recruited with the understanding that after basic training they would go to OCS; if they were not selected for OCS during basic training or if they entered OCS and did not receive a commission, they could resign from the army and return to civilian life. By the end of 1942, about 38,000 volunteer officer candidates had been accepted into the army, of whom about 27,000 were already enrolled in officer candidate schools. When the demand for officers eased in 1943, the Volunteer Officer Candidate program was reduced, and by late 1943 it had been eliminated. Meantime, the VOC program had recruited many men whose intellectual talents, on average, exceeded those of enlisted men admitted to OCS from the ranks. The VOC program led to the commissioning of many men of education and talent who otherwise might have secured direct commissions in the AAF or navy.

All branches of the army, especially those requiring technical knowledge, complained throughout 1942 and early 1943 about the poor quality of candidates sent to OCS from the ranks. The Signal Corps wanted to recruit men with degrees in engineering, but only 2 percent of its OCS trainees held engineering degrees. There was close correlation between academic failure and scores on the AGCT (Army General Classification Test), not only in technical fields such as signal and ordnance but in infantry and artillery OCS courses, as well. All branches of the army enrolled more men in OCS in 1942 with lower AGCT scores and less education than they desired. The problem was that more talented men had volunteered for the navy and the AAF, leaving the army with scarce talent for leadership, forcing OC schools to admit men of lower intelligence because of the desperate need for officers. Army unit commanders were pressed to send talented men to OCS but were often reluctant to do so since it meant losing the most capable noncommissioned officers and possibly subjecting the commanders to criticism for failure to meet performance targets.

Prior to 1942, most of the new commissions in the army consisted of ROTC graduates called to active duty. By contrast, psychologist Samuel A. Stouffer and his research group, in studies of opportunities for advancement in the army, found that in the last half of 1942, 89,922 commissions were awarded through officer candidate schools, and in the first half of 1943, OCS accounted for 90,868 officers commissioned, together almost two-thirds of all OCS graduates during the war.

In early 1945, army historian Willard W. Hansen analyzed records of officers who graduated from OCS between December 9, 1942, and June 3, 1943, and found that only 51.8 percent of those who graduated from OCS had completed one year of college or more. Presumably, of those who were admitted to OCS but did not graduate, the percentage who had attended college was much lower. The educational level was particularly low in some branches of the army. At the tank destroyer OCS, only 28.2 percent of the graduates had attended college; 21.0 percent had not graduated from high school. Only 12.6 percent of the graduates of the armored force OCS had attended college; on the other hand, 43.3 percent of the graduates of the infantry OCS had attended college.

Although Hansen does not elaborate, a partial explanation for the low percentages of college men completing armored force and tank destroyer OCS lay in the fact that the latter had been created as a branch of the army just a year or so earlier, and the armored force, following the great success of tanks in Louisiana maneuvers in 1941, had launched a crash expansion program. The armored force was also relatively new, having been formed in July 1940 by combining the fledgling tank corps and the mechanized cavalry. Both recruited regular army sergeants from other branches of the army, most of whom had many years of peacetime service, to form the cadre of new units, from which the most promising were later sent to OCS. Since virtually no peacetime enlisted men had attended college, it can reasonably be concluded that this group constituted a substantial portion of non-college men and non–high school graduates who completed tank destroyer and armored force officer candidate schools in the period studied.

Infantry OCS graduates included ROTC men who had completed

eight semesters of ROTC or the equivalent between December 1942 and March 1943 and had attended OCS in lieu of summer camp, which was canceled after war was declared. Hansen's sample included a considerable number of ROTC engineers and men in infantry, field artillery, coast artillery, cavalry, and other branches found in ROTC units, but, except for a few ROTC men who had transferred from other branches, none in the armored and tank destroyer branches, neither of which was offered in college ROTC.

After June 1943, the educational level of OCS graduates rose sharply for several reasons: the numbers admitted to OCS declined rapidly due to a temporary oversupply of junior officers, which allowed better selectivity; more men with some college education were drafted after the draft age was lowered from 20 to 18 in November 1942; and after May 1943 a high percentage of OCS classes consisted of advanced ROTC students or graduates—in many classes more than 75 percent—who had completed three or four years of college. When they had enrolled in advanced ROTC, the army had assured them that they would have a chance to earn a commission and thus was obligated to send them to OCS.

Table 4-1 summarizes the sources of male officers for the period July 1, 1940, through June 30, 1945. It includes those who were awarded commissions or were already commissioned and were called to active duty during this period, but does not include female officers—WACs, nurses, physical therapists, dietitians, and other women who were commissioned during this period. It does include AAF officers—both OCS and aviation cadet graduates—who often are not included in army totals. Further, the number of commissions awarded through OCS shown in Table 4-1 includes more than 20,000 advanced ROTC cadets who were called to active duty before graduating from college and attended OCS. (In some tallies, they are included with numbers of officers furnished by ROTC.) The table does not, of course, include those officers already on active duty as of June 30, 1940, nor those commissioned after June 30, 1945. The size of the officer corps was substantially less at any one time than the total in the table.

Direct Commissions

Early in the war the army, the navy and the AAF all mounted large officer training programs which, by late 1943 to early 1944, had largely filled the need. In the meantime, however, the services were desperate for officers, particularly those with specialized skills, which led to direct commissioning from civilian life of large numbers of individuals, many of whom were older—between 30 and 45. As of June 30, 1943, the army—including the AAF—had commissioned from civilian life 47,000

TABLE 4-1
SOURCES OF MALE COMMISSIONED OFFICERS, U.S. ARMY, JULY 1, 1940–JUNE 30, 1945

Source	Number	Percent
Officer candidate schools	280,949	32.7
Direct commissions to enlisted men	44,399	5.2
Aviation cadet training	246,810	28.8
Direct commissions to civilians	112,355	13.1
Reserve Officer Training Corps	87,112	10.2
Officers Reserve Corps	16,622	1.9
Officers Military Training Corps [CMTC]	5,773	.7
National Guard	22,543	2.6
Former warrant or flight officers	19,561	2.3
Former World War I officers	17,486	2.0
Regular Army [West Point]	4,157	.5
Total	857,767	100.0

Source: Stouffer, Samuel A., et al. *The American Soldier: Adjustment During Army Life*. Vol. I. Princeton, NJ: Princeton University Press, 1949. Reprinted by permission of Princeton University Press.

professionals and specialists of various kinds and 12,000 former officers, in addition to 23,000 physicians, 8,000 dentists, and 4,200 chaplains.

Early in the war, small numbers of direct commissions were awarded to enlisted men on active duty, mostly to master sergeants and technical sergeants with long years of service. In the latter part of the war, direct commissions to enlisted men rose sharply; in the first six months of 1945, 16,447 enlisted men received direct commissions, most of them battlefield promotions. Due to the acute shortage of officers throughout 1942 and early 1943, the various services worked diligently to locate enlisted men who were qualified for OCS and to identify civilians whose qualifications fitted them for either leadership or technical positions in the military services.

On July 13, 1943, the acting secretary of war ordered that direct commissions to civilians no longer be awarded, except in the cases of medical personnel, chaplains and limited numbers of highly specialized personnel. In the 12 months beginning July 1, 1943, the army awarded direct commissions to 13,747 civilians, of whom 58 percent were in the Medical Department, which included 147 physical therapists and 440 dietitians, in addition to physicians and dentists; 13 percent were chaplains; and the remainder were primarily specialists for the AAF and the Transportation Corps. After July 1, 1944, few direct commissions were awarded to civilians, and only to physicians and other health specialists, chaplains, and persons with specialities particularly needed by the army.

The Medical Department of the army awarded direct commissions to physicians, dentists, veterinarians, nurses, dietitians, pharmacists, sanitary engineers and other specialists. The Medical Administration Corps officer candidate school, first at Carlisle Barracks, Pennsylvania, and later at Camp Barkeley, Texas, trained thousands of MAC officers, in addition to those awarded direct commissions from civilian life and from the enlisted ranks. For example, in the spring of 1942 the surgeon general authorized the direct commissioning into the MAC of 200 specialists from civilian life, including hotel and restaurant managers, who would serve as supply officers in large hospitals. In the last half of 1944, 85 enlisted men and warrant officers in the Fifth Army in Europe and another 30 in North Africa were awarded direct commissions in the MAC. The Surgeon General's Office estimated that between 1,300 and 1,400 enlisted men and warrant officers serving overseas received direct commissions as second lieutenants in the MAC, in addition to an uncounted number commissioned directly from the ranks in the United States. Several times during the war, representatives of chiropractors, optometrists, and podiatrists requested that they be commissioned in the Medical Department, but of the three only optometrists were awarded commissions and then only after the end of hostilities.

Essentially all of the officers in the Judge Adjutant General Corps had qualified for the practice of law in civilian life, and most were awarded direct commissions, although during the war the JAG Department did conduct an officer candidate school at the University of Michigan for individuals who already held law degrees. Automotive and diesel engine specialists, explosives specialists, law enforcement officers and persons with a variety of other specialities were commissioned directly. Persons with broad experience in the telephone industry and in radio were commissioned into the Signal Corps. Some in public relations and journalism were commissioned directly to apply their civilian expertise in the army. The army awarded a few direct commissions to individuals from most of the professions and business and industry. Frederick Osborn, a friend of both President Roosevelt and Secretary of War Stimson, former president of a railroad and in 1940 an investment banker, was named chairman of the Army-Navy Joint Committee on Morale; later he was given a direct appointment as brigadier general, and was subsequently promoted to major general.

The navy and AAF commissioned larger percentages of their officer corps directly from civilian life than did the army (Ground Forces and Service Forces), for a number of reasons. The navy's ROTC program had been authorized by Congress in 1925, but only 27 colleges and universities had navy ROTC units when World War II began (three times as many as in 1939) and there were only 2,000 NROTC graduates in the naval reserve. Thus, the navy sought other means—primarily direct commissions—to meet its officer needs. To a greater extent than the army, the navy's officer needs called for expertise possessed by civilian professionals. In February 1942 the navy set up officer procurement offices all over the country and hundreds of thousands of individuals applied for navy commissions.

As in the case of the army, a high percentage of those awarded direct commissions in the navy were physicians, dentists, nurses, chaplains, and lawyers, but the list also included diesel engine experts, personal experts, engineers, and persons with seagoing experience such as merchant marine officers and yachtsmen and dozens of others with expertise needed by the navy. The commissioning of men who had experience with yachts and other pleasure boats resulted in the awarding of direct commissions to a large number of men from privileged backgrounds, like future President John F. Kennedy, and contributed to the fact that navy officers, on average, were better educated than army officers and came from more socially and culturally advantaged backgrounds.

With the outbreak of war, the navy recognized that it would need to increase vastly the number of personnel skilled in the construction industry. The Seabees (construction battalions) were created on December 28, 1941, and the navy immediately set out to recruit men with construction experience in some 60 trades and professions. Those recruited were given direct appointments as officers and petty officers; ratings or commissions were awarded commensurate with their experience, qualifications and usefulness to the navy. Seabees built airfields, runways, docks, bases, bridges, and other installations needed by the navy and marines.

As shown in Table 4-2, the largest source of naval officers during World War II was direct commission from civilian life, and the next largest number was of individuals sent directly to midshipmen's school from civilian life, including men from the V-12 program who had not previously served in the navy. As Admiral Julius A. Furer noted in his comprehensive study of the *Administration of the Navy Department in World War II*, the basic educational requirement for a direct commission in the Naval Reserve was a college degree, although "this was eased somewhat later in the war, particularly for those with highly specialized qualifications and experience." Nonetheless, the navy had among its officer corps the highest percentage of college graduates of all of the military services.

TABLE 4-2
SOURCES OF NAVY OFFICERS, WORLD WAR II

Source	Number	Percent
Commissioned directly from civilian life	129,795	49.07
Entered officer training directly from civilian life	84,016	31.76
Temporary appointments from enlisted ranks	33,583	12.70
Officer training from enlisted ranks	5,325	2.01
Officers from U.S. Naval Academy	2,702	1.02
WAVES officers appointed from civilian life	8,123	3.07
WAVES officers appointed from enlisted ranks	953	.37
Total	264,497	100.00

Source: Furer, Julius Augustus. *Administration of the Navy Department in World War II.* Washington, DC: Navy Department, 1959.

All legal services officers in the navy had qualified for legal practice in civilian life and been awarded direct commissions, but most lawyers who received direct commissions in the navy became communications officers, personnel officers, training specialists, deck officers and other specialties. In fact, the navy commissioned from civilian life persons with postgraduate degrees in many fields of study.

Direct commissions for sea duty ended on August 17, 1944; thereafter, most of the officers were commissioned from midshipmen's schools, following completion of a V-12 college training program. In the year ending in February 1945, 91 percent of the male officers receiving commissions were graduates of V-12 programs. (For a more extensive examination of the V-12 program, see the author's book on *Colleges and Universities in World War II.*) Most of the WAVES (Women Accepted for Volunteer Emergency Service) officers shown in Table 4-2 as commissioned from civilian life were, in fact, appointed to midshipmen's school directly from civilian life and received their commissions after completion of officer training.

The Marine Corps relied to a considerable extent on its Platoon Leaders program for officer candidates immediately prior to and following the outbreak of war. Established in 1935, it allowed young men in colleges to attend summer camps at the end of their sophomore and junior years and, if they qualified, to receive commissions upon graduation from college. After war was declared and summer camp was abolished, college men could enlist in the Marine Corps reserve and be sent upon college graduation to Marine Officer Candidate School, along with enlisted marines from the ranks. Like the other services, the Marine Corps also commissioned officers directly from civilian life, particularly those who had completed army ROTC and subsequently resigned their commissions, plus persons with special skills. In 1942, when all of the services were short of officers, almost one-third of the general duty officers receiving commissions in the Marine Corps were commissioned directly in the field, mostly in combat zones.

In July 1943 when the Navy College Training Program (V-12) began operating, it absorbed the Platoon Leaders program and the Marine Corps began to rely on trainees from the V-12 program for officer candidates. For the 12-month period beginning July 1, 1943, 80 percent of those attending Marine Corps officer candidate classes were from the V-12 program.

Of all the services, the AAF faced the most difficult task of recruiting and training an adequate number of officers in the shortest period. Early in the war the AAF requisitioned a large number of hotels in Miami Beach and used them for training administration officer candidates and officers. Lacking adequate numbers of regulars to serve as a cadre, the AAF recruited a number of field artillery officers from Fort Bragg, North Carolina, and Fort Sill, Oklahoma, to get its training programs off the ground.

Applicants who qualified were awarded commissions directly from civilian life and sent to Miami Beach where they received training similar to that provided officer candidates. A total of 13,000 persons completed the officer training school at Miami Beach, the last class completing its training in June 1943, after which training schools were conducted at stations and bases by respective commands. As in the Army Ground Forces and Army Service Forces, officers commissioned in the AAF directly from civilian life tended to be older and were commissioned because of special training or talents.

Seven Air Corps ROTC units had been established in colleges and universities in 1921 but were abolished in 1935 due to lack of funds. The Air Corps was left without a reservoir of reserve officers to draw on, so it sought individuals with special talents wherever it could find them and awarded them direct commissions.

The AAF recruited and commissioned many persons with experience in advertising, public relations, journalism, communications, and the entertainment industry, including movie producers, directors and writers. The Air Corps and, to a lesser extent, the navy awarded direct commissions to a great many celebrities, and while the army also awarded commissions to celebrities, the percentage was much smaller. Many of those awarded commissions in the Army Signal Corps were assigned to the AAF.

The Signal Corps and the Air Corps awarded direct commissions to several directors and producers in the film industry. Anatole Litvak, the director, and producers Jack Warner and Hal Roach were commissioned in the Air Corps, with assignment to the Army Pictorial Service of the Signal Corps to make training films for the army and AAF; both ended the war as colonels. William Wyler, the director, reported that he simply walked into a general's office in Washington and said he was interested in joining up, to which the general said, "How would you like to be a major in the Air Corps?" Wyler, who actually went on bombing raids over Europe and received the Air Medal (awarded for completion of five combat flights), directed several documentary films for the AAF, including *The Memphis Belle,* a film of actual bombing raids which was shown in civilian movie houses to high praise and was remade in 1990 under the same title.

Director John Huston was appointed a lieutenant in the Army Signal Corps, rising rapidly to major while heading a photography unit in North Africa. Director Frank Capra was appointed a major in the army, later rising to colonel, to head a movie unit producing morale movies, the best known of which was the "Why We Fight" series. Capra's unit took over the Hal Roach Studios in Hollywood, which became known unofficially as "Fort Roach."

Among the celebrities receiving direct commissions in the navy was John Ford, the movie director, who was named head of the Field Photographic Branch of the Office of Strategic Services with a direct commission as lieutenant commander, finishing the war with the rank of captain, later rising to rear admiral in the navy reserves. Robert Montgomery, the actor, joined up in 1941 before Pearl Harbor, secured a commission as a navy lieutenant and was posted to the office of the naval attaché at the American embassy in London. Douglas Fairbanks, Jr., also joined in 1941 with a commission in the navy, rising during the war to commander. Fairbanks was awarded medals for valor in combat by the governments of Great Britain, France and Italy, as well as the navy's own silver star.

Not all Hollywood notables entered the service with direct commissions. James Stewart, the actor, entered in 1941 as a private, took flight training and ended the war a full colonel commanding a bomber unit. Henry Fonda received a direct commission as a lieutenant (j.g.) in the navy but by a circuitous route; he volunteered after Pearl Harbor, went through boot camp in San Diego, then four months of quartermaster school, and after several months was sent to New York where he was awarded a commission without applying. Actor Tyrone Power entered the Marine Corps as a private, completed the Officers Candidate School (infantry) at Quantico, Virginia, then after several months attended flying school and became a pilot. Clark Gable entered the AAF as a private, receiving a commission after completing the AAF administrative OCS at Miami Beach, Florida.

People from the film industry who were awarded direct commissions received more publicity because of their prominence, but other well known figures were also awarded direct commissions. Elliott Roosevelt, the son of the president, was commissioned captain in the Air Corps reserve, completed flight training, and by the end of the war was a colonel. Some direct appointments were for brief periods to perform special assignments; for example, Walter Winchell, the New York gossip columnist, was appointed a lieutenant commander in the navy to undertake a secret mission to Brazil.

Some leading celebrities were unsuccessful in their quest for high rank in the military service. Fiorello LaGuardia, mayor of New York City, who had been a major in the air service in World War I, volunteered early. He asked President Roosevelt to appoint him a brigadier general, but the army protested and he was offered the rank of colonel instead. LaGuardia found the rank insufficient and refused it. Later, President Roosevelt named LaGuardia the first national director of civilian defense.

BOTH GERMAN AND JAPANESE intelligence were fully aware of America's poor military posture in the 1930s, which helps to understand how the planners of the Japanese attack on Pearl Harbor underestimated the potential strength of the United States. When President Roosevelt wrote to Hitler in 1939 and asked him to assure the world that Germany had no claim on a long list of countries, Hitler went before the Reichstag and ridiculed FDR's request, to the merriment of the audience, for his intelligence agency had assured him that America's military was weak.

The speed with which the armed forces were mobilized, equipped and trained was nothing less than spectacular. At the time of the Pearl Harbor attack, some military leaders were thinking in terms of three or four years to prepare, and while the armed forces were not fully mobilized until early 1944, they were engaged in serious warfare within months after the attack on Pearl Harbor.

Chapter V

Government Mobilizes

After the war, the Bureau of the Budget prepared a list of agencies created during the period from 1939 to 1945 to help prosecute the war. The number totaled 162, in addition to the prewar departments and agencies that were involved in the administration of defense activities. Many of the wartime agencies were created as subsidiary organizations of existing departments and agencies of government, but a large number were independent of existing agencies, responsible only to the president or to a board or commission.

The war brought a large number of individuals to Washington to staff these agencies and to fill expansions in existing agencies and departments to manage the civilian production functions of the war. Many of them were highly talented persons who did not plan to become career government workers and who had strong opinions about how their agencies should perform their functions. It was perhaps inevitable under such circumstances that conflict would develop. Even so, the large amount of intrigue that did develop within the various agencies is perplexing—doubtless due in part to large egos, but also to the fact that the individuals involved were sincere and dedicated persons, many of whom came from the business world, were accustomed to direct action and were frustrated with the way the bureaucracy worked.

Congress passed the First War Powers Act on December 18, 1941, just days after the attack on Pearl Harbor, when the sentiment in Congress favored giving the president whatever powers he needed to prosecute the war. The act essentially authorized the president to create such agencies as he determined necessary to manage the war. The Second War Powers Act, passed on March 27, 1942, added further to the president's powers to act without congressional authority.

These acts came well after defense preparations had begun, and in the meantime the president had already established several agencies to direct defense activities. The Government Reorganization Act of 1939, which President Roosevelt had requested two years earlier, led to major shifts of offices in the executive branch, strengthening the president's ability to control and direct the government. This act provided some of the legal basis for later executive orders creating, revising and abolishing government agencies.

The German invasion of Poland on September 1, 1939, and the declaration of war on Germany by France and Britain two days later led President Roosevelt to issue an executive order on September 8 declaring a limited national emergency and proclaiming the president's authority to establish "such offices for emergency management as the President shall determine."

With the passage of the two war powers acts, Congress gave the president authority to control all production of materials related to the war effort from the mining of metals to the delivery of finished products and supplies. The government opened mines, took over some industries and services, and stockpiled raw materials of various kinds, yet it assumed direct management of few industries. Unlike the British government, it left the running of the railroads and the operation of manufacturing plants to private companies.

This chapter examines how the government organized to manage wartime production and some of the problems it faced in doing so. No attempt is made to describe all of the government agencies created to deal with defense and war matters; only some of the more significant and, in some cases, more visible ones are discussed.

Government Organizes

Aside from the permanent agencies responsible for the government and the defense of the country, the first agency created to direct defense preparations was the War Resources Board, formed jointly by the navy and war departments on August 9, 1939. It consisted of a committee of civilians whose task was to provide guidance on industrial mobilization for war, more specifically to advise the Army-Navy Munitions Board. Those who hoped to see the board grow into a major component in preparing for defense were soon disappointed. The military had created an Industrial Mobilization Plan in 1930, and issued a third revision of the plan in 1939, which called for placing immense wartime powers in the hands of the military. It would have virtually turned over management of the total economy to the military. The main work of the WRB was to review this plan and make a recommendation to the President. The antiwar movement protested the establishment of the WRB, as did labor and farm interests, liberals in Congress, and especially the isolationists in the

Senate. It became clear that the public would not sit still for a military takeover of the entire economy in case of war and that President Roosevelt, as later events showed, expected to retain control of government agencies himself. He allowed the War Resources Board to expire on November 24, 1939.

Defense preparation and the organization of government agencies to expedite it proceeded throughout the autumn of 1939 and spring of 1940, but the pace quickened sharply following Germany's invasion of the low countries and France on May 10, 1940. Relying on the executive order of September 8, 1939, as his authority, the president created the Office of Emergency Management by administrative order on May 25, 1940. The OEM was an umbrella organization under which several agencies were later created and which allowed the president to retain direct control over them. If anyone questioned the president's authority to create the Office of Emergency Management by administrative order, their objections were overshadowed by the deep concern that swept the country as a result of the German invasion of the low countries and France and their surrender within days.

On May 27, 1940, in a national radio address that reportedly drew an audience of 85 million people, President Roosevelt declared an unlimited national emergency which remained in effect until canceled by President Harry Truman in 1952. President Roosevelt explained that it was necessary to establish a number of agencies to direct defense preparation, that while the United States had no intention of becoming involved in the European war, it was essential that the country be better prepared militarily and industrially.

On May 29, 1940, the president established the National Defense Advisory Commission under legislative authority approved during World War I that had not been repealed. The term "advisory" was a misnomer, for in fact the commission members also became operating heads of the divisions for which each was responsible, under the direction of the president. By creating the commission the president was able to move ahead with industrial mobilization without raising the issue with Congress, where isolationist sentiment remained strong despite developments in Europe. The commission consisted of seven members, each heading one of the following operating divisions: the Industrial Production Division, Industrial Materials Division, Employment Division, Agricultural Division, Price Stabilization Division, Transportation Division, and the Consumer Division. Later, Donald M. Nelson from Sears, Roebuck & Co. joined the commission with status equivalent to a member, but he was not officially a full member since the number on the commission was set by law. Nelson's position was coordinator of national defense purchases. The Division of State and Local Cooperation and Division of Defense

Housing Coordination were headed by non-commissioners. All divisions were, in due course, transferred to other agencies as they were created.

A major task of the NDAC was to coordinate and rationalize purchases of defense equipment and supplies by the army, Army Air Corps, navy, Maritime Commission and other agencies. To head the Division of Industrial Production, the president chose William S. Knudsen, a Danish immigrant who had risen to president and production chief of General Motors. Knudsen later became head of the Office of Production Management, and when it was abolished he was appointed a lieutenant general in the army, its top adviser on industrial production.

The NDAC was not considered a success, and on January 7, 1941, the Office of Production Management was created and most of the NDAC functions transferred to it. Other components were transferred later to other agencies and departments. The president named two individuals from the NDAC to share direction of the OPM. Knudsen was to serve as director-general, and Sidney Hillman, president of Amalgamated Clothing Workers of America and head of the NDAC Employment Division, was named associate director-general. Roosevelt emphasized that they were co-directors, an arrangement which provoked a testy but amusing interchange at a press conference when a reporter asked Roosevelt why he did not name one responsible head of OPM. Roosevelt insisted that he had done so and that the post was filled by two men; the press persisted that he had two heads and FDR said he had one head of OPM, shared by two men. Many in Congress and the press claimed that Roosevelt created a two-headed OPM because he wanted to keep final control of its work in his own hands. But it also gave parity of power to two important representatives of industry and labor.

The president had hoped that the Office of Production Management would overcome the problems faced by the National Defense Advisory Committee, but OPM was organizationally weak and lacked authority to command cooperation among the various agencies. The Washington press corps began to criticize and ridicule the manner in which different agencies seemed to be going off in all directions, awarding contracts for defense supplies without coordination, while at the same time little progress was being made in developing the stockpiles of raw materials that industry would need to fill orders. But the problem was not lack of staff; by December 1941, OPM had 8,000 employees.

In August 1941, when it became apparent that OPM was having difficulty scheduling production orders, the president created the Supply Priorities and Allocations Board (SPAB) which in its brief life worked to allocate available materials among military needs, defense assistance to other countries, and civilian needs. In point of fact, SPAB had little authority and its board members, who had fulltime jobs as heads of other government agencies, could do little more than act in an advisory capacity.

War Production Board

When war came, it became apparent that better coordination of war production activities was needed, and on January 16, 1942, the president established the War Production Board, which absorbed the functions of the Supply Priorities and Allocations Board and the Office of Production Management, both of which were abolished. The president named Donald M. Nelson chairman, giving the WPB broad powers to coordinate and control virtually all industrial production and procurement. Quickly dubbed "Production Czar" by the press, Nelson described the job as more than any one man could do.

Nelson had been executive vice president of Sears, Roebuck & Co. in Chicago, where for ten years he was in charge of buying all of the products Sears sold. Because of his experience in helping to plan production of materials needed by Sears, he was considered an expert on locating production facilities, a talent greatly needed by the government throughout the war. He had gone to Washington initially in May 1940 on a two-month assignment at the request of the secretary of the treasury to assist with the scheduling of airplane purchases by the French, British and American armed forces, a job the president had handed temporarily to the treasury secretary. Nelson headed the SPAB from its creation in August 1941 until its demise in January 1942. When the president appointed Nelson to head the WPB, businessmen breathed a sigh of relief for it was known that the president had been considering Supreme Court Justice William O. Douglas, an ardent New Dealer, for the job.

The War Production Board was given full powers over industry, production, raw materials, factories, machine tools, priorities, allocations and rationing, absorbing in the process many other agencies or their functions. The authority of the WPB was limited to war production and procurement, however; it did not have authority over the entire economy, which produced ambiguity and conflict with other agencies charged with other responsibilities and confused manufacturers who were not sure whom to heed when they got conflicting instructions.

Independent agencies concerned with food, rubber, aviation gasoline, coal, transportation and civilian requirements managed their own programs with autonomy, weakening the authority of WPB branches responsible for those sectors. Several agencies that dealt with a single commodity, such as the Petroleum Administration for War and the Solid Fuels for War, were virtually left alone. The WPB also basically ignored some of the permanent agencies such as the Bureau of Mines and the Federal Power Commission.

Friction developed quickly between WPB and the army and navy, both of which wanted autonomy in procurement matters. The army and the navy took the stance that the WPB was overly interested in maintaining production of goods for civilian consumption. Long before the WPB was created, the army and navy had accrued to themselves, primarily through the Army-Navy Munitions Board, considerable autonomy in contracting with civilian industries, including the allocation of raw materials, and they were not willing to allow WPB to take over that function in 1942. In addition the military lacked confidence in the ability of WPB to do the job, or at least to do it as efficiently and effectively as it was already being done by the military. The military argued that procurement involved more than simply letting a contract. They contended that they had tried to work with the NDAC, and then with OPM, but that both organizations had been ineffective. The primary reason, of course, was that by the time WPB was established the army and navy had already established their own procurement procedures and saw no reason to relinquish them.

The WPB was particularly interested in establishing priorities in the manufacturing and use of raw materials, but the military argued that its needs were more critical than civilian needs and made little effort to prioritize its procurement. The military's position had been known since the 1939 revision of the Industrial Mobilization Plan called for the army and navy to have control of all aspects of the national economy in time of war. The problem with this concept was that it gave complete authority to the military to pre-empt all other government agencies in the choice of plants and to give the plants priority in obtaining raw materials, equipment, and labor needed to fill contracts—all elements for which WPB or other agencies of government were responsible—with no consideration for essential civilian, industrial, and foreign wartime needs.

Conflict over construction was commonplace. The WPB would authorize the construction of a gasoline plant, a synthetic rubber plant, a raw materials processing plant, or some other kind of war plant only to discover that the army or navy had begun construction of a base that would absorb all of the available labor and most of the other services needed for the WPB construction project. The military took the position that nothing was more important than its construction or production, yet in some cases other production was more important not only to other purposes but indeed to the military itself.

Despite problems it would entail, Nelson decided to leave procurement to the military, with the proviso that they operate within WPB's policies and guidelines for mobilization of the entire economy. He appointed several military personnel to key posts in WPB to help facilitate its limited oversight of military procurement. The military shrewdly named William Knudsen, the former OPM co-director, as its top adviser on industrial procurement when OPM was abolished and its functions absorbed by WPB, naming him to the rank of lieutenant general so that no one could say it was not a significant appointment. Roosevelt was a strong supporter of Knudsen; indeed, there was strong suspicion that Knudsen's appointment as lieutenant general was solely the work of Roosevelt.

Nelson's decision to allow the army and navy virtual autonomy in procurement was doubtless due in part to his feeling that the job of director of WPB was "too big for one man." He demonstrated it by gradually surrendering control over an array of responsibilities to other government agencies, sometimes willingly and sometimes as a result of pressure or political maneuvering. For example, he voluntarily gave up authority over the Office of Price Administration, which became an independent agency. Further, when the president created the War Manpower Commission on April 18, 1942, he offered to place it under the WPB, but Nelson rejected it. All policies and programs related to labor under the various divisions of government were brought together under the WMC. In due course, lack of control over WMC inevitably led to problems for Nelson's War Production Board.

Nelson essentially surrendered authority over purchasing activities of the army, AAF, navy, Maritime Commission, and Treasury Department, at least the contracting for and purchasing of finished products. The WPB retained authority over allocation of raw materials, which gave it some indirect control of production priorities. To facilitate coordination, the former head of the Army-Navy Munitions Board was appointed to a senior position in the WPB. The Army-Navy Munitions Board was largely an army activity; its office was located in the War Department, and the navy participated little in the activities of the board, preferring to handle its own procurement.

The WPB was an extremely busy organization. In early 1942, as many as 130,000 applications a week arrived from manufacturers requesting allocation of raw materials their plants needed, such as cement, wire, lumber, steel and other metals plus motors, valves, machine tools, and various production equipment. The board eventually established 100 district offices and 14 regional offices, with some 4,000 employees, which at first were engaged largely in explaining WPB regulations and processing applications to be forwarded to Washington. In early 1943 these offices gained authority to make priority decisions, within certain limits, but continued to inform Washington about problems in the field.

The early days of the WPB were chaotic. The organization was seen as disorganized and uncertain of its role throughout the war, although especially so during the first 18 months of its existence. The businessmen who had flooded into WPB in its early days could not get answers to many of their questions and little happened. They were accustomed to getting things done promptly and made their irritation with the WPB known to the press and Congress.

While much of the WPB's difficulty was due to the ambiguity of its role and to conflict with other agencies, it suffered mainly from the fact that there was disagreement within WPB about most matters and lack of the kind of staff support for the top leaders found in traditional government agencies and among civil service employees. In short, Nelson could never be sure that all employees were pursuing the same goal or were in accord with the policies he approved.

When the War Production Board was created, several of its offices were responsible for allocations of rubber and other rubber activities designed to maximize the availability of rubber for military purposes and consumer use, yet there was widespread discontent in Congress and the public with the coordination of rubber programs. Several departments of government were concerned with rubber, in addition to offices within WPB. On September 17, 1942, the president directed the WPB to assume responsibility for all of the government's rubber programs and to create a rubber director. Nelson appointed William B. Jeffers, president of the Union Pacific railroad, who was soon labeled "Rubber Czar" by the press. All of the offices in the WPB concerned with rubber were merged into the rubber office. Technically the rubber office was under WPB, but because of authority delegated to the rubber director by the president, Jeffers functioned with virtual autonomy until he resigned in September 1944 to return to his civilian post, at which time his office was replaced by a Rubber Bureau under the WPB. Among the many activities of the rubber director, the public knew him best for establishing a nationwide auto speed limit of 35 miles per hour, violation of which could result in loss of ration permits for gasoline and tires.

One of the many continuing problems of the WPB was the tendency of other agencies to submit requests that inflated their requirements. Most of them figured out that whatever they requested would be trimmed, so they inflated their requests. The WPB knew this and engaged in a guessing game, trying to decide what the agencies' real needs were.

The WPB retained responsibility for mobilizing production of raw materials—metals, fibers, chemicals and other raw materials, both domestic and imports—and managing their allocation. One of its most difficult tasks was to see that scarce raw materials arrived at plants when needed and in adequate quantities. There were constant shortages of raw materials, which meant that somewhere plants were idle. For example, during 1942 there was a serious shortage of aluminum.

It was perhaps inevitable that the various agencies did not provide close supervision of subcontracting. When an agency let a contract to a prime contractor, it tended to allow the contractor almost total freedom in choosing subcontractors. On the one hand, this strategy usually allowed the contractor to expedite subcontracting, it allowed the choice of subcontractors who were known to do good quality work and to deliver on time, and it was more likely to speed the job. On the other hand, it allowed contractors to reward subcontractors with a view to better post-war relationships and resulted in the overlooking of hundreds of small manufacturers whose plants had closed or would close, throwing employees out of work because of shortages of materials or government limitations on what could be manufactured.

By the end of 1942 the WPB had 23,000 employees, a huge number for an organization assembled in less than a year. In addition, many of its branch and office heads were business executives, often on leave from their companies for only three or six months. With such turnover, it was difficult to maintain stability and continuity. Many of the executives who came to Washington, particularly those working for $1 a year, threatened to resign and return to their permanent jobs if they did not get their way. It was impossible to discipline such people or to threaten them with demotion or other punishment that might be used on career employees.

The WPB, as did the NDAC and the OPM before it, was organized into industry groups or divisions, each of which specialized in an industry or associated industries. The industry divisions, which were charged with both regulating and helping their respective industries to achieve their mission in production, were usually headed by "$1 a year men,"* especially in the WPB and its predecessors. The $1 a year jobs had started much earlier, however; I. F. Stone, the muckracker journalist, reported that as early as September 1939 Treasury Secretary Morganthau had named three prominent bankers and financial executives to $1 a year posts to advise him.

Although many people were not bothered by the presence of business executives working in government for $1 a year while still on the payroll of their business employer, some saw it as a conflict of interest. It was often charged that since they were still on the payroll of their companies, they favored those companies in letting contracts, but others contended that businesspersons who were not on leave but were looking ahead to future jobs in industry were probably no more objective. A large portion of the population nonetheless looked at the $1 a year men and their companies as patriots, trying to help win the war.

**The business executives who worked in Washington for $1 a year were so termed since the large majority of them were male. The phrase is used here for historical accuracy.*

The Truman Committee (Senate Committee to Investigate the National Defense Program) was troubled over the ethical aspects of the government hiring $1 a year men while they were still on the payroll of their civilian employers, particularly since there were so many of them—300 in the WPB at the beginning of 1942 and 805 at the end of the year. In testimony before the committee, Nelson said that it was a matter of necessity, that it was impossible to attract anyone with the experience the WPB needed at salaries paid by the government. The Truman Committee concluded that while there was a danger of the $1 a year salaries' fostering improprieties, they were a necessary evil. The ethical problem with $1 a year men also applied to the industry advisory committees, of which there were about 750, or one for nearly every industry. It was solved by assuring that the committees were *advisory* and by not paying the members for their services, nor reimbursing their expenses, and by not allowing them to see any confidential documents.

Prior to the establishment of the Office of War Mobilization, many of the agency heads that were supposed to report to or work with the WPB actually bypassed the agency and dealt directly with the president. In many cases they were civilians who had come from high positions in industry to contribute to the war effort and felt it was their right to deal with the president; they also were frustrated with the ways in which career bureaucrats operated. Further, they knew they would be in Washington for a limited period and feared no retaliation for violating the chain of command. Finally, Roosevelt often encouraged not only these individuals but indeed many others to report directly to him. His doing so caused problems for the WPB; frequently the president would approve an idea without knowing that it had been turned down by the WPB.

It was characteristic of Roosevelt to go outside the chain of command and communicate directly with government employees and individual servicemen overseas. Throughout the war, Roosevelt suggested to several lower ranking members of the diplomatic service and the military, usually civilians in uniform, that they keep in touch with him directly, and he carried on correspondence with some of them. For example, Roosevelt was scheduled for an unofficial conference on April 13, 1945, the day following his death, with the actor Douglas Fairbanks, Jr., then a lieutenant commander in the navy, about a plan Fairbanks had developed for ending the war with Japan diplomatically.

By the middle of 1944, the nation's industrial might had caught up with demand and only needed to maintain momentum in production. Also, it had become apparent that it was only a matter of time before the war would be won, and Nelson began to argue for gradual reconversion of industry to production of civilian goods. He was strongly opposed by the military, which maintained an "all-out" stance throughout the war for fear that any shift to the production of civilian goods would lead industries and the work force to relax their commitment to the war effort. The president solved the dispute by dispatching Nelson as his special emissary to China and appointing Julius Krug to succeed him.

The War Production Board functioned until November 1945 when it was redesignated the Civilian Production Administration.

Office of Price Administration

The Office of Price Control and Civilian Supply was created by executive order in April 1941, but it could only cajole, jawbone and persuade, none of which was very effective in controlling prices. Its name was shortened to Office of Price Administration in August 1941. The passage of the Emergency Price Control Act in late January 1942 was a first step in setting price controls and rationing regulations with teeth.

Fearing runaway inflation, the president assigned primary responsibility for price stabilization to the OPA. In March 1942, the OPA issued price ceilings for most commodities, along with regulations covering fuels, paper, equipment, and other items. At the same time, it invoked rent controls in 302 areas of the country where significant defense activities were taking place. Violations could bring the culprit a year in jail or a $5,000 fine. The OPA was also responsible for rationing. Between the summer of 1942 and the end of the war, the number of rationing boards fluctuated between 5,300 and 5,700. In August 1944 there were 5,520 rationing boards with 18,033 rationing panels (individual boards were divided into panels to deal with different commodities) and 98,641 panel members, plus about 75,000 of what the OPA called paid volunteers, with backup support provided by 94 district OPA offices. Among the major tasks of the OPA were printing and distributing nationally the vast number of regulations it promulgated, printing and issuing millions of ration books, and managing the billions of stamps people submitted for purchases that were rationed.

The first head of the OPA was economist Leon Henderson, a longtime government employee and ardent New Dealer. The job immediately put him in conflict with anti–New Deal members of Congress; the clashes only got worse month after month, until he resigned in December 1942. Successor Chester Bowles, a journalist and successful advertising man, developed somewhat better relations with Congress, but the OPA remained highly controversial throughout its existence.

In addition to irritating the public, the OPA had difficulty working with other agencies of government. It was frequently necessary for staff members of the OPA and the WPB to work together, but they did not do so without difficulty. The WPB staff largely came from business and industry; the OPA was populated largely by academicians. Staff members in the two organizations simply disagreed or did not understand one another. The academicians included a high percentage of Keynesian economists with advanced degrees who were dedicated to social planning and an activist government. Rationing administrator Paul O'Leary called them "public welfare minded," but the businessmen regarded them as socialists. There were exceptions, to be sure, such as future president Richard Nixon, who served as an attorney in the OPA prior to entering the navy.

The conflict was especially acute between the OPA staff members in charge of rationing and the office of Petroleum Administration for War, which was composed largely of petroleum industry executives who were strong believers in free markets. It was the job of PAW to determine the supply of petroleum products, then turn the job of rationing over to the OPA, but the businessmen in PAW were never willing to trust completely the OPA rationing staff and tried to set rationing policies themselves.

A similar situation existed between the OPA rationing staff and several other offices, such as the Office of the Rubber Director and the Office of Defense Transportation (ODT). The Office of War Information would contact representatives of the rubber director, PAW, or ODT for assessments of supplies of commodities or services for which they were responsible and issue news releases based on this information. The commodity organizations tended to be overly optimistic about supplies available or expected, while the OPA rationing staff tended to understate available supplies in order to justify rationing and price regulations. This conflict led to much public distrust of the rationing system and many violations of its regulations.

The OPA staff felt that once a commodity agency had made its determination of supplies and rationing was turned over to the OPA, all information concerning supplies should be controlled by OPA staff, but that view was not shared by several of the commodity agencies, and conflict continued between them and the OPA throughout most of the war. On several occasions, various government officials discussed the possibility of turning over all rationing and price control of rubber to the Office of the Rubber Director, petroleum products to the PAW, and food to the War Food Administration, leaving to the OPA the rationing of such items as shoes, clothing, bicycles, typewriters, and stoves. But this idea never got far, primarily because the commodity agencies did not have the field organization to handle the job, while the OPA had more than 5,000 local rationing boards in place. The rationing of trucks was switched to the ODT, but the OPA retained control over the allocation of new automobiles.

Farmers and businesses tried to abolish the OPA, in the belief that the country would be better off if prices could rise to the market level. And legislation was passed several times in one house of Congress to abolish the OPA, but each time the agency was saved by the other house.

During its first year, the OPA expected to be able to control prices through regulation alone. John Kenneth Galbraith, deputy administrator for prices, argued that local boards should not be involved in "spying" on merchants to see if they were abiding by price control regulations. But within one year the OPA became convinced that for price regulations to work effectively, local volunteer boards would have to be involved. That proved to be the case; the public was more amenable to accepting decisions made by local volunteer boards than those made by paid government officials. For the last two years of the war, rationing and price controls worked about as well as could have been expected, thanks in large measure to local, unpaid, volunteer board members.

War Manpower Commission

Before the War Manpower Commission was created in March 1942, some 20 offices and departments in government were responsible for various aspects of the national workforce. The WMC was primarily concerned with development of policies relating to labor supply and utilization; in several cases agencies concerned with labor supply were brought directly under WMC control. For example, in September 1942, the U.S. Employment Service and several smaller labor agencies were transferred to the WMC, but the collection of all such agencies under one head never became reality. Within a month responsibility for agricultural labor was assigned to the Agriculture Department. In December 1942 the president directed that the Selective Service System be brought under the WMC. The change actually had little effect on the work of the national office of Selective Service, and volunteers serving on the 6,500 draft boards around the country were only vaguely aware of the change. But the lack of autonomy rankled the leadership of Selective Service, and one year later Congress made Selective Service autonomous again. The Civil Service Commission continued to recruit workers for the federal government, the Railroad Retirement Board continued to handle recruitment for the railroads, and the War Shipping Administration continued to supply crews for the merchant marine.

Thus, WMC control over labor was limited. Unlike the control over raw materials, which could be shipped to any point where they were needed, labor was not so mobile. Proposals to draft workers and move them to sites where they were needed created a political firestorm and were never seriously considered.

The WMC and various divisions of the WPB were continually in conflict. Divisions of the WPB thought they should have some authority over how labor was allocated to industries with which they worked, while the WMC argued that it was responsible for labor allocation. The fact that many industries worked on a cost plus fixed fee basis meant that they had little incentive to use labor most efficiently.

With its power over the hiring, dismissal, and transfer of labor, the WMC should have been effective in labor allocation, but it was not. In a nation with such a militant dedication to freedom, it was not possible to enforce WMC regulations. The workers ignored or disobeyed them, and employers evaded them. After the Office of War Mobilization was created in 1943 and given supervisory powers over all the wartime agencies, the WMC lost clout. When a serious labor shortage developed on the West Coast in mid-1943, the WMC developed a plan to regulate allocation of labor among West Coast industries, but it was pre-empted by a plan advanced by the new head of the OWM.

Office of Defense Transportation

The declaration of war was followed by the rapid creation of several special agencies to manage various sectors of the economy. Since transportation would be critical to the war effort, an Office of Defense Transportation was created on December 18, 1941, replacing and absorbing the functions of the Transportation Division of the National Defense Advisory Commission. The president's executive order gave the ODT responsibility for coordinating "transportation policies and activities of the railroad, motor, inland waterway, pipe line, air transport, and coastwise and intercoastal shipping industries." The ODT was also concerned with maintaining supplies of coal, collecting iron and steel scrap, obtaining iron ore, easing port congestion, preventing sabotage of transportation facilities, and several other functions.

The ODT, which served primarily in a coordinating capacity but was given the authority to force compliance if necessary, set policies to maximize the efficiency of transport, including an order preventing the shipment of partially filled boxcars. Railroads were the mainstay of transportation throughout the war. The nation's heavy reliance on large trucks for shipping came after the war; during the war the shortages of tires, gasoline and serviceable trucks combined with the lack of a good interstate highway system relegated trucks to local delivery and short-haul transport. Trains had begun to shift to diesel fuel, although many still burned coal, and the network of rail lines was in relatively good shape. Railroads were left in private ownership, but the ODT worked closely with railroad managements to ensure the most efficient use of rail services.

The ODT relied largely on the Association of American Railroads to see that freight transport met the needs of the military services and other war demands, with ODT surveillance. The ODT also monitored passenger travel. As a result of reductions in auto travel and a sharp increase in total travel, passenger travel on railroads rose from some 2.4 billion passenger miles per month in early 1942 to more than 8 billion per month in the middle of 1943.

In early 1942 German submarines were sinking so many tankers transporting oil from Gulf ports to the East Coast that alternative transportation had to be found. This led to the construction of two pipelines from Texas to the East Coast. The first, known as the "Big Inch," was a 24-inch pipe that carried crude oil from Longview, Texas, north to Norris City, Illinois, then east to Phoenixville, Pennsylvania, then through smaller lines to refineries near Philadelphia and Linden, New Jersey. The Big Inch was in partial operation by February 1943 and fully serviceable by August of that year. A 20-inch line, known as the "Little Big Inch" originated in southeast Texas, joined the Big Inch at Little Rock, Arkansas, and paralleled it from there to the East Coast. Completed in early 1944, the Little Big Inch carried gasoline and other refined petroleum products. Both were constructed and operated by War Emergency Pipelines, Inc., with financing by the government, through the Defense Plant Corporation (which funded the construction) and the Defense Supplies Corporation (which financed the line's operation). The lines were sold after the war to Texas Eastern Transmission Corporation in a blind bid process for more than it had cost to build them.

The ODT controlled the use of rental cars, limited the number and services of taxicabs and canceled auto racing. It also encouraged a variety of other steps to conserve fuel and transportation facilities, including restoration of streetcars, extending streetcar services and reducing services based on rubber.

The main barrier to automobile travel was the shortage of rubber. On December 11, 1941, the sale of new tires was halted; tire rationing began on December 27. Because of the sinking of oil and gas tankers by German submarines, gasoline rationing was introduced on the East Coast on May 15, 1942. For political reasons, the president was reluctant to extend gasoline rationing nationwide, but a study by a committee composed of financier Bernard Baruch, President Karl T. Compton of the Massachusetts Institute of Technology, and President James B. Conant of Harvard University reported on September 10, 1942, that the rubber shortage required nationwide gasoline rationing. The administration of tire and gasoline rationing was assigned to the OPA.

The loss of more than 90 percent of the rubber supply when Indonesia and Malaya were occupied by the Japanese presented the United States with a serious problem. Raw rubber from South America supplied only a small fraction of the need. Construction of synthetic rubber plants had begun earlier, but time was required to build an adequate number. In fact, only one synthetic rubber plant was operational at the beginning of 1942, having produced only 8,383 long tons of rubber in 1941. By 1944 several other plants were operational, with total production that year of 753,111 long tons.

Commercial truckers had to qualify for a Certificate of War Necessity and abide by the 35 mile per hour speed limit in order to be eligible for gasoline, tires, and parts. The Certificates of War Necessity issued to truckers and other commercial vehicles by the ODT led to a conflict with the OPA, which accused the ODT of issuing the certificates too liberally and upsetting the balance of rationing of motor fuels.

Barges on lakes and canals that were idle before Pearl Harbor stayed busy throughout the war, although in many cases war materials that could have been shipped by water more cheaply were shipped by train to save time.

Office of War Mobilization

The lack of coordination among the various agencies continued to frustrate not only the members of the various agencies but the president himself. On October 3, 1942, the president created the Office of Economic Stabilization, charging it with preventing inflation by coordinating the activities of agencies that had been created to control wages, costs, profits, rationing, subsidies, and rents. The president persuaded James F. Byrnes, a former congressman and senator from South Carolina who had been appointed to the Supreme Court only the year before, to resign from the court and become director of the OES.

The conflict among various other agencies, particularly between the WPB and the military services over allocation of scarce raw materials and production facilities, continued to hamper productivity and efficiency. In many cases, no one could resolve differences but the president. As a result, he spent a disproportionate share of his time trying to iron out disagreements between various agencies or vetoing projects. But more often such disagreements never reached him, were never solved, and continued to thwart efficiency.

Even though the Office of Economic Stabilization, among all

agencies, probably did most to bring inflation under control, the responsibility for OES allowed Byrnes to supervise only selected agencies and programs. The press and members of Congress continued to call for an overall manager of agencies prosecuting the war. Members of the press said there were too many "czars." Several bills were introduced in Congress to address this concern, and one was on the verge of passing when on May 27, 1943, Roosevelt issued an executive order establishing the Office of War Mobilization with authority over essentially all war-related activities except military strategy. The president chose to establish the OWM through executive order rather than rely on legislation for several reasons, but primarily because it allowed him to change the responsibilities as needed; it also permitted him to avoid some of the transfers of agencies that the legislation would have required.

The OWM provided a central office to which wartime agencies could turn for approval of ideas, for confirmation that they were not invading the province of others, for adjudicating differences between individuals and agencies, and for resolution of other conflicts that had permeated the government agencies involved in war production. Thanks to the OWM the role of the WPB was better defined by late 1943, and many of the difficulties and conflicts the WPB had experienced earlier began to settle down.

The president chose Byrnes to head the OWM. Byrnes was a master at human relations and a superb strategist in dealing with Congress. Although a self-effacing man, Byrnes soon came to be called assistant president. In contrast to many wartime agency heads, Byrnes accumulated a staff of only 10 professionals, calling on experts from inside and outside the government from time to time to help with technical problems. His credibility with Congress, the president, and the press was such that he was able to accrue to himself the control authorized in the executive order. Byrnes's primary role was to referee when there was conflict between two or more agencies; because of his prestige and the fact that he enjoyed the confidence of the president, he was able to settle matters which had previously drifted. His skills as a politician paid off as head of the OWM. He often managed to settle difficult problems between strong-willed agency heads to the satisfaction of both, with the result that both agencies performed their jobs better. His role was not the direct management of agencies, but on occasion he overruled agencies and set policy for them. The fact that his office was in the White House and that he usually required agency heads to meet in his office provided the symbolic authority he needed.

One example will illustrate Byrnes's wisdom and value in the OWM. In January 1945 the navy sent to President Roosevelt a plan to begin construction of 84 new ships; the president approved the plan, as the navy assumed he would, considering his history as a strong supporter of the navy. When news of the decision reached Byrnes, he worked with the director of the Bureau of the Budget to persuade Roosevelt that since the ships would not come off the production line until 1947, it was highly unlikely that they would be needed. By this time it was apparent that the European war was virtually over, so some of the ships in that theater could presumably be transferred to the Pacific soon. Roosevelt relented, construction of the 84 ships was canceled, and hundreds of millions of dollars were saved.

Of course, Byrnes did not resolve all conflicts. In fact, President Roosevelt was a great believer in allowing agencies to fight on some matters, rather than solving the differences. The president was famous for not only allowing but sometimes stimulating conflict between agencies and individuals in the belief that it could contribute to greater productivity. However, with the establishment of the OWM, the president was relieved of the multitude of problems related to war production that had consumed so much of his time.

The president had created the OWM by executive order, but in October 1944, Congress one-upped the president by creating the Office of War Mobilization and Reconversion, which absorbed the OWM and had the additional responsibility of directing activities related to winding down war production and converting America's productivity to civilian purposes. Byrnes was named director of the OWMR. At that time, additional staff members were brought in, including Major General Lucius D. Clay, who later served as commander of American occupation forces in Europe. Byrnes stayed with the OWMR until April 1945, when he was succeeded by Fred M. Vinson, former congressman and federal judge, who had earlier succeeded him as director of the OES.

Selected Agencies

Several other agencies concerned with the management of the war economy merit mention, though some of them existed for only short periods before being abolished or merged into other agencies. The administration became increasingly conscious in early 1940 that the country was inadequately equipped for the production of instruments of war and the stockpiling of raw materials that would be needed. When Germany invaded the low countries and France in May 1940, Congress was prodded into activity. It passed and the president signed on June 25 a bill which gave the Reconstruction Finance Corporation authority to create as subsidiaries what became the Defense Plant Corporation, the Defense Supplies Corporation, the Rubber Reserve Company, and the Metals

Reserve Company. The legislation also authorized loans to private industry to achieve the purposes of the bill, and instead of requiring competitive bidding, it authorized negotiated contracts, which made it possible for the four agencies to move more rapidly.

The Defense Plant Corporation was established on August 22, 1940, to develop defense production capability. Private industry was not yet committed to conversion from civilian to defense production, for it had no assurance that defense production would be needed for long. In addition, the civilian economy was on the upturn and most industries were reluctant to abandon their civilian markets. So the government built several hundred war plants, particularly for the production of explosives, metals and heavy construction, and contracted with private industry to operate them.

The Rubber Reserve Company and the Metals Reserve Company were created on June 28, 1940. The Rubber Reserve Company was responsible for building up supplies of rubber and beginning the construction of synthetic rubber plants since, if war with Japan occurred, the source of natural rubber would likely be cut off. After the attack on Pearl Harbor, the supply of rubber from Southeast Asia, which accounted for more than 90 percent of the country's natural rubber supply was indeed cut off.

The Metals Reserve Company was charged with procuring and stockpiling strategic metals, and it was authorized to open and operate mines. Congress had approved the Strategic Materials Act on June 7, 1939, and within months had provided $70 million for the stockpiling of such materials. By May 1940 significant amounts of chromium, manganese, quartz, tin and tungsten had been accumulated under the direction of the Army-Navy Munitions Board. Substantial quantities of the metals especially bauxite, lead, tin, nickel and copper, were imported from South America and the Caribbean. In April 1941, the Metals Reserve Company bought 500,000 tons of copper from Chile, Peru and Mexico, in addition to 100,000 tons it had bought the previous November. The company also subsidized the expansion of mines in Latin America. It reopened copper mines in the United States that had earlier been closed because they were uneconomical, and reactivated metals processing plants that had been closed.

The Defense Supplies Corporation, created on August 29, 1940, assumed the task of stockpiling strategic materials not specifically covered under other legislation, including aviation gasoline, manila fiber, cork, teak, quinine and other drugs, plus burlap, wood, silk and other fibers, drugs and chemicals.

The National Defense Mediation Board had been established in March 1941, but its powers were limited. On January 12, 1942, it was replaced by the National War Labor Board (WLB), which consisted of four representatives each from labor, industry and the public, with "final jurisdiction over all labor disputes and over wage and salary rates except as to railroads." The executive order establishing the WLB said that "the Board shall finally determine the dispute, and for this purpose may use mediation, voluntary arbitration, or arbitration under rules established by the Board." On September 1, 1942, the president gave the WLB authority over all wage rates, which were administered by its Division of Wage Stabilization, not solely those in dispute. The representatives of the public on the 12-member board essentially decided issues that separated industry and labor. For instance, union representatives on the WLB pushed for a union shop ruling (i.e., a decree that all workers in a unionized shop had to belong to the union). The board voted that new workers in unionized plants would automatically become union members, but during the first 15 days of employment they could decide to opt out of the union if they wished. However, fear of punishment or harassment by union members discouraged most new workers from opting out.

The WLB had no direct enforcement mechanism itself, but it could bring to bear a number of punitive actions to force a company to comply with its rulings, including requesting the army or navy to withhold contracts, the WPB to deny raw materials, and the IRS to deny certain tax deductions. Finally, if a company or its labor force refused to comply with WLB rulings, the WLB could ask the president to direct the army or navy to take over the company temporarily and operate it to ensure compliance.

Early in the war, food production and distribution was scattered among more than a dozen agencies. Prior to its abolition, the National Defense Advisory Commission's Farm Products Division monitored food production. Other agencies concerned with food included the War Shipping Administration, the War Production Board, the Lend-Lease Administration, the Office of Education, the Food Requirements Committee, and several others, both within and outside the Department of Agriculture. To consolidate and coordinate matters relating to food and fiber, the War Food Administration was established April 19, 1943, under the secretary of agriculture. The OPA continued to be responsible for food rationing and price control. The WFA did not absorb the functions of all of the other agencies but did provide greater coordination.

The War Shipping Administration was created on February 7, 1942, to oversee the American shipping industry. It operated ships owned by the U.S. government and set priorities for all ships sailing under the American flag. The Maritime Commission, which had been established in 1936 and charged with supervision of ship construction, worked closely with the WSA. This was accomplished smoothly, largely because Admiral

Emory S. Land, Chairman of the Maritime Commission, was given an additional appointment as administrator of the WSA.

As war plants sprang up, an influx of workers poured into nearby towns to fill the newly created jobs. Unfortunately, almost all of the towns lacked sufficient housing to care for them. This crisis led to the creation on February 24, 1942, of the National Housing Agency, superseding the Division of Housing Coordination, with the purpose of centralizing all government activities having to do with the financing, management and construction of wartime housing. The government built thousands of housing units near war plants for rental to defense workers, but this was not the first effort of the federal government to support housing. Congress had included $100 million for defense housing in an appropriations bill passed September 9, 1940; then, just over a month later, on October 14, it had passed the Community Facilities Act, better known as the Lanham Act, that added another $150 million for the purchase of land and construction of housing, utilities, nursery schools, child care centers, transportation and other community facilities.

The Office of Scientific Research and Development, created June 28, 1941, was established to conduct research on weapons of war and problems specific to the war. It conducted little research itself but contracted with universities, independent research foundations, private industry and hospitals to conduct research. The OSRD began a year earlier as the National Defense Research Committee and was the first example of the application of science in a major, organized way to the development of weapons of war.

The Committee on Fair Employment Practice was created by executive order on June 25, 1941, to prohibit racial discrimination in defense industries. It was briefly a component of the WPB, when first established, but in the summer of 1942 was transferred to the WMC. The FEPC was a political football throughout the war. The House of Representatives voted to reduce its budget and later to eliminate its budget altogether, but in each case its appropriations were saved by the Senate. The committee and its work represented the beginning of equal opportunities for minorities in industries doing business with the government.

The War Ballots Commission, one of the more obscure wartime agencies, deserves mention only because of its unique responsibility. Few military personnel had voted in the 1942 national elections, for to do so they had to cast absentee ballots in their home districts. In 1944, Congress passed a bill to permit service personnel to vote in national elections wherever they happened to be stationed, beginning with the 1944 presidential election and continuing until six months after the war, and set up the War Ballots Commission to administer it. The army and navy did a remarkable job of persuading soldiers and sailors to vote. Of the

3 million service personnel who voted, the overwhelming majority voted for the re-election of President Roosevelt.

Censorship

Two agencies that were not involved directly in industrial production played important roles in the government's management of the war. The Office of Censorship was created by executive order on December 19, 1941, just 12 days following the declaration of war, with the task of concealing from the enemy any information that would aid in its war effort. Censorship offices were soon established at ports, post offices, and telephone and cable companies throughout the country. But the press reacted against the idea of censorship, so the president wrote a letter on December 27, 1942, authorizing the censorship office to establish "voluntary censorship" of radio and the press. Newspaper and radio broadcasters voluntarily followed guidelines set by the Office of Censorship and indeed voluntarily submitted many stories for censorship before publishing them.

The Censorship Office remained open at all times to answer queries from editors concerning whether specific stories might be published without harming the war effort. The code prohibited publication of information about troop movements, war production figures, locations of military installations, and other information that would be useful to the enemy. Thus, the sinking of large numbers of American merchant ships off the East Coast of the United States in 1942 was not fully reported. The atom bomb project remained unreported until the first one was dropped on Hiroshima in August 1945.

The main jobs of the Press Division and the Radio Division were to set guidelines and codes for the press and radio to follow in keeping with voluntary censorship, a process that seemed to work fairly well. There were exceptions to voluntary censorship; reporters covering army maneuvers were required to submit all stories for approval by the censorship office. According to the Office of Censorship, violations were few, usually in small-town newspapers, due to lack of information rather than intention to violate censorship guidelines. Nor did the media object strenuously to the restrictions, for they agreed that they had an obligation to support the government's attempts to withhold information that might benefit the enemy.

Office of War Information

The Office of War Information, created on June 13, 1942, was the culmination of several steps by the government to inform the public about the war and about defense preparations and government policy concerning national security. It was not a new idea: during World War I there had been such an organization known as the Committee on Public Information, directed by the journalist George Creel.

The OWI grew out of the efforts of two men. Archibald MacLeish, a lawyer by training, former editor of *Fortune* magazine, and by the late 1930s the librarian of Congress, was better known as a poet. A Division of Information in the Office of Emergency Management had been created in March 1941, but the coordination of government information began with the creation of the Office of Facts and Figures (OFF), with MacLeish, who continued as librarian of Congress, as its head. The name of the office was intended to mollify members of Congress who feared the establishment of a propaganda agency.

The other was Robert Sherwood, the noted playwright (*Idiot's Delight, Abe Lincoln in Illinois, There Shall Be No Night*) who had become a speech writer and adviser to President Roosevelt in mid–1940. In August 1941, Sherwood persuaded the president that the United States needed to provide information about the American government's position on the war to people in countries not allied with Germany. His intent was to bolster their spirits by providing factual information, in contrast to the raw propaganda they heard from Germany. Sherwood was named head of the Foreign Information Service, as it was called, and assembled an able staff, including such notable literary figures as Stephen Vincent Benét, John Houseman, and Thornton Wilder.

By the spring of 1942, with America in the war, President Roosevelt decided that a centralized office of government information was needed, and the OWI was created. The term "propaganda" was not used in the creation of OWI, but in the pure definition of the term that was the agency's product. MacLeish's OFF became the Domestic Branch, with a new director, and Sherwood's FIS became the Overseas Branch. The new director of the OWI was Elmer Davis, the well-known broadcaster whose nightly news program on CBS radio was one of the most popular of the day. His reputation for presenting the news objectively and his flat nasal voice reflecting his Indiana roots were reassuring to his listeners, with the result that he was one of the most trusted newsmen in the country. A former Rhodes scholar, Davis was a bland on-air personality, accentuated by his trademark black bowtie.

A brilliant journalist and writer, Davis gave the new office credibility with Congress and the press but was not a strong administrator, and conflict within OWI and between OWI and Congress festered throughout the agency's existence. The OWI attracted some of the best known writers of the day but also some highly controversial people, including several who had been identified with the Communist Party in their writings and public statements.

The OWI wrote special articles and other material for newspapers, magazines and radio, and prepared brochures, flyers, posters, newsletters, films, and other material to inform the public about the war effort. Millions of posters, openly propagandistic and often in cartoon form, decorated government buildings and were distributed to grocery stores and other private businesses which posted them in prominent places. The OWI prepared postcards with propaganda cartoons on half of the address side of the card, and they were sold through post offices (postcards sold then for one cent, including postage). One of the largest collections of reproductions of propaganda postcards appears in Stan Cohen's illustrated book *V for Victory: America's Home Front During World War II.*

The OWI staff was especially effective in persuading writers for radio serials and movies to insert information in their scripts focusing on support of national defense. Some of the "progressive" materials the OWI issued raised the ire of members of Congress, however. The *Chicago Tribune* called it a haven for Communists and draft dodgers, and many members of Congress thought it unduly oriented toward propounding New Deal philosophy and serving as a propaganda agency for the Roosevelt administration.

In early 1943 the Domestic Branch recruited a considerable number of staff members with backgrounds in advertising and public relations. The original staff considered their material objective and were offended by what they considered to be sales promotion material prepared by the people from the advertising world. This perception led to considerable internal friction, on top of friction already existing within and from outside the OWI. A month earlier, Davis had asked the writers to alter copy for a brochure that conflicted with Agriculture Department policies. They refused, he banned publication of the brochure, and the writers quit amid loud protestations concerning the integrity of OWI. This incident helped to convince several members of Congress that the OWI was a hotbed of ideologues, and when the 1943-44 appropriations bill for OWI was approved, funds for the Domestic Branch had been cut by almost 75 percent, effectively eliminating most of its programs.

The Overseas Branch also drew criticism from Congress. The greatest flap had to do with the American recognition of Admiral Jean Darlan as head of government in North Africa in November 1942, and recognition of King Victor Emmanuel III and General Pietro Bagdolio as leaders of the government of Italy after its surrender in September 1943. The liberal staff of the Overseas Branch was shocked that its government would embrace fascists or those formerly identified with fascism and proceeded to issue broadcasts contrary to American government policies.

The Overseas Branch redeemed itself with superb work in psychological warfare, persuading many Italians and, later, Germans to surrender. It survived intact and ended the war with 8,400 employees, half of whom were immigrants and other foreign nationals.

The Overseas Branch's primary medium for reaching other countries was radio. It was called "Voice of America," and in that form survives today, broadcasting in many different languages. Along with the British Broadcasting System, it was the most objective source of information for occupied countries all over the world, both during and after the war.

Paying for the War

About 45 percent of the cost of the American war effort was paid with taxes; the remainder was borrowed, primarily through the sale of bonds. The *Statistical Abstract of the United States* shows that the national debt totaled $43 billion on June 30, 1940, and by that date in 1945 had risen to $259 billion.

The Treasury Department conducted eight War Loan drives, the first beginning in November 1942 and the last ending December 31, 1945. The first ones lasted three to four weeks each but the later ones were extended to six to eight weeks. Individuals purchased $49 billion in war bonds, including some $35 billion of E bonds, in addition to larger denominations sold to banks, insurance companies and other financial institutions. (See Chapter IX for more about E bonds.)

For most people, income taxes were relatively low. Historian Henry Pringle calculated that under the revenue act of 1941, a married man with two children, earning $5,000 a year (a large salary then) paid $271 in federal income taxes; under the 1943 revenue act, the same man paid $773. The present system of tax withholding was introduced during the war; previously all personal income taxes were paid annually in March.

Taxes were raised every year during the war. In 1944 a marginal tax rate of 92 percent was established on personal incomes over $200,000 a year, though after the war the threshold was raised to $400,000. The marginal rate was 91 percent from 1951 until 1964 when Congress lowered it to 77 percent. Marginal rates were lowered to 70 percent in 1965, to 50 percent in 1982, to 38.5 percent in 1987 and to 28 percent in 1988, with income levels to which the marginal rates applied reduced significantly. In 1993, Congress raised the marginal rate to 39.6 percent for personal incomes over $250,000 a year.

Change in tax law, along with increased incomes, resulted in thousands of people becoming taxpayers during the war after having never paid taxes before. In 1940, approximately 4 million individual income tax returns were filed; this number rose to 42 million in 1944. In 1941 only 3.4 percent of personal income went to federal taxes; this figure had grown to 12.2 percent in 1945. Personal income taxes accounted for $1.4 billion of the national budget in 1941, but had increased to $18 billion in 1945. While taxes on personal income were raised sharply, the increase in the number of taxpayers resulted in part from a reduction in personal exemptions, as for example from $2,000 for a married couple in 1940 to $1,200 in 1942.

Tax policy was directed not only at paying for the war but also at helping to control prices and limit inflation by reducing the purchasing power of consumers. In addition to taxes, measures to control inflation included limitations on credit, restrictions on the purchase of consumer goods, wage controls, price controls, rationing and the sale of war bonds.

In view of all of the conflict that existed within and between agencies created to conduct the war, how was it possible for the country to have been so productive? The reasons were several, not least of which was the near total dedication of all segments of society to winning the war. Even those in government who were engaged in conflict were almost always focused on achieving the most production possible. As far as government was concerned, the issues that drew most criticism were the very ones that deserve credit for much of the productivity. The $1 a year men drew a great deal of criticism, but in fact they knew the country's industries, which plants could do specific jobs, where to find raw materials, and how to get them to plants as fast as possible. The nature of government purchasing, which drew so much criticism, also accounted for the rapid buildup of industry and its astonishing productivity. Moving from the bidding process to negotiated contracting was more expensive but resulted in a massive output of goods in the shortest time possible. Finally, the considerable autonomy of the military services in their procurement programs, even though it came at some expense to other priorities, gave the army and navy the materials to fight the war.

Was the great proliferation of agencies necessary during the war? Perhaps not. It arguably resulted in large part from the fact that President Roosevelt, a charismatic leader, was not highly skilled as a manager. He found it difficult to dismiss people; instead he would sometimes create a new agency to handle a task without abolishing the agency that had been doing the work. He created several agencies to handle labor matters that some argued should have been handled by the Labor Department, and several to do other work that logically came within the domain of the State Department.

Although most of the regulatory agencies responsible for prosecuting the war had authority to force compliance, that authority was used rarely and usually only in egregious cases. The more common "enforcement" method was to appeal to patriotism.

Chapter VI

Industrial Mobilization

America's industrial production during World War II has appropriately been called a miracle. At the Yalta conference of Allied war leaders in February 1945, Stalin toasted American industrial production, asserting that without it the war would have been lost. It was, to be sure, an astonishing feat of productivity, accomplished in a relatively short period. With full credit to the military forces, they could not have been successful without the monumental productivity of American industry, which turned out thousands of airplanes, ships, tanks, guns, and other munitions in short order.

Before the war the army had six arsenals that produced most of its munitions. Within a year after war was declared, thousands of plants were engaged in war production. Typewriter factories produced machine guns and automobile plants manufactured bombers, tanks and airplanes. Once the government halted production of civilian goods, or restricted the availability of critical raw materials, conversion to war production moved quickly. In Illinois, the Pullman Standard Car Company began to build tanks and airplane parts, Stewart-Warner manufactured artillery fuses, Buick and Studebaker turned to making airplane engines, International Harvester manufactured artillery gun carriages, the Elgin Watch Company manufactured time fuses, and a manufacturer of girdles and corsets turned to making parachutes. Almost every industry was engaged in war work. Even convicts were used to inspect bombs, cartridge clips and gun parts.

Although most industries involved in war production were manufacturing items that were related to their prewar manufacturing, such as the bedspread factory that made mosquito nets, in a great many cases they were not. For example, a factory that processed and canned citrus fruit converted to manufacturing parts for merchant ships, a mill that processed cotton switched to manufacturing guns, a mechanical pencil factory manufactured bomb parts and precision instruments, a piano manufacturer converted to building airplane wings, a tire manufacturer built airplane fuselages, and a pickle plant made airplane skis.

On February 1, 1942, automobile production ceased, and automobile manufacturing plants that were not already engaged in war production began to convert to it. Employees of automobile manufacturing plants remained employed, manufacturing war equipment, but thousands of automobile dealers across the country went out of business. Automobile production had already begun to downsize, albeit with great reluctance on the part of manufacturers who had been relishing the increased demand for cars, as people had more money to spend.

The government had begun to pressure automobile manufacturers to cut back production of cars in the spring of 1941. That April the government directed that for the year beginning August 1, 1941, production of the 1941-42 model be reduced 20 percent. But the growing scarcity of raw materials and the need for the auto industry to produce war materials led the Office of Production Management to order further reductions, beginning with 26.5 percent for August through November and increasing to 50 percent by the summer of 1942. The cutoff of civilian auto production in February 1942 made the earlier plan moot.

Prior to the Pearl Harbor attack, American industry approached defense production with what journalist I. F. Stone has called a "business as usual" attitude. Government contracts were taken on largely in addition to, not instead of, production for the consumer market. Congress had made appropriations for a modest expansion in the number of naval and merchant ships in the mid– to late 1930s, but when Germany invaded Poland in 1939, setting off World War II, America's industrial preparation was still on a peacetime footing. A few days after the invasion, when President Roosevelt declared a limited national emergency, some increase in defense production occurred. But it was not until Germany invaded Denmark and Norway in April 1940 and the low countries and France in May that Congress began to appropriate significant amounts of money for defense production. Thereafter, appropriations for more tanks, guns, planes and ships seemed to come almost monthly.

Even then, manufacturers were reluctant to terminate or reduce production for the civilian market. The country was not yet in war, and business executives had no way of knowing how long their plants would be needed in war production. If they retooled for war production, would their civilian markets be taken over by competitors?

Another factor influencing defense production was the attitude of business toward the New Deal. When the Roosevelt administration came to office in 1933 it quickly launched a social and economic revolution that the business community regarded as repressive and antibusiness. Business leaders were enraged and mounted campaigns against the New Deal and its programs. Yet, as the Roosevelt administration saw it, business was simply opposed to its efforts to ease the hunger and deprivation that gripped the country. Business leaders believed that the New Deal administration was dominated by enemies of a free market economy, that the self-proclaimed social democrats were actually socialists or communists. Later revelations confirmed that several New Deal staff members were members of the Communist Party or sympathizers to it and that others were intellectual socialists.

Antipathy and distrust between President Roosevelt and the business community ran deep. For almost six years, before the beginning of defense production, Roosevelt had referred to businessmen as "economic royalists" and "money changers," and constantly vilified business in speeches and press conferences. Not only opponents of the New Deal but some of its supporters acknowledged that the administration was using business as the whipping boy, a scapegoat for the Depression. Following the Democratic national convention in 1936 when FDR was nominated by his party for a second term, even the liberal *Washington Post* took him to task for bashing business so hard in his acceptance speech.

The antibusiness climate in the New Deal frightened businessmen, who had little confidence in the administration and would not undertake the expansion that could have solved the unemployment problem and revived the economy. In fact, at the time when industrial expansion was urgently needed to provide jobs, industries closed factories or reduced output, and retreated from growth, waiting until the attitude of Washington toward business changed or until the future appeared more predictable. Historian Gary Dean Best has charged that the policies, and particularly the rhetoric, from Roosevelt and the New Dealers not only failed to encourage private industry to create jobs that were necessary to end the Depression, but in fact had exactly the opposite effect, and prolonged severe unemployment and lack of economic development. In his book *Pride, Prejudice, and Politics: Roosevelt Versus Recovery, 1933–1938*, Best argues that the Depression and severe unemployment would have ended long before World War II if the business community had trusted the New Deal, and that the persistence of unemployment right up to the war was an effect of the antibusiness attitude of the Roosevelt administration.

Best contends that this was not unplanned but rather was a carefully calculated scheme of the New Deal to provide an excuse for the creation of government welfare programs. When New Deal policies came into force in 1933 with a commitment to end the Depression, unemployment had reached 25 percent, but according to the Bureau of Labor Statistics, 17.2 percent of the workforce was still unemployed in 1939. Unemployment in the years immediately following World War II never rose above 11.7 percent.

It was not only rhetoric that discouraged business expansion. Several laws which industrialists considered antibusiness were passed rapidly and indeed were intended to punish business. To be sure, a half century later most businesspeople viewed many of those highly controversial laws as necessary or benign, but at the time they were revolutionary and viewed by many as socialistic, the enemy of the free market.

There is little question that some laws did deter the expansion of plants and the purchase of new machinery. For example, Congress passed a law in 1936 that placed a surtax of 27 percent on undistributed profits, funds that could otherwise have gone into plant expansion and modernization, and the acquisition of new tools. This tax no doubt contributed to the fact that America's manufacturing facilities were sorely deficient in 1939 when the country entered the defense preparation period. The surtax was repealed in 1939.

As the defense buildup got under way, President Roosevelt recognized that he had to work with industry and toned down his bashing of business. Business and industry gradually moved into defense production but never forgot their longtime feud with FDR. As late as November 1941, three out of four businessmen surveyed by *Fortune* magazine believed that Roosevelt would use the war emergency to promote social programs.

America's industries were slow to move into defense production throughout 1940 and much of 1941 for several other reasons. It meant major changes in the way they worked. They would have to discard or mothball their tools and retrain their labor force. And instead of having control over their production and the conditions of work, industries would be subject to the dictates of government bureaucrats. At the same time, businesses were not unaware of a new law that could *require* them to produce for defense needs. Included in the Selective Service Act of August 1940 was a section, little publicized but well known among major manufacturers, that authorized the secretaries of war and the navy to require any manufacturer to produce war materials, if needed.

The German invasions of Denmark and Norway in April and then France and the low countries in May 1940 jolted Congress into the realization that the country needed to step up preparedness. Appropriations in May and afterward provided funds for substantial increases in war production, and by the fall of that year several major corporations were heavily engaged in war production: Chrysler manufacturing tanks, General Motors making diesel engines for navy ships, Hudson making parts for guns and torpedoes, Willys-Overland making shell cases, International Harvester producing artillery ammunition, General Electric making radios for the Air Corps, and Westinghouse manufacturing various parts for navy ships.

America geared up for war production sooner than would otherwise have occurred because of munitions orders from Great Britain and, to a lesser extent, France before it fell in June 1940. The British contracted with American industry to build planes, tanks, guns, ships, and other war materials and provided manufacturers with British designs and plans, plus technical assistance. The British government financed the construction of 61 war production plants in the United States at a cost of $171 million. By the end of 1940, Britain had placed orders for approximately $2.7 billion worth of production with American industry, including 12,950 airplanes, 3,650 tanks, more than 1,000 artillery pieces, 3,700 tank and anti-tank guns, 124,500 machine guns, 750,000 rifles, 362 million artillery rounds, merchant vessels totalling 300,000 gross tons, and hundreds of thousands of other munitions. With the approval of lend-lease legislation in April 1941, the shipment of American war materials, food, and other supplies to Britain grew rapidly.

The famed P-51 fighter plane was originally built on order for the British, who dubbed it the Mustang. Later, when the Rolls-Royce Merlin engine was installed in the P-51, it became the premier American (and Russian) fighter plane of the war. With the addition of wing tanks it was able to accompany American bombers all the way to their targets, and it sharply reduced bomber losses. In 1940, Dixwell Corporation, a small plant in Connecticut, created a subsidiary called High Standard Manufacturing Corporation, to make machine guns for Britain. By the middle of 1941, it was producing machine guns in volume. The British also contracted with a manufacturer of locomotives to build tanks, and by the end of 1941 it was producing M-1 tanks at a rapid pace.

During the preparedness period, before the United States joined the war, it became apparent that if the government was to prepare as rapidly as necessary, it would have to underwrite much of the cost of war plant construction, conversion of plants and equipment, and retooling. In addition, it would need to guarantee industries a reasonable profit to persuade them to convert from consumer to defense production. This led to cost plus fixed fee contracts, in which the government would pay the manufacturer all approved costs plus a maximum of 8 percent profit. Congress had enacted legislation on June 28, 1940, limiting profits on defense production contracts to 8 percent, and had granted authority for the executive branch to negotiate defense production contracts, rather than going through the slow and expensive bidding process. The fixed fee might be considerably less than 8 percent, depending on such factors as production in government-built plants and bonuses and penalties for early or late delivery.

One of the reasons for the phenomenal productivity of American industry during the war was the government policy of constructing defense/war plants and then contracting with established industrial firms to operate them. The Defense Plant Corporation, created in August 1940, built or financed construction of more than 900 war production plants. The government recognized that companies experienced in industrial production could begin production of defense materials more quickly and produce more rapidly. For example, when it became apparent that ALCOA, which had a monopoly on aluminum production, could not meet the demand, the Defense Plant Corporation built a $250 million aluminum plant and turned it over to the Reynolds Metals Company to operate. Most of the plants were operated by well-established companies with sound records of management, such as Dupont, the major automobile companies, established airplane manufacturers, manufacturers of metals, and other leading manufacturing corporations. A sizeable number of them were built to produce explosives, since prewar demand for explosives was so small that few companies were manufacturing them. The Defense Plant Corporation built most of them or paid for their construction. While several companies built plants to manufacture explosives, a single company was responsible for the construction of 54 gunpowder factories.

Although the government's program to construct and equip new plants got most attention, vast sums were also supplied to upgrade equipment in existing plants. Many plants were willing to convert to war production, but to do so would require pushing existing equipment aside (where it would be mothballed until after the war) and installing equipment for producing war materials. Some simply did not have the capital that would be required, but more often they were reluctant to invest in such equipment when they had no assurance that it would be needed long enough to pay for itself. In addition, it was no small task to retool. The limited number of machine tool makers in the country were overloaded with orders until near the end of the war.

Conversion

After Pearl Harbor, the attitude of industry changed markedly. Manufacturers went all out to exceed production goals. In fact, considering the reluctance of industry to convert to defense production in the two years before the United States entered the war, the zeal with which war production was launched is astonishing. Patriotism flooded out of industries all over America. Reports to shareholders were larded with stories of the company's dedication to the war effort. Many corporations seemed willing to undertake without question the production of anything the army or navy wanted, and not always with careful calculations of potential profit. Their patents and other manufacturing secrets, which had been carefully guarded, were turned over to the government or passed on to competitors who were manufacturing the same war materials.

The key factor in the rapid conversion, however, was the increase in federal contracts. After Pearl Harbor, Congress let loose a deluge of money for war. In 1941 Congress appropriated just over $20 billion for defense, but early in 1942 it appropriated $100 billion, then later that year added another $60 billion. Most of that was on a lump sum basis; that is, the military was able to determine what would be purchased without congressional instructions. As a result, over $100 billion worth of contracts were placed in the first six months of 1942, including $68 billion for military equipment and supplies, $12.6 for industrial expansion and $6.9 billion for military construction.

Conversion took on added impetus when the WPB began to put into effect its L and M orders in the early spring of 1942. The L orders required termination or restriction of manufacture for the civilian market of a long list of items that used scarce metals and other materials in their manufacture. The M orders stopped the use of critical raw materials for "nonessential" purposes. The manufacture of gambling machines was the first to be terminated, in January 1942. In the last two weeks of March and the first week of April, L orders stopped the manufacture of metal home furniture, vacuum cleaners, metal toys, phonographs, washing machines, lawnmowers, refrigerators and a long list of other appliances made of metal, and sharply reduced the manufacture of dozens of others.

Some industries had already closed, scaled back or converted to war production due to shortages of raw materials. In May 1941, aluminum was the first metal to become scarce, followed by tungsten, zinc and manganese; the shortages forced some industries to close or convert to war production then. The construction of office buildings had been curtailed by government order in September 1941.

By mid-March 1942, industries had switched to war production in large numbers and the manufacture of war materials stepped up markedly. By the middle of May the manufacture of most durable consumer goods had ended. A government survey found that as a result 24,308 manufacturing plants would close by October 1942 if they did not get war production contracts. By the summer of 1942 almost all of the major manufacturing industries had converted to war production. All of the automotive manufacturers became major producers of war materials; in fact, no other industry converted so fully and expanded as much as the auto industry. It produced not only trucks, jeeps, tanks and engines for all kinds of military vehicles, but also airplanes and airplane parts, artillery and naval guns, rifles, mines, helmets, bullets and artillery shells, and hundreds of other items having no identifiable relationship to automobile manufacturing. Chrysler alone produced 35 different items of war matériel.

Approximately 80 percent of the tanks manufactured in World War II were built by the automobile industry, although non-auto manufacturers such as the Pullman–Standard Car Manufacturing Company, Baldwin Locomotive Works and Lima Locomotive Works were heavily involved. Chrysler became a major contractor in tank production, but involved hundreds of large and small companies in the production of tank components. In his exhaustive study of wartime industrial production, Francis Walton states that the automobile industry built a third of the machine guns, half of the diesel engines, and nearly 40 percent of the aircraft engines produced in the United States during the war.

While most major industries converted to war production gradually, the majority of plants, particularly small and medium sized plants and subsidiaries of major corporations, converted at one time. One day the plant would be producing goods for the civilian market; the next day it closed to convert and tool up for producing war materials. For some workers, this meant days and weeks of unemployment, waiting for the plant to resume operation. In some cases, the switch to defense production involved a long wait, when the plant closed due to lack of raw materials or had no defense contract that would authorize allocation of a quota of such materials.

Among the strange conversions was General Mills, which operated several food processing plants. Its first production contract was to produce dried eggs, but due to a shortage of raw materials some of its plants faced closure and unemployment for its workers. Thus, its division that made milling equipment and packaging machinery boldly bid for contracts making weapons, and throughout the war it manufactured gun sights, gyroscopic control devices, torpedo directors, ammunition, and a machine to provide smoke-screen for a large area quickly.

Conversion was often followed by more conversion and conversion again. For example, one automobile plant converted to the manufacture of artillery shells, but later converted to the manufacture of artillery barrels for tanks, then to antiaircraft artillery and later to bazookas. Although some of these changes required less than complete conversion, some required major retooling. The plant was converting to other manufacturing as late as 1944.

When the government requested manufacturers to build additional facilities to produce war materials, the companies usually wanted to build them near or adjacent to existing plants so that they could utilize skilled workers and management from nearby plants in the new facility, among other advantages. The government, however, wanted to spread the establishment of new facilities all over the country, or as President Roosevelt put it, "between the mountains" (meaning the Appalachian and Rocky mountains). Congress insisted on this plan, which definitely made sense from a security standpoint. Further, it took jobs to where workers lived, reducing dislocation of the population and the attendant problems of housing, transportation, schooling, and other public services. As a result, manufacturing firms on the East Coast, West Coast, and in the upper Midwest ended up with branch factories in Texas, Kansas, Mississippi, Tennessee, Georgia, Arizona and several other states where, prior to the war, industrial development was limited.

Prior to the outbreak of war, labor availability had been the major factor in determining where the army would place a new war production plant. Frequently lack of labor would eliminate a town as a possible site and a plant would be located in an area that was lacking in other ways but had a labor surplus. After the United States entered the war, labor availability became only one of several factors in determining where to locate new plants. There were advantages in locating additional airplane manufacturing in Southern California, and construction of the new plants led to increased demands for employees and mass migration from the South and Midwest to the Los Angeles area. Yet aircraft plants were also scattered all over the central part of the country, in addition to Buffalo, Hartford, Seattle, and Southern California.

Although the National Defense Expediting Act of July 2, 1940, authorized the army to award contracts based on negotiation rather than bids, contract officers often continued to call for bids. Contract officers were authorized to award contracts on a cost plus fixed fee basis to plants in labor surplus areas, even though their bid might be as much as 15 percent above the lowest bid. Calling for bids ended in 1942, when the WPB directed all government agencies engaged in contracting for war production to negotiate contracts.

Business and industry had long been careful not to get too closely involved with their competitors lest they be subject to prosecution for violation of antitrust laws. But wartime problems required that they work together, so Congress authorized the WPB to provide immunity to certain industries which it thought should be able to work together on production problems. One of the most productive cooperative endeavors occurred in the automobile industry. In January 1942 representatives of all the automotive industry met and formed the Automotive Council for War Production, which served as a clearinghouse for information, equipment, blueprints, and designs and helped to solve bottlenecks in war production for its members.

The antitrust matter was one of serious concern until mid-1943. Thurman Arnold, head of the antitrust division of the Justice Department, was an aggressive trustbuster who, in the late 1930s and early 1940s, had indicted a large number of leading American industries for violation of antitrust laws. These cases caused the management of those companies to be cautious about cooperating with competing manufacturing companies. By 1943, Arnold realized that Congress wanted industries to cooperate and that his zeal in prosecuting antitrust cases was not supported. He accepted a federal judgeship, and thereafter antitrust prosecutions were pursued less vigorously.

Airplane Manufacturing

When one views pictures of airplanes, artillery, trucks and other materials used in World War I, it is impossible not to be impressed by the progress in design and development of military equipment that occurred between the two world wars. In no industry was progress greater than in the design of airplanes. By the time World War II began, the United States was producing the B-17 bomber, which had been developed in 1935 and was the mainstay for carrying bombs throughout the war. The B-29 bomber, a spinoff of the B-17, emerged later in the war and was used primarily to bomb Japan. It carried the atom bombs that were dropped on Hiroshima and Nagasaki, but B-29s had done far more damage to Tokyo and other Japanese cities through months of conventional bombing, particularly fire bombing.

In no industry did the production explosion surpass that of airplane manufacturing. On May 16, 1940, when President Roosevelt asked Congress for funds to produce 50,000 airplanes, it meant, in effect, that manufacturers of aircraft were to increase production from fewer than 200 a month to 4,000 a month. This seemed an impossible task to most people, including leaders in the aircraft manufacturing industry. A vice president of airplane manufacturer Curtiss-Wright said it would take five years for the airplane industry to gear up for that level of production. In 1935 U.S. aircraft manufacturers produced only 1,586 airplanes of all kinds. In 1939 they produced 5,856 planes, of which 3,500 were light private planes; only 2,141 were military planes, most of which were manufactured for other countries, principally Britain and France.

In January 1942, President Roosevelt called for 60,000 airplanes to be built in 1942 and 125,000 in 1943, of which 100,000 would be combat planes. Airplane output did not meet President Roosevelt's announced goals; only 47,836 were built in 1942. But production increases were impressive. In the month of September 1939, only 117 planes were delivered to the military; this number had grown to 5,013 in January 1943 and to 8,800 in November 1943. A total of 85,898 aircraft were completed in 1943 and 96,318 in 1944.

Prior to the war, airplane manufacturing plants assembled planes in the traditional way—craftsmen assembling each component individually. Ford Motor Company volunteered to build airplanes using an assembly line, similar to the way it built automobiles. Henry Ford was told it could not be done, that airplanes could not be built that way, but he insisted that it could be done. At the Willow Run airport near Detroit, he proceeded to construct an airplane assembly plant that was one mile long and one quarter mile wide, all under one roof. Nine months after construction began, the first B-24 bombers rolled off the assembly line, although production was hampered throughout most of the war by a steady succession of design changes requested by the Army Air Forces, a total of more than 500.

The first plane was scheduled to fly away on July 1, 1942, but due to delays was not completed until September. Indeed, labor shortages and turnover and other production problems interfered with production until April 1943 when the plant began to produce more efficiently. Because of so many changes requested by the AAF, rather than delay the assembly line Ford finally decided it was more efficient to turn out planes according to a single design, then send the planes to a center where they were modified to meet the most recent changes requested by the AAF. Some of the changes were required to cope with severe weather conditions: for example, if planes were being manufactured for the Southwest Pacific and the AAF needed to send a quota to Alaska, several modifications were necessary.

Although Ford's B-24 assembly line took a while to smooth out its production, most manufacturers of war materials moved with astonishing speed, as illustrated by the Grumman Aircraft plant. On December 19, 1941, just 12 days after Pearl Harbor, the navy approved an experimental model of the Avenger, a torpedo bomber. Six weeks later, Avengers began to come off the production line at Grumman.

How was the United States able to increase its output of airplanes exponentially in such a short period of time? The construction of new airplane manufacturing plants tells part of the story. The number of airplane (mainframe) manufacturing plants in the United States, by year, was as follows: 1938, 9; 1939, 17; 1940, 25; 1941, 38; 1942, 51; 1943, 67. At the end of 1938, about 24,000 workers were employed in the aircraft industry. This number grew to 28,000 by the end of 1939; to 471,000 by the end of 1942, and to 1,326,000 at the end of 1943. These numbers account for the manufacture of mainframes alone, not subcontractors producing engines and parts. Altogether the industry employed at its peak more than 2,102,000 men and women.

Another factor was the sharing of information among industries after the WPB was authorized to certify industries with immunity to antitrust action. And some companies cooperated without requesting immunity. For instance, the eight major airplane manufacturers on the West Coast—which were highly competitive, secretive and suspicious of one another, even to the point of open hostility—had relaxed by 1942 to the reality that they could be more productive if they cooperated, or at least communicated. The heads of the companies met periodically to share problems, and in due course, other groups such as engineers and production staff began getting together to share problems and solutions.

One of the main outcomes was the sharing of parts. One plant might be prevented from completing planes by the lack of a single part, which another company might have in surplus and might lend a supply of so that production could continue. As Walton points out, this collaboration was probably illegal, but all agreed that it was mutually beneficial and clearly in the interest of the country.

Shipbuilding

Following its creation in 1936, the Maritime Commission approved a ten-year program of cargo ship construction, with 50 fast-moving, sophisticated ships to be constructed annually. But it moved with little urgency. With the fall of France in 1940, Congress realized the seriousness of the cargo ship situation and began to increase authority for construction. The shipbuilding industry soon shifted its methods of construction and began production of a new type of merchant vessel, the Liberty ship.

The Liberty ship was one of the miracles of World War II. The construction of cargo ships in the traditional manner was too slow and too expensive, both of which problems were addressed by the design of the Liberty ship, a vessel of 10,000 (later 13,000) dead-weight tons, based on an old British model which did not require the complicated propulsion machinery used in many naval vessels. Part of the ship was prefabricated, and its parts were welded together instead of riveted, which cut construction time in half. This innovation, which had been in use in Germany for several years, including in the construction of battleships, soon became standard in ship construction. A simple ship, the Liberty moved at only 11 knots per hour and lacked much of the sophistication found in modern ships, but it could be mass produced quickly at low cost.

The first Liberty ship required 244 days to build, but by the summer of 1942 the average had declined to 105 days, and in the spring of 1943 construction time was less than 60 days, although there was considerable variation among the shipyards that built Liberty ships. Later, the Oregon Shipbuilding Corporation in Portland, one of Henry J. Kaiser's several war production plants, in an effort to set a record, completed construction of a Liberty ship—the *Joseph T. Neal*—in 14 days.

By shifting to welding instead of riveting, not only the Liberty but other ships were produced more quickly and at less cost. But Liberty ships began to break up in late 1943; more than 20 experienced cracked hulls, and one broke in two and sank, with a loss of ten crewmen. Researchers at Pennsylvania State College and the University of California at Berkeley were enlisted to determine the cause. They traced the problem to the fact that the Liberty had been designed for riveting and adjustments had not been made when welding was substituted.

As simple as the Liberty ship was, it required 7,500 different types of components and involved some 6,000 different industries in their production. The task of coordinating production such that each item was available in needed quantities at the proper time required careful planning. Although it lacked "class"—it was dubbed the "Ugly Duckling" and the Model T of cargo ships—the Liberty ship was hailed as a major factor in the ability of the United States to supply its armed forces overseas and ensure them the supplies needed in combat. By the end of the war, Liberty ships had been modified to transport personnel as well, and after the war they were used to bring back the large number of servicemen from Europe and the Pacific who were eager to return home and resume civilian life as soon as possible. The manufacture of standard cargo ships continued throughout the war, although the first Victory ship came off the shipway in 1944. The Liberty ship accounted for about half of all cargo ships produced during the war.

American shipbuilding, both naval and cargo, benefited from orders by the British and French. Before Hitler invaded Poland, both the French and British were placing orders in America for a variety of ships, as well as for weapons. Orders from Britain, in particular, resulted in the American shipbuilding industry being far better developed when American entered the war.

As noted already, the construction of navy ships during the interwar years was modest, but the rebuilding of the fleet proceeded rapidly after July 1940. In 1941, according to Navy Department figures, new construction totaled some 14,000 vessels of all sizes; in 1942, it was 31,000; in 1943 about 44,000; then in 1945 down to 28,000. The following summary of U.S. naval ships constructed after the declaration of war illustrates the productivity of U.S. shipyards.

Battleships	8	Submarines	203
Heavy cruisers	15	Mine layers	12
Light cruisers	3	High speed transports	55
Aircraft carriers	18	Patrol craft	1,828
Light aircraft carriers	9	Large landing craft	4,094
Escort aircraft carriers	114	Small landing craft	79,125
Destroyers	352	Small boats	19,366
Destroyer escorts	504	Other craft	5,229

Prior to the attack on Pearl Harbor, the schedule called for 39 months to complete construction of a battleship; in 1943, the schedule was down to 32 months. For aircraft carriers, the time was reduced from 32 to 16 months; for submarines 14 months down to 7; and destroyers, from 13.5 to 5.5 months.

One of the most impressive examples of war production was set by Andrew Higgins, a boat builder in New Orleans. Before the war Higgins had designed a small boat whose special value lay in the fact that the propeller was installed in a tunnel in the keel, making it possible for the boat to operate in very shallow water. The military version was ideal for landing over coral on Pacific islands. The LCVP, which he produced by the thousands for the military services, was probably his most famous boat, but he built several types of landing boats, plus small interisland freighters diesel engines, and parts for other defense manufacturers. By the end of the war Higgins had built more than 20,000 boats for the military. Hard driving and combative, Higgins loved a challenge, and over and over again filled contracts for boats in less time than others thought possible.

News media of the period gave ample publicity to the production of merchant and naval ships, but one of the little known facts of World War II is that the army operated a larger number of ships and watercraft than did the navy during the war. In his 1987 book *U.S. Army Ships and Watercraft of World War II,* David H. Grover describes the astonishing number and variety of vessels operated by the army during the war. They included 1,665 ships larger than 1,000 gross tons: 212 troop ships, 1,345 cargo ships, and 108 ships of a variety of types including hospital ships, repair boats, tankers, and others. It operated 12,379 vessels of less than 1,000 tons, including 511 FS/coastal freighters used primarily for interisland shipping, 4,343 tugboats, 4,697 launches and similar small craft. The vessels used in the greatest numbers by the army were 88,366 amphibious assault craft and 25,383 nonpropelled crafts—8,596 barges and 16,787 pontoon sections. Referring only to vessels that were large enough to have a name or number—excluding barges, small landing craft and the like—the army had 14,044 vessels and the navy 13,734. The army fleet, perhaps more than that of the navy, included ships constructed for the Maritime Commission, such as Liberty ships and other cargo carriers; ships and boats leased or purchased from private owners; and vessels confiscated from the enemy. Fifty small freighters were chartered from their Filipino owners. Few of the larger ships in the army's fleet were owned by the army.

Small Plants

In the early period of defense buildup, almost all contracts went to larger companies, and small companies continued to manufacture for the consumer market and their industrial customers. But as the government began to ration raw materials and close down plants producing for the civilian market, small businesses began to suffer. Many closed, laying off workers who did not always find other work immediately.

Between June 1940 and December 31, 1941, the 100 largest manufacturing firms in the country received three-fourths of the war production contracts. Politicians argued for spreading the war production work among as many manufacturing firms as possible. As early as July 1941, the Truman Committee criticized the military for awarding a disproportionate share of contracts to large industries, and a congressional committee found that up to September 1944, 67.2 percent of the prime contracts had gone to the 100 largest corporations in the country. The military argued that large corporations, to a greater extent than small manufacturers, had the machinery and technical personnel to do the job. Small plants could not manufacture tanks or airplanes or ships, and as one military officer pointed out, all of the small plants in the country combined could not produce the army's daily need for ammunition. Government procurement personnel not only found it easier to negotiate with large corporations but felt more secure in doing so, perceiving that large corporations were more likely to be able to deliver the product in keeping with the contract. It was also easier to write a contract with one large company and monitor it than to find several small companies which could do the job, write contracts and monitor them. As a result, many small plants continued to produce items for the civilian market long after larger plants had converted to war production. As of January 1942, only 10 percent of the small plants had war production contracts.

To be sure, all of the large corporations subcontracted pieces of each contract, normally for parts, to smaller companies. This accounted for several thousand plants, but there were thousands more that initially did not have government contracts and did not know how to go about getting them. Many small plant owners went to Washington to try to find out how to secure a contract, and often they left empty-handed when their hotel reservations expired, unable to find lodging any longer.

Many small plants were able to secure contracts or subcontracts manufacturing items similar to what they had produced for the consumer market—or sufficiently related so that their equipment could be used and their workers could be retrained easily. A toy maker found that its equipment and personnel who made electric motors for toy trains could manufacture equipment to stabilize planes while releasing their bombing loads. A plant that made cases for cosmetics produced cases for explosives.

The shortage of raw materials had begun to close small plants by the summer of 1941, and owners complained to their congressmen, who made speeches on the floor of the House and Senate, calling on the president and the OPM to involve small plants in war production. The government did in fact take several steps toward involving small plants in war production. As early as October 1941 the importance of small plants to war production had been recognized with the creation of a Small Business Committee in the SPAB. In late 1941, the Office of Production Management ruled that at least 2 percent of raw materials must be allocated to small plants engaged in war production.

The problems that small plants faced in obtaining war production contracts were, to a considerable extent, due to their inherent limitations, as the army and navy had argued. Many of them, especially the very small plants with fewer than 20 employees, lacked tools and equipment, research and development capability, and capital. The government could do something about their lack of capital. In March 1942 President Roosevelt signed an executive order authorizing the War and Navy departments to make loans to small businesses that wanted to be involved in war production. Then, in June 1942, Congress established the Smaller War Plants Corporation, primarily to make loans to small plants, and provided $150 million for that purpose. Unfortunately, the SWPC did not get moving until September. The first director was Lou Holland, a manufacturer from Kansas City. Donald Nelson, chairman of the War Production Board, hoped that Holland's appointment would appease Senator Harry Truman, whose Senate investigating committee had been monitoring the WPB closely, but Holland was replaced in January 1943 by Col. Robert Johnson, a reserve officer and former executive with the pharmaceutical firm that bore his name. A year later Johnson was succeeded by Maury Maverick, the populist ex-congressman from Texas, who was named chairman of the SWPC and concurrently vice chairman of the WPB. Maverick, who had been a controversial figure in Congress, brought aggressive leadership to the SWPC. The War Production Board, which had assumed most of the functions of the OPM, created a Smaller War Plants Division to help small plants to become involved in war production, but it was troubled by administrative difficulties and in March 1943 was absorbed by the SWPC.

The military services also made a special effort to involve small plants. In November and December 1941, Defense Special Trains toured the country with exhibits of 60,000 parts needed by the army and navy; reportedly 50,000 manufacturing firms, large and small, inspected the exhibits. And the military services worked at directing contracts to small plants. In the last two months of 1942, the army awarded more than 43,000 contracts to plants having not more than 500 employees.

But unless a company had a lobbyist in Washington—which small plants did not—or in some other way knew where to go and whom to talk to, it often had little chance of gaining a manufacturing contract directly from the government. This problem led to the emergence of the "five percenters," men who knew their way around Washington and could help manufacturers land contracts, for which their fee was 5 percent of the contract. They were widely condemned by Congress and the White House, but many small plant operators turned to them for assistance when they were unable to land a manufacturing contract. Eventually the army and navy set up field procurement offices which had lists of items needed and could help businessmen apply for contracts. War Information Centers in leading college and public libraries received publications from most offices in Washington listing materials needed and how to apply for contracts.

One of the most innovative approaches used by small businesses to get war production contracts consisted of pooling. In hundreds of towns, particularly in the East and Midwest, small plants faced extinction unless they could come up with some way to get government contracts. Someone came up with the idea of pooling, a system in which the managers of small plants in a given area got together and analyzed what they could provide and worked together to bid for contracts. One of the first was in York, Pennsylvania, where there were 110 small plants, most of which employed fewer than 100 workers each. They banded together as the Manufacturers' Association Defense Committee of York, and by the Pearl Harbor attack almost all of them were engaged in war production. Almost every contract the committee obtained involved dozens of small plants in York. They produced shell forgings, gun carriages, armor plate, Bofors guns, turbines, trench mortars, fuse parts, and a variety of other munitions.

Other cities adopted the York plan, frequently led by the local chamber of commerce, and by the end of the war there were dozens of such pools all over the country in both small towns and large cities. The companies were working together, each plant manufacturing one or more parts for a weapon or other materials needed by the army or navy. In San Jose, California, 37 small manufacturers pooled their resources in order to participate in war production. But not all pools were located in a single town or area. When steel and other materials were cut off, 36 companies that manufactured washing machines joined in a version of pooling to produce war materials. In late 1941, with its three largest members serving as prime contractors and farming out parts work to the other members, the pool began manufacturing machine guns, which then launched the companies into producing other munitions, the kind of conversion and cooperation that Donald Nelson, head of the War Production Board, was promoting. In the unlikely location of Denver, several companies formed a pool and manufactured cargo ships which they shipped in sections to the West Coast where they were assembled and launched.

There were hundreds of examples of small plants that not only stayed in business during the war but made significant contributions to war production. Francis Walton relates several examples of small to medium sized manufacturing firms that exemplified the imagination of so many small plants in converting to war production. For example, the Talon Company, famous for zippers in clothing, remodeled its tools and plant to produce fuses for bombs. A company in the Midwest that built merry-go-rounds for carnivals secured a contract to make towers on which mechanics stood to work on airplanes. Gradually the plant started to take on the manufacture of airplane parts, which in time became its main production. The Armstrong Cork Company in Pennsylvania, which had produced tile, bottles and brick, switched to the manufacture of aluminum parts for planes and, in due course, expanded into the manufacture of a variety of airplane parts. Many of the tools required were fabricated by modifying those used in the production of tile.

Walton unearthed a particularly intriguing story concerning the Beatrice Steel Tank Manufacturing Company in Nebraska. When its supply of steel was cut off and directed to war production, the plant was about to go out of business. Without knowing what his factory might build for the government, the owner visited several government agencies in St. Louis, Louisville, and finally in Washington. After visiting various offices he chanced into the office of a navy officer who asked if he could build a type of depth charge the navy used for antisubmarine work. The plant owner had no idea whether he could, since his plant did not have a trained engineer, but after examining the blueprints, he assured the navy officer he could. And he did. Contracts for other munitions followed. An engaging part of the story is the fact that, because of the labor shortage, he turned to the Beatrice Institute for Feeble-Minded Youth. By breaking the manufacturing tasks into short, simple segments, they were able to do the work, a happy combination for all concerned.

Fortune magazine reported another case typical of companies that converted to war production. In 1928 a man in California bought a small plant that manufactured orchard sprayers. By the time war began it was known as Food Machinery Corporation and had expanded to 11 plants. In the summer of 1942, eight of the plants were involved in producing a variety of items for the army, including amphibian tanks, ammunition boxes, and a fog driver to put out fires in airplanes, based on the original orchard sprayer.

Despite the sterling performance of many small plants, there was a dark side to their role in war production. There were many cases of fly-by-night companies securing war production contracts, largely because they were small, and failing to fulfill them properly. Government agencies, responding to politicians' demand that small plants be awarded contracts where at all possible, were sometimes not sufficiently discriminating in awarding contracts to small plants. In addition, small plants were the subject of investigations for kickbacks and other forms of corruption.

Labor

By 1944, some 18.7 million more Americans were employed than had been in 1939; 10 million were new entrants into the work force, of whom close to 8 million had been unemployed, plus some 2 million who had come of work age. But 11 million of the additional jobs were in the armed forces, and only 7.7 million in the civilian work force.

The normal work week of 40 hours disappeared during the war. By December 1942, war plants averaged 90 hours per week. The day shift continued to account for most of the production, but in the spring of 1943, 39 percent of war plant workers were on second or third shifts. (The country changed to war time, what is now called Daylight Saving Time, on February 9, 1942.) Six and seven day work weeks became routine in plants manufacturing war materials. By 1944, with only 1.2 percent of the workforce unemployed, the country was experiencing a severe labor shortage. President Roosevelt issued an executive order setting the standard work week at 48 hours in areas where there was a shortage of labor. And, as noted earlier, in some cases government contracts were shifted to areas where there were ample supplies of labor.

The nature of war production often resulted in a massive concentration of workers in a single locality, indeed in a single plant. For example, 50,000 worked at the Curtiss-Wright airplane plant in New Jersey, 100,000 at the Douglas airplane plants in El Segundo and Long Beach, adjacent to Los Angeles, and 40,000 at the Ford bomber factory in Michigan. Many of the factories were under one roof, like Ford's B-24 bomber plant at Willow Run, Michigan, which as noted earlier was one mile long and a quarter mile wide. But it was Chrysler that built the largest plant under one roof, just outside Chicago, where it manufactured tanks.

Labor problems plagued every war production industry. Turnover was unusually high, averaging 5–8 percent a month in both the aircraft and munitions industries. But the main problem was that most of the workers had no prior experience at their jobs. During the 1930s, half of the workers hired in shipyards already had the skills needed for their jobs, but in 1942, 90 percent of the new employees had to be trained for their jobs. Hence, in most plants training programs were continuous. In addition, jobs had to be broken into small steps that could be taught quickly so that a new worker could learn the job with little instruction. Many workers lacked basic skills, talent or intelligence for their work. A factory foreman in Detroit said that he would not have hired most of the new workers before the war.

Shortly after war was declared, Donald Nelson, head of the War Production Board, met with industry and labor leaders in Pittsburgh to develop a model for labor-management committees. Nelson thought that labor disputes could be settled by such committees, and more than 4,000 were eventually formed. The committees were helpful in reducing absenteeism, building patriotism, increasing productivity, and promoting war bond drives and other government campaigns, but they were supposed to steer clear of matters that fell within the purview of collective bargaining. Avoiding such situations was not always easy to do. Nelson said at the end of the war that the committees had been effective, but R. J. Thomas, the labor leader, commented that neither labor nor management was willing to give up on fundamental issues lest they become a part of postwar labor contracts.

In view of the dedication of all Americans, including factory workers, to the war effort, one might expect that there were few or no strikes during the war, but such was not the case. At the beginning of the war, leaders of the major unions and industry met with President Roosevelt and made a "no strike, no lockout" pledge, yet there were more than 14,000 strikes during the war. As historian Alan Clive has noted, in 1944 the number of strikes hit a peak of more than 5,000, resulting in a loss of 8,721,000 worker hours. Most of them were wildcat strikes that did not last long, and more often than not involved a small group, sometimes not more than 100 workers who struck over a minor grievance, often for only one shift. In many cases, strikes were in response to disciplinary action against one worker by a foreman or plant manager. Many of the strikes were precipitated by migrants from the South who were slow to adjust to the demands of industrial work and had little understanding of union discipline, while others were led by shop stewards, sometimes to imbue the new workers with the union ethos. Referring specifically to factory workers in Michigan, Clive wrote that the "cost of living, fatigue, intransigent management, restrictive government policies, union rivalry, and worker suspicion of labor leadership all contributed to a mounting wave of wartime strikes."

The main grievance, however, was the fact that industry profits rose sharply, while worker wages did not. To be sure, workers had more job security and slowly increasing wages, but only a little over one-third of the 42 percent wage increase seen by the average American worker between 1939 and 1944 was due to higher wage rates; the remainder was accounted for by increased employment. In addition, workers saw prices rising in spite of price controls, often exceeding increases in earnings.

The matter of wages was a subject of major contention throughout the war. The administration wanted to hold wages steady to control inflation but labor thought it was treated unfairly. Steel workers pointed out that between January 1, 1941, and May 1, 1942, the cost of living had increased 15 percent, and they had not had an increase in wages during that period. The WLB approved their request for 15 percent increase on July 16, 1942, justifying it on the assumption that most other workers had received increases. Other workers whose wages had not increased that much were allowed comparable increases.

Since price controls on most commodities had been instituted by May 1, 1942, the WLB took the position that the cost of living would not increase beyond that date, and therefore wages should remain stable. This became known as the "Little Steel" formula and, with a few exceptions, wages were generally stabilized industry-wide at the 1942 level for the rest of the war. Exceptions included coal miners, industries in which wages were particularly low such as the textile industry, and wage adjustments in 1943 at the Boeing aircraft plant in Seattle. The adjustment at Boeing was due to the fact that starting pay at Boeing had been 67.5 cents per hour, although starting pay at shipyards a few miles away was 95 cents per hour and in other industries in the area, 88.5 cents an hour. In all industries the WLB also allowed pay adjustments for workers on the swing shift (4 P.M. to midnight) and the graveyard shift (midnight to 8 A.M.).

John L. Lewis, head of the United Mine Workers, called his coal miners out on strike four different times in 1943, demanding among other things "portal to portal" pay, which would amount to an increase in wages contrary to WLB guidelines. He eventually coerced the government into wage concessions that violated the Little Steel formula. The first walkout, in April 1943, drew heated condemnation from newspaper editorialists, servicemen, and the public in general, and provoked Congress into passing the Smith-Connally Act in June of that year. The act gave the War Labor Board statutory powers, authorized the president to seize war plants and mines where there were illegal strikes, banned strikes by union leaders in war plants seized by the government, and banned political contributions by labor unions. It also required local unions to give a 30-day notice of a strike, followed by a cooling off period of 30 days, then to submit the matter to its membership for vote under the supervision of the National Labor Relations Board. President Roosevelt argued that the 30-day cooling off period was an invitation to strike, since the unions could declare a strike and have 30 days to pressure management to settle without actually having to go on strike and lose pay for an unknown length of time. Labor leadership opposed the ban on political contributions from membership dues, particularly since it would limit their ability to help re-elect Roosevelt as president in 1944. Unions solved the problem by establishing some of the first of the political action committees whose proliferation would come to figure so prominently in American politics. Roosevelt vetoed the bill, but irate congressmen, supported by thousands of letters of outrage from servicemen overseas, overrode the veto. The bill had strong public support, thanks to both the negative public image of UMW head Lewis and a series of strikes in war production plants in Detroit, Akron, Chicago, and several other manufacturing facilities, which had fueled public resentment against strikers.

President Roosevelt put the antistrike legislation to use in 1944 when railroad workers were threatening to strike. Pointing out that a rail strike would interrupt war production and disrupt the entire country, he awarded temporary army commissions to the top management of the railroads and directed them to keep the rails operating. Roosevelt might not have been so ready to seize the railroads had the railroad workers not talked about striking almost constantly throughout the war.

Between November 1, 1943, and V-J Day, the government took over about 50 companies, mostly because of illegal strikes. The most publicized takeover involved Montgomery Ward in late 1944 and early 1945. When Sewell Avery, the company president, refused to yield on a labor matter, the army seized the company, and when Avery refused to vacate his office in Chicago, two military policemen picked him up and packed him out the street door. A picture of him being ejected from the building appeared on the front pages of newspapers all over the country.

In addition to strikes against management, there was serious strife between unions and between different factions within unions. In 1937, the United Mine Workers had been expelled from the American Federation of Labor because of its role in the founding of the competing

Congress of Industrial Organizations, and because Communists dominated the UMW leadership. Although John L. Lewis was not a Communist, he tolerated them in the belief that they could be helpful to the union, and he would oust them when they were no longer needed. Communists were in control of the electrical workers' union and very influential in the United Auto Workers. Communists had stirred up a great deal of labor unrest before the war, and even though American Communists urged that the United States enter the war when Germany attacked Russia on June 22, 1941, they continued to foment internal srife in unions. In 1943, a serious fight broke out in the UAW between a strong Communist-led faction and the non–Communists led by Walter Reuther.

Rivalry between labor unions was keen throughout the war. The CIO and the AFL were constantly raiding one another's membership. As new war production industries were established, the zealous efforts of union leaders to unionize the new plants and new workers often resulted in struggles between competing unions, clashes with management, and harassment of new workers, many of whom were opposed to joining a union. In fact, the struggle to bring about union shops was a major cause of strikes and much of the violence in war production plants.

Another factor was race. President Roosevelt had signed an executive order on June 25, 1941, forbidding discrimination based on race, creed, color or national origin, and several work stoppages ensued. One of the most publicized involved streetcar operators in Philadelphia, where the union had written into its contract with the company a provision that blacks could not hold platform (operator) jobs. The company was willing to promote blacks, but when it attempted to do so, the union called a wildcat strike. Finally, the army sent in soldiers of the 102nd Division from nearby Fort Dix to operate the system until the dispute was settled. A teamsters strike in Chicago in May 1945 led the president to send a field artillery battalion from Oklahoma to drive the trucks until the strike could be settled.

In most cases, wartime strikes did not affect war production seriously, but they had several side effects that were detrimental to the war effort. Some consumers felt that if union members could strike, they could cheat on rationing and other war effort activities. Strikes abated following the Battle of the Bulge in December 1944, at least for a couple of months. The public wrath made it unwise to strike while Americans were battling to survive in Belgium. Still, factory workers remained frustrated and believed that they were being treated unfairly. As a result, the year following the end of the war saw the largest number of serious strikes in the history of American unions. Union membership grew by more than 50 percent during the war, establishing precedent for the expansion of organized labor in the years following the war.

The draft had severely reduced the labor supply in certain industries, some of which were critical to the war effort. On several occasions, at the request of the War Manpower Commission, men with special civilian skills were released from the army to return to their civilian jobs. In the fall of 1943, due to reduced production of copper, zinc and other metals, 4,300 soldiers were released to return to the mines. In several other industries, soldiers were allowed to return to their civilian jobs because of labor shortages. In most cases, they were placed in the Enlisted Reserve Corps. In 1943, the army also released 1,000 former seamen to replace seamen lost in merchant vessels that had been sunk. The army allowed selected numbers of soldiers to be furloughed for 90 days to work in war plants, keeping some of them on full army pay while they were engaged in war production. Soldiers in several parts of the country were encouraged to help with crop harvests on weekends and other free time; in fact, soldiers from Fort Dix, working on weekends, saved the New Jersey tomato crop in 1943. In several cases, the army allowed temporary leave for several days or weeks to help with crop harvesting and the operation of canning plants.

Laborers were imported from Caribbean countries and Mexico. Some 60,000 Mexicans worked in agriculture and another 50,000 on railroads. Some 26,000 workers from Jamaica and the Bahamas were brought in for farm work. By late 1943, however, prisoners of war from North Africa were being used in crop production and in nonsensitive industrial work to ease the labor shortage.

In plants where the War Department had contracts and severe labor shortages existed, or where war production was slowed by labor unrest short of strikes, the army sent special project teams of two or three officers to do troubleshooting. As Fairchild and Grossman explain in their exhaustive treatise, the teams were given authority to cut through red tape and expedite solutions. They often arranged for housing, child care, transportation, adjustments in working conditions, and changes in food service and work schedules; they also persuaded draft boards to defer workers, convinced military recruiting offices to suspend recruitment of workers from war plants, and shifted contracts to other areas that had an ample labor supply. Between September 1943 and June 1945, the army formed 15 such teams, most aimed toward not a specific city but an entire industry such as aircraft, aluminum, or railroads.

The Works Progress Administration, the National Youth Administration, and the Civilian Conservation Corps had been created in the 1930s to provide work for the unemployed. The CCC was terminated in 1942, and in 1943, with labor already becoming scarce, Congress abolished the WPA and the NYA and sharply curtailed several other of the New Deal social programs.

Profits

It was widely believed that manufacturing corporations earned huge profits during the war, and it is true that many did so. On average, corporate profits before taxes more than doubled. Corporate executives point out, however, that during the Depression years many companies were reaping small profits and some were making no profit at all, so any increase in profits could be large on a percentage basis. And large profits were substantially reduced through taxes, as will be seen shortly.

Large profits were due in part to the government's lack of efficiency in contracting for war production. With cost-plus contracts, there was little incentive for a plant to economize. Workers were often given a variety of free or highly subsidized fringe benefits such as cafeteria meals, child care, health care, transportation, housing, fully paid pensions, vacation pay, paid holidays, recreation and entertainment. Because wages were controlled, corporations used fringe benefits to enhance compensation for workers—with the approval of the WLB—and since all such costs could be included in charges to the government, they cost the corporation nothing. In one notorious case described by Walton, the company provided its employees free insurance, free Turkish baths, free Florida vacations, and wristwatches at Christmas time. The president's secretary was paid 20 times a typical secretary's salary.

The excess profits tax contributed further to inefficiencies in manufacturing. Prior to World War II federal taxes on corporations had been moderate, at least compared with taxes a half century later. During the war, corporate income taxes were raised to 25–40 percent, depending on profit level, but more important was the excess profits tax. Companies that earned more than "normal" profits were taxed at 80 percent initially (eventually 90 percent) on all profits above "normal." Companies that earned a large profit, recognizing that part of it would be taxed at 90 percent, sought ways to charge expenditures to manufacturing costs and thereby reduce excess profits. This practice led to conspicuous consumption and waste in war plants and contributed to the perception of huge profits. And, as noted, some firms were less than discreet with their wasteful spending, providing unheard-of luxuries to executives and leaving the impression that all war production plants were reaping large profits.

For many firms, profits were less than the public thought. "Normal" profits, computed either of two authorized ways, turned out to be fairly low for some companies. The Department of Commerce reported the following average after-tax profits for all wartime manufacturing firms:

	After tax profits as a percent of assets	After tax profits as a percent of sales
1940	2.2	5.8
1941	2.8	6.2
1942	3.1	4.5
1943	3.1	4.1
1944	2.8	4.0
1945	2.4	3.1

With cost-plus contracts, speed in production, and the loose management often found in war production, it was not surprising that waste, fraud, and dishonesty were commonplace. Nothing was so important as getting production under way, producing planes, tanks, ships, guns, and other war materials in large quantities and as rapidly as possible. By early 1941, Congress had come to believe that it needed to keep an eye on war production contracts, so in March of that year the Senate established its Special Committee to Investigate National Defense Programs with obscure Missouri senator Harry S Truman as chairman. Truman's handling of the investigations got Roosevelt's attention and resulted in Truman's being selected as FDR's runningmate in 1944; Truman would succeed to the presidency shortly after assuming the vice presidency. The Truman Committee served a policing function through its investigation and reporting on war profiteering. It reported on malfeasance in manufacturing, manpower utilization, distribution, and other aspects of the wartime economy.

Although dishonesty in war production attracted much press attention, most informed observers at the time agreed that the overwhelming majority of factories producing war goods made every effort to produce quality materials at the lowest cost possible and treated the government fairly. Like other Americans, the management of those industries and its workers were patriotic citizens, dedicated to helping the country win the war. Factory workers frequently wrote patriotic slogans or messages on artillery shells and other items manufactured for combat.

Most plants had suggestion boxes to collect ideas from workers on how to do a job more efficiently. The War Production Board awarded prizes to workers who came up with ideas for saving labor and improving the manufacturing process, and reported that such efforts had saved more than 15 million hours of labor by the end of the war. The General Electric Company and Eastman Kodak actually returned some profits to the government voluntarily, and the Dupont company charged the government only $1 above expenses for its work on the atomic bomb.

Stories of inefficiency and waste in war plants do not tell the whole story. In fact, most industries became more efficient as they gained experience and reduced the cost of manufacturing war materials. Worker productivity increased about 25 percent between 1939 and 1944, resulting in part from the longer work week but also from the introduction of new equipment and especially from greater worker efficiency. As the Boeing Company gained experience in manufacturing the B-17 bomber, the number of hours required to build each plane was cut in half, and the cost was reduced from an average of $301,221 during the 1939–1941 period to $204,370 in 1944. Over the same period, the cost of producing the C-47, the AAF workhorse transport, dropped from $128,761 to $88,574. Henry Kaiser's shipyard in Oregon reduced the hours required to produce a Liberty ship by more than 75 percent, and in 1943, a tank cost 27 percent less than in 1942.

AMERICAN DEFENSE PRODUCTION was meager during the 1930s, but two years after the attack on Pearl Harbor, the United States was producing as much as Germany, Italy and Japan combined. In 1939 war production accounted for 2 percent of American manufacturing; in 1943 and in 1944, it accounted for 40 percent. Total manufacturing production tripled between 1939 and 1944, mining output increased 60 percent, and the importation of raw materials doubled. Between July 1940 and V-E Day, American industry produced 299,300 airplanes; 86,700 tanks; 5,400 merchant ships; more than 100,000 naval vessels including landing craft and small boats; 20,086,061 rifles, pistols, machine guns and other small arms; 4 million tons of artillery shells; 2.4 million trucks and jeeps; 41 billion bullets; 372,431 artillery guns; and millions of other war-related items.

By the fall of 1944, the military services were already canceling war production contracts. The army had canceled its contract with Chrysler for the manufacture of Bofors guns in late 1943, having already achieved a stockpile that would last the rest of the war.

Throughout the war, there was real fear in Congress and the executive branch that the country would slide into a recession or return to a depression after the war, and indeed when the defense industries closed there were temporary problems of unemployment. Within hours after Japan surrendered, billions of dollars' worth of government contracts were canceled, including $1.5 billion in the Detroit area alone, and hundreds of thousands of people were thrown out of work. But the disruption was temporary. Anticipating it, the government authorized automobile plants to begin building cars again in July 1945. They built 216,000 in the last half of that year, and 2,146,000 in the 1946 fiscal year. On August 20, 1945, the WPB canceled controls on the production of 210 items, including radios, refrigerators, stoves, washing machines, electric fans, motorcycles, photographic film, and construction machinery.

Those who feared massive unemployment did not reckon with the vast amount of pent-up demand that had developed during the war and during the Depression when people did not have money for the things they wanted to buy. Accumulated savings coupled with pent-up demand for consumer goods fueled a healthy economy following the war, and the anticipated recession never occurred.

CHAPTER VII

Women at War

AT THE BEGINNING of World War II, the role of women in American society differed markedly from that of a half century later. The 19th Amendment to the Constitution extending national suffrage to women had been in effect for only two decades. A smaller percentage of women than men attended college, fewer women worked outside the home and few women were involved in politics. During the Depression, it was considered inappropriate in some circles for married women to work outside the home, especially middle and upper class women. Within certain classes and cultural groups, a woman's taking a job outside the home suggested that the husband could not support his family and reflected negatively on him as a man.

Legislatures in 26 states considered laws during the Depression to forbid married women to work outside the home, in an effort to give employment to as many breadwinners as possible. A national poll in 1936 found that 82 percent of respondents thought that if a husband was employed, his wife should not work outside the home; 75 percent of the women surveyed agreed. Many school systems, private businesses and government agencies, in an attempt to spread work among as many families as possible, would not employ married women. Historian D'Ann Campbell found that, "In the 1930s, 84 percent of the nation's insurance companies, 65 percent of the banks, and 63 percent of public utilities had restrictive rules preventing married women from holding *any* jobs. Furthermore, 77 percent of the nation's city school systems refused to hire married teachers and 63 percent routinely fired a teacher if they discovered she had married." And some companies had a policy that if layoffs were required, those who had working spouses were the first to be laid off; under such rules married women usually went first.

World War II changed the employment patterns of women, both in numbers and types of employment, and the roles of women in society. According to the Census Bureau, the number of females over 14 years of age employed in nonagricultural jobs increased from 11.4 million in the middle of 1941 to a peak of 16.5 million in the middle of 1945; with the addition of those employed in agriculture, the numbers were 12.9 million and 18.8 million, respectively. In 1940, 17 percent of working women were employed in professional positions, most of them in school teaching. The majority of working women were employed in low wage jobs, but a large percentage of them later shifted to high wage jobs in war production plants.

A major employer for women was government—federal, state and local. Employment in the federal government grew from about 1 million in 1940 to almost 4 million when the war ended. As the nation began to mobilize, thousands of young women flocked to Washington, D.C., to become government workers, replacing longtime government employees in all types of jobs and then filling most of the new positions created to meet the new demands of the wartime economy and government. To be sure, around a million of the civilian jobs in Washington were clerical. These jobs, which existed primarily in the War and Navy departments, were occupied mostly by women after military leaders decided that many of the jobs in the Army and Navy departments could be performed by women, thereby making men in those jobs available for combat. But women also moved into professional jobs formerly filled by men—biologists, economists, sociologists, nutritionists, geologists, statisticians, attorneys, and more. The number of female employees in the War Department increased four times as fast as the number of male employees during the war years. Historian William H. Chafe notes that by the end of the war 38 percent of all civilian government employees were women.

Women entered virtually all sectors of the workforce by the hundreds of thousands during the war and were symbolized by "Rosie the Riveter," whose image adorned the covers of magazines and was featured in magazine and newspaper ads and in movie news reels; her name even provided the title for a movie. She became the personification of the working woman in wartime, and indeed more than 2.5 million women were employed in shipbuilding, aircraft plants, and other war industries. Most of the popular magazines published stories with pictures of women working in blue collar jobs as welders, riveters, sheet metal workers, lathe operators and pipefitters.

When expansion of war production began, most factories were leery of employing women on production lines and in other manufacturing jobs, but due to lack of manpower they did so in all industries. The growth of women employees in General Motors plants was typical. At the beginning of 1942, GM employed 19,197 women, 9.5 percent of its total workforce, in hourly wage jobs; at the end of 1943, this number had grown to 114,772 or 30.7 percent. In shipbuilding, the employment of women rose from less than 1 percent in 1941 to 10 percent in 1944, and from 7 percent to 18 percent in the steel industry. In aircraft production the number of women in blue collar jobs rose from 4,000 to 310,000 in 18 months; in the fall of 1943 some 478,000 women were employed in the aircraft industry.

Government munitions plants were the first to employ large numbers of women in blue collars jobs. In early 1941, 40 percent of the workers in plants that made small arms ammunition were women. The largest increase in the employment of women in defense plants came in 1943, however. Unemployment among women who wanted to work virtually disappeared, except in rural areas and towns with no war production manufacturing.

A survey in the middle of 1942 to assess receptivity to hiring women in manufacturing found that the large majority of managers said they would hire women in not only skilled and semiskilled jobs but in supervisory and managerial positions as well. In some industries, primarily those with assembly jobs that required nimble fingers, women workers were preferred. Plant managers also believed that in jobs involving repetitive tasks women were more efficient and reliable than men. Women were often preferred as inspectors; many managers found them to be more careful than men and less likely to allow faulty parts to get by undetected. Women inspectors took their task seriously, and those who had husbands or brothers in combat seemed to be especially meticulous as inspectors. While it was assumed that younger women would be more productive workers, many supervisors preferred older women, whom they found to be more reliable and less likely to be injured. According to the April 1943 census almost one quarter (23.1 percent) of women workers were 45 years of age and older; 1.9 percent were 65 or older.

Employment of women in war plants was not without problems. Some women were ineligible for jobs due to lack of strength or size. According to D'Ann Campbell, one study showed that a "150 pound man was two and one-half times as strong as a 100 pound woman and one and one-half times as strong as a woman his own weight." In some cases, it became necessary to break tasks into small components or separate steps that women could handle, though this strategy often tended to make the work less interesting.

Absenteeism was much greater among women, especially those with children. Although women were less prone to accidents than men, due in part to the fact that most of the dangerous jobs were filled by men, women who did suffer injuries required longer to heal or to return to work, sometimes due to factors such as home demands. Illness accounted for more absences among women workers than men. Women also suffered exhaustion more than men and found it necessary to be absent to recuperate. As one observer noted, sheer exhaustion accounted for more absenteeism of married women who tried to continue managing households, caring for children, standing in lines to shop, and coping with rationing and shortages, all while working 40 or more hours a week in a defense plant. In addition to absenteeism, turnover among women workers in defense plants was greater than among men.

Child care was a major problem for many women workers. The government set up some 3,000 child care centers that cared for approximately 130,000 children, and private child care facilities emerged as demand grew, often providing supplemental income for homemakers. Kaiser shipyards, several aircraft manufacturers and other plants set up child care centers for their women employees as a fringe benefit; if the plants had cost-plus contracts they could pass the cost on to the government. Child care more often became the responsibility of an older female relative at home, but "latch-key" children nonetheless became a serious social problem during World War II. Between the end of the school day and the time when parents arrived home, teens had ample time to become involved in delinquent activities, which became a major problem for law enforcement personnel and social workers.

As before and since, women usually earned less than men for doing similar or identical work, although many defense plants adopted a policy of equal pay for men and women. In many cases it was made easier because the plants were producing defense materials on a cost-plus basis, and it cost the company no more to pay women an equal wage. Nonetheless, wage differentials remained a sore point with women workers. Equal pay was more common on the West Coast where there was a labor shortage throughout most of the war than, for example, in the South, where labor was more plentiful. Part of the income differential was due to the fact that men routinely accepted overtime work, while women were more likely to refuse it because they were exhausted or needed the time for home demands. Compared with prewar pay, women employed in factories realized an average wartime wage increase of 70 percent, contrasted with 15 to 30 percent increase for those in clerical work. Many women switched jobs when they found that they could increase their income by 50 to 100 percent in manufacturing as compared to clerical or retailing work.

The Fair Employment Practices Committee prohibited racial discrimination in the federal government and in industries with federal contracts. Although the order was not always enforced rigorously, it resulted in the employment of hundreds of thousands of African Americans, including many women, in war production plants. The order did not apply to women, but as labor became increasingly scarce, few women who wanted to work were denied employment.

The major opposition to equal pay often came not from management but from labor unions whose leaders were reluctant to institutionalize equal pay, fearing the implications for postwar labor relations—notwithstanding the fact that women helped to swell union membership during the war years. On the other hand, some union locals supported equal wages for women lest plants hire women instead of men to save money. Union membership increased by approximately 50 percent during the war. Prior to the war, women accounted for less than 10 percent of union membership, but by 1944, women made up more than 20 percent of the total. Even so, there were very few unions in which women achieved leadership roles commensurate with their membership.

Far more women were employed as secretaries, stenographers, and in clerical and retailing work than in manufacturing, but they did not garner as much publicity as women working in war-related jobs. The press found nothing novel about women working as clerks. Employment in retailing almost doubled between 1939 and 1944, with almost all of the new jobs being held by women. Despite shortages, people were now working and had money to spend on consumer goods, thereby providing a boost in retailing.

Publicity in magazines, newspapers, and films was effective in inducing women to join the labor force. In addition to general recruitment of women for defense work, special campaigns emphasized the need for middle and upper class women to take laboring jobs, portraying it as the patriot thing to do. However, the cultural prohibition against married women, particularly well-to-do women, working outside the home remained among both women and men, particularly among men. Married women who worked outside the home were more likely to work in a white collar job, probably for less pay than they could have earned in a manufacturing job.

As men left jobs to enter the armed forces and it was impossible to find male replacements, women filled a wide variety of jobs that either had not been open to women before or that were held predominantly by men. Many educated women who had not worked before took jobs in advertising, radio, journalism, banking, securities, and other areas of commerce previously closed to them or otherwise restricted.

Why did women who had not worked outside the home choose to do so during the war? For many the primary reason was money. Wives of soldiers often needed to supplement the income they received from the government. (In June 1942, Congress provided that an enlisted man could have $22 of his monthly pay sent directly to his wife, and it would be supplemented by $28; later the government contribution was raised to $50 a month, with additional allotments for children and other dependents.) About half of servicemen's wives worked outside the home at some time during the war.

Many magazine articles, often written by the Office of War Information, featured newly married women, whose husbands had gone overseas shortly after marriage, who were working as therapy for loneliness. The war could be an exciting time for young women, opening opportunities for recreation and entertainment they had not known before, but for many young wives who were living with their parents or in-laws while their husbands were away in the military service, it was a confining experience. By taking a job in government or in a defense plant they were able to develop a circle of friends of their own age.

Finally, it was patriotic to work. Hundreds of thousands of women took wartime jobs because they felt it their duty to do so. The country needed their services. Many young women whose parents would not have approved of their working in a factory before the war (parental approval was a factor for single women well into their early twenties at that time) were willing for their daughters to accept jobs that would contribute to winning the war. For the young women, it provided the chance to meet people, especially men, and a way to have a more interesting social life.

The Women's Land Army

Some 750,000 women joined the Women's Land Army, also known as the Land Corps, to assist with farm labor, particularly harvests. The Women's Land Army was modeled after similar organizations that had been created earlier in England, Canada and Australia. The program was coordinated by the Agricultural Extension Service, and in many states agricultural colleges and schools such as the Agricultural and Technical Institute at Farmingdale, New York, trained women for work in the Women's Land Army. Their prescribed uniform consisted of blue denim overalls, a bright blue shirt and a cap with a visor bearing the name "Women's Land Army." (The uniform was optional, however.) The Farm Cadet Victory Corps, also sponsored and trained by the Agricultural Extension Service, consisted of high school–age youths who agreed to help ease the shortage of farm workers. In the summer of 1942, women constituted 14 percent of farm workers nationally, 24 percent in Florida.

Yet not all married women became war workers; in fact 58 percent reported that they thought they could best serve the war effort by remaining at home. The Census Bureau reported 35.5 million "non-worker" females 14 years of age and over at the beginning of 1944, about twice the number in the labor force. So, while the WACs, the WAVES and Rosie the Riveter got the publicity, most married women were homemakers during World War II.

Most women who entered the workforce during the war returned to their traditional roles afterward, but their work experience had changed their perspective. Many had relied on their husbands to handle the family money before the war, but during the war they had become experienced in managing money, paying bills, budgeting, saving, and making financial decisions while their husbands were in the service. Men returned from the service to find that their wives had learned how to change a tire, mend a faucet, repair an electrical connection, and take care of many of the household chores that the men had handled previously.

Of those women who chose volunteer service rather than employment for pay, their experiences helped prepare them for leadership in their communities, some of which led to political activity including standing for public office. Like women who worked outside the home for pay, these women viewed themselves differently because of the war. Their experiences had given them self esteem and confidence to take on new and different roles. War work sometimes led to postwar marital difficulties. Servicemen returning home expected to find their wives unchanged, to pick up where they had left off, but working wives had experiences that profoundly affected their outlook on life and their relationships with their husbands. It was inevitable that those experiences would affect marriages, resulting in a leap in the divorce rate after the war.

Although the women's movement may be said to have been a product of efforts in the 1970s and 1980s, in fact much that happened during World War II contributed to allowing women to assume roles that had previously been denied them. For example, in 1943 legislation was enacted in Oklahoma permitting women to hold elective political office, thus opening politics to women in the final state where prohibitive legislation existed.

Thanks to the war and labor shortages, women gained power and greater freedom in jobs men had traditionally filled. The onus against married women in teaching disappeared and the many restrictions placed upon women teachers eased. Prior to the war, school districts in some states would dismiss teachers, mostly women, after two or three years to avoid increasing their salaries or awarding them tenure, and hire new ones at lower pay. Wartime shortages changed this practice; it was often not possible to find new teachers, so school districts were forced to keep experienced teachers. And prewar prohibitions against unmarried teachers dating, wearing cosmetics, or living alone disappeared, as did strict dress codes.

Military Services

Each of the military services created women's divisions during World War II, and in addition to the women's branches of the army, navy, Marine Corps and Coast Guard, women served in several other related capacities. As a result of legislation passed in April 1943, a limited number of women physicians were awarded direct commissions in the Army Medical Corps and the Navy Medical Corps. Women performed most jobs in the military services except for combat positions; they were particularly valuable in filling administrative and clerical positions, freeing men for combat assignments.

Mothers with children under 14 could not enlist in the WAC, and those with children under 18 could not enlist in the WAVES, SPARS or women marines. All of the women's services initially required women to be 21 years of age to join (later it was lowered to 20) although men were drafted at age 18 and the Marine Corps and navy permitted enlistment of males at age 17. Most of the officers in all of the women's military services had at least two years of college, and enlisted women, all of whom were volunteers, were better educated than men in the services.

Although women did not serve in combat during the war, the governing board of the American Association of University Women voted to recommend that women be used in combat if the defense establishment felt it was necessary. Shortly after Pearl Harbor, a poll showed that 63 percent of the men and 73 percent of the women approved of drafting single women 21–35 years of age; 91 percent of those who would have been affected favored it. Most people favored a program, similar to the British plan, under which the government would decide where each person could best serve the war effort. The question of drafting women was considered several times during the war, not necessarily for military service but as part of a larger national service plan to require both men and women to serve in war work or in other service that the country needed.

The motivations for women to join the women's branches of the armed services were varied. Without question, patriotism was a major factor, but not the only one. Joining also represented an opportunity for adventure, excitement, travel, and meeting interesting people; it might offer a cure for a hum-drum life or a chance to get away from an unpleasant situation at a time when social convention limited or precluded other options; and certainly serving in the military opened the door to experiences that would never have occurred back on the farm or in small-town America. Susan Goodson found that service women claimed they had "more dates and a better time" than before joining the military. Lt.(j.g.) Frances S. Miller, an officer in the WAVES and a former teacher, wrote in 1944 that for her money was an important factor in addition to the usual reasons. As a navy officer she was paid a salary of $1,800 a year, plus an allowance for food and housing that brought her income to $2,595.50 a year, and a $250 uniform allowance. Her pay was equivalent to that of a full professor in college. She pointed out that some schoolteachers then earned as little as $900 a year, and the average teacher's salary nationally in 1940 was only $1,441. Indeed, historian Mary Martha Thomas found that in 1940-41 an elementary school teacher with two years of college earned $800 per year in rural Alabama and a college graduate earned $950; the starting salary for high school teachers was $1,150. It is little wonder that so many college educated women deserted teaching to enter the military services or seek employment in war-related industries that paid far higher salaries.

Throughout the war, the women's divisions of the military services were all of a temporary nature, but in May 1948 Congress passed the Women's Armed Services Integration Act giving women permanent status in the military services, with the exception of the SPARS which was disbanded on June 30, 1946. With the creation of the Air Force as a separate arm in 1948, the WAF (Women in the Air Force) was born, replacing the Air WACs.

In addition to women in uniform, the military services hired many civilian women to do specialty jobs, such as automotive and aircraft mechanical work, and the full range of staff duties. The Army Air Forces hired 150,000 and the Army Corps of Engineers hired over 80,000—not only in clerical jobs but as architects, cartographers, engineers, and technicians of various kinds.

Army

Congress approved legislation establishing the Women's Army Auxiliary Corps in May 1942, but its auxiliary status meant that it was not an integral part of the army and created several difficulties. This led to legislation on July 2, 1943, making the organization an integral part of the army, effective September 1, 1943, and designating it the Women's Army Corps. The main training center for the WAAC/WAC was Fort Des Moines, Iowa. Other training centers were later established at Daytona Beach, Florida; Fort Oglethorpe, Georgia; Fort Devens, Massachusetts; and Ruston, Louisiana. Officer training was also conducted at Fort Des Moines but was moved to Fort Oglethorpe in the spring of 1943.

The first group to complete training went into the field in November 1942 to a variety of jobs, including clerks, stenographers, typists, postal clerks, teletype operators, dietitians, and linguists. In January 1943, a detachment of WAACs was sent to North Africa to serve in General Eisenhower's headquarters, including specialties listed above plus drivers

TABLE 7-1
WOMEN IN THE MILITARY SERVICES AS OF JUNE 30, DESIGNATED YEARS IN WORLD WAR II

Service and role	1941	1943	1945
Army:			
WAAC or WAC Officers	–	4,917	5,733
WAAC or WAC enlisted women	–	55,326	90,780
Nurses	5,433	30,316	53,291
Women physicians	–	–	72
Other health personnel	–	989	2,796
Navy:			
Officers	–	3,827	8,385
Enlisted women	–	21,717	73,813
Nurses	671	5,431	11,086
Marine Corps:			
Officers	–	244	831
Enlisted women	–	3,399	17,606
Coast Guard:			
Officers	–	235	867
Enlisted women	–	2,956	8,877

Source: Grace, Alonzo G. *Educational Lessons from Wartime Training.* Washington, DC: American Council on Education, 1948.

of staff cars and bilingual telephone operators. Members of the WAC also served as Link trainer operators, camouflage technicians, parachute riggers, cartographers, cryptographers, control tower operators, electricians, mechanics, musicians, and chaplain's aides, among other noncombat jobs, relieving men for combat duty. The largest number of WAC officers served in administrative posts, but they also served as personnel, supply, mess, and special services officers, in addition to those commanding WAC units.

Initially about 30 percent of the WACs, and eventually almost 40 percent, were assigned to the Army Air Forces, of whom a large percentage were posted to the AAF Aircraft Warning Service up and down the East Coast. At the end of the war more than 7,000 Air WACs were serving overseas. Before the war was over, WACs served in Europe, China, Africa, India, Australia, and New Guinea, and afterward in Japan and Korea. Although the WAC sent thousands of enlisted women and officers to specialty schools, it relied on civilian skills to a much greater extent than did the other women's services.

The director of the WAAC/WAC until July 1945 was Oveta Culp Hobby, who was responsible for planning and organizing the corps. Initially appointed with the title of director, with privileges equivalent to those of a colonel, she was awarded the actual rank of colonel when the WAC was created and received considerable praise for the professional manner in which she planned, organized and managed the WAC. In the WAAC, enlisted women were known as "auxiliary" instead of private, but the title lieutenant was routinely used instead of third officer. After the WAC was created, all enlisted women and officers held the same enlisted and officer ranks as males.

The WAC thrived, in part because of the strong support the organization and Col. Hobby enjoyed from army Chief of Staff Marshall, who concluded the organization fully justified his initial confidence in its potential value to the army in replacing thousands of men who could now assume combat roles.

Unlike the other women's services, the WAC did not commission officers directly from civilian life, with the exception of Mrs. Hobby; she had wanted to be a member of the first officer candidate class, but her request was denied by General Marshall. Officers entered the service as privates and, if qualified, were sent to officer candidate school at Fort Des Moines. The exception was the first class, members of which went directly to OCS from civilian life. In the summer of 1942, review boards composed of women deans, personnel directors, YWCA executives and others with administrative experience interviewed hundreds of candidates for the first class of officer candidate school. The first class of 360 was chosen from 30,000 applicants. Ninety percent of the first class had attended college and many had advanced degrees, although only a high school diploma was required for admission to officer candidate school. After the first class, officer candidates were selected from the enlisted ranks, and the educational level of officer candidates declined.

Later, exceptions were made to the rule against direct appointments of officers. In August 1944, the army encouraged enlisted personnel who could qualify as bacteriologists, parasitologists, medical entomologists, serologists, and industrial hygiene engineers to apply for direct commissions in the Sanitary Corps. Among those who did so were a few members of the WAC who were not commissioned in the Sanitary Corps but were in the WAC and detailed to the Sanitary Corps. By the fall of 1943, the Medical Department faced a shortage of physical therapists. Qualifying WACs were admitted to the physical therapy training program; upon successful completion of the training program, they were discharged from the WAC and appointed second lieutenants in the Medical Department.

About 20 percent of the enlisted WACs had attended college; another 42 percent were high school graduates. In 1943, D'Ann Campbell notes,

70 percent of the WACs were single, 15 percent were married and 15 percent were divorced, widowed or separated. By the end of the war, 16 percent were engaged to be married and half were single.

For specialist training WACs were sent to a variety of locations, often in classes with men. For administrative specialist training, six colleges in the Southwest were chosen; radio operator training was given in colleges and universities in Missouri, New Jersey and Pennsylvania. In November 1942 the AAF issued a directive that Air WACs could attend the same specialty schools for positions open to them as men, and were integrated with men in work situations. The term "Air WACs" was officially discouraged by the WAC but nonetheless became standard in the AAF.

When the WAAC became the WAC in 1943, members were permitted to resign, and more than 14,000 of the enlisted WAACs did so. Many had enlisted without understanding fully what was involved and were disenchanted with the WAAC. The army policy against fraternization between WAC enlisted women and male army officers, plus uniforms that were less attractive than those of other women's services, contributed to morale problems in the WAAC. And initially the lowest rank in the WAAC was paid $21 per month, while those in SPARS, WAVES, and the MCWR, which were created originally as military organizations, received regular military pay of $50 per month.

Many had joined to get away from home, a boring job, a boyfriend, or family problems, and resigned from the service when given the chance. And in many cases they were assigned to jobs that were less interesting, or in some cases more demeaning, than they had expected. Resignations of WAACs assigned to the Army Air Forces were lower than among those in the Army Service Forces or Army Ground Forces. Few officers resigned.

For whatever reasons, the WAC did not enjoy the good public image that the other women's services—WAVES, SPARS and women marines—enjoyed. As Mattie E. Treadwell, a WAC officer, pointed out in her definitive volume on the WAC, fairly early in the history of the organization its members got a reputation for loose morals. Samuel A. Stouffer and his team of psychologists found in a survey of 3,400 male enlisted men in November 1943 that 43 percent agreed that becoming a member of the WAC was "bad for a girl's reputation"; 70 percent said they would not want their sister to join the WAC, and 77 percent disagreed with the statement that a woman could do more for her country by joining the WAC than working in a war industry. Most of the gossip about WACs did not see print, but in the spring of 1943 *New York Daily News* columnist John O'Donnell repeated it in his column, which seriously damaged the organization's recruiting efforts.

A heavy recruiting campaign to enlist WACs began in January 1944, using newspapers, radio, magazines, billboards, short films in movie houses and other media. The abundant talents of the Office of War Information were brought to bear on the problem, and a New York advertising agency was hired to assist with the drive. Morale and enlistments in the WAC rose in the summer of 1944 when the army adopted new uniforms for WACs and allowed them to wear high heel shoes when off duty. Even though the maximum age for enlistment was raised to 50, however, the WAC was never able to recruit its authorized maximum of 150,000; its peak strength reached approximately 100,000.

Navy

Congress enacted legislation to establish the WAVES in June 1942, but this was not the first time women would serve in the navy. Near the end of World War I, the secretary of the navy had authorized the enrollment of 11,275 women to become yeomen, with service limited to shore duty.

All WAVES were required to have had two years of high school or two years of business school, to be 20–36 years of age (18 with parental consent), stand at least five feet tall, weigh at least 95 pounds, be of "good reputation" and pass an aptitude test. Married women were accepted but not if they had children under 18 years of age. Enlistment was for the duration of the emergency plus six months.

Initially, WAVES recruits were sent directly to specialty training schools, but their lack of understanding of the navy proved to be a problem and at the end of 1942 the navy decided to send them through a short indoctrination course of basic training. Beginning in January 1943, enlisted WAVES received their basic training at Hunter College in New York City, which in many ways seemed an unlikely location for enlisted WAVES to undergo boot training: it had no dormitories, no large auditorium, and no indoor drill arena. There were, however, several advantages in using a college for WAVES training and for selecting Hunter specifically. For one, it made it possible to establish a training center quickly and at less cost than opening a military base. The social standing of colleges was a big asset, both in attracting young women to enlist and in relieving parents of apprehension. The navy used the Hunter College name as a decided recruiting advantage, promising enlistees, "You will be trained in a leading women's college." Hunter's location in New York was another attraction in recruiting, and transportation was simple—two subway stations were within three blocks of the campus.

The need for housing was solved by taking over 13 apartment buildings next to the campus. The attorney general of New York, at the navy's request, brought condemnation proceedings on January 13, 1943, and the apartments were empty by January 30. The takeover caused no little inconvenience to the occupants, but there was a surplus of vacant apartments in New York at that time and the navy subsidized relocation costs. The problem of an assembly hall for large meetings was solved by renting the 1,399-seat auditorium in Walton High School, next door to the college; and the 8th Regiment Armory of the New York National Guard, which was located one block from Hunter, was used for drills, parades, and reviews.

The initial objective was to graduate 1,600 WAVES every two weeks in what started as a six-week course but was reduced to four weeks after the third class, due to the pressing need for trained personnel. When demand eased in September 1943, the program returned to a length of six weeks. When demand eased further in early 1945, numbers enrolled were reduced (the last class had fewer than 1,000) and the training program was extended to eight weeks. When the school closed on October 10, 1945, it had trained 80,936 WAVES, 1,844 SPARS and 3,190 women marines.

Following boot training, most of the WAVES went to specialty training at 19 locations all over the country. The largest number entered training as yeomen or radio operators at colleges and universities: the University of Wisconsin and Miami University in Ohio for radio operator training; Oklahoma A&M College, Georgia State College for Women at Milledgeville, and Iowa State Teachers College at Cedar Falls for training as yeomen (clerks); and the University of Indiana for training as storekeepers (supply clerks). Thousands were sent to many other specialty training schools, some of which were conducted solely for WAVES, SPARS and women marines, but most went to navy bases where they attended schools with men, and were trained to become bakers, pharmacist's mates, photographers, chauffeurs, telephone operators, mail clerks, and chaplain's assistants.

Some 23,000 WAVES were assigned to the Bureau of Aeronautics, of which the largest number became machinists (airplane mechanics) after completing training at naval aviation schools at Memphis, Tennessee, or Norman, Oklahoma. Others were trained as aviation metalsmiths, Link trainer instructors, control tower operators, parachute riggers, and specialists in other aspects of aviation.

Those WAVES who had appropriate training could be accepted into the Hospital Corps upon enlistment and, following six weeks of basic training, would be assigned as a hospital apprentice or pharmacist's mate. Those who lacked professional preparation could apply upon conpletion of basic training for a special Hospital Corps course, following which they would be assigned to duty in the Hospital Corps as a hospital apprentice. They could then apply for specialty schools to qualify for work in neuropsychiatry, dental technology, operating rooms, X-ray operation, laboratories, and other specialties.

Elizabeth Reynard, a professor of English at Columbia University, had been engaged by the navy to assist with planning before legislation establishing the WAVES was approved; she later served as assistant director of the WAVES. It was she who coined the acronym WAVES (Women Accepted for Volunteer Emergency Service). The acronym preceded the organization's establishment and remained its usual name; only rarely was the service identified by its full name.

On June 7, 1942, Professor Reynard called the president of Smith College in Northampton, Massachusetts, about using the school for training WAVES officers. With growing enrollment, Smith was crowded but agreed to make three dormitories plus classrooms and administrative space available. Arrangements were made with the nearby Northampton Hotel to house some of the trainees and to feed all of them. The college built a permanent wing onto the infirmary plus a temporary wooden annex to take care of the WAVES, but Smith still could not accommodate all of the trainees. Arrangements were made for the overflow (initially 320 WAVES) at nearby Mt. Holyoke College, which could provide living quarters, food service and classrooms.

Initially, all of the trainees arrived as commissioned officers, mostly ensigns, who had been awarded direct commissions from civilian life based on education, professional experience, and aptitude. This was consistent with the policy of commissioning qualified male officers directly from civilian life and sending them to indoctrination schools. After the third class of trainees who arrived with direct, probationary commissions, virtually all trainees were designated V-9 (officer candidates) and required to completed the training program before being commissioned as ensigns. Officer candidates continued to be recruited solely from civilian life, however, until the summer of 1943 when women who had served at least six months in an enlisted status were accepted as officer candidates. The latter route accounted for about 1,000 officers by the end of the war.

The first course for 600 enlisted WAVES officer candidates began on October 6, 1942, along with an indoctrination class of 125 officers. Except for the officer candidates accepted from the ranks, those receiving direct appointments as officers and those selected to attend midshipmen's school were required to have at least two years of college or two years of post–high school business training. In fact, most of the first ones were college graduates; many were recruited from senior classes. Upon completing indoctrination or officer candidate school, some went directly to job assignments, but the majority went to one of 16 different specialty schools.

In addition to serving in command positions in the WAVES, officers filled a variety of specialist posts, particularly in communications, after completing communications training at Mt. Holyoke College. A number of WAVES officers qualified as navigators and flew in transports within the United States and its territories. Some who were trained in mathematics worked in ordnance, helping to design and manufacture guns, and others worked on secret war plans.

The director of the WAVES was Mildred McAfee, president of Wellesley College (to which post she returned after the war). She was appointed lieutenant commander, and received promotions to commander and, in November 1943, to captain. Following her appointment on July 21, 1942, she chose and had commissioned directly sixteen other women, including seven college officials, to assist in establishing the WAVES. The makeup of this group probably accounts for the fact that the WAVES placed greater emphasis in officer selection than did the WAC on academic training and the use of colleges and universities for personnel training.

The navy recognized early the importance of an attractive uniform in recruiting WAVES and enlisted the famous couturier Mainbocher to design the WAVES uniform, which was dark blue with light blue stripes. A white uniform was designed for summer wear. Both were dressy and attractive. Thanks to a number of factors—the dressy uniform, the use of colleges for boot and officer training, the filling of leadership positions with college educated women, selectivity in recruiting, and others—the WAVES were able to recruit intelligent young women and maintain generally high morale throughout the war.

When the war ended, approximately 86,000 WAVES officers and enlisted women were on duty, filling a variety of jobs. By then 38 of the 62 enlisted ratings in the navy were open to women, and about 80 percent of the navy's mail was handled by WAVES.

Marines

Since the Marine Corps is a component of the navy, when women were allowed to become yeomen in the navy in World War I, the Marine Corps also accepted women. Some 272 women marines were on active duty on November 11, 1918, and the number grew eventually to 305. They served in capacities similar to the navy women.

Women served in the Marine Corps in World War II under arrangements comparable to those of the WAVES, inasmuch as the authority for their service was contained in the same legislation that established the WAVES. At peak strength, 18,838 officers and enlisted women marines were on duty. During the war they served in administration, supply, motor transport, communications, recruiting, public information, photography, mess administration, post exchange operation, educational services and aviation. About 62 percent served in clerical and supply positions. The distribution of women marines among specialties paralleled that of the WAVES, including aviation specialties. Schaffter cites a study of 21,051 women marines which showed that 13,734 had worked in clerical and sales positions in civilian life, of whom 11,020 were assigned as clerks in the Marine Corps Women's Reserve. More than 2,100 completed specialist training in aviation, including 957 as aviation machinists.

The members of the Marine Corps Women's Reserve did not gain a pronounceable acronym but were known simply as women marines or the MCWR. The first appointee to the MCWR was Ruth Cheney Streeter of Morristown, New Jersey. The mother of four grown children, three of whom were in the military services, she was active in health and welfare activities and was a licensed pilot. Streeter was originally commissioned a major but was promoted to lieutenant colonel and later to colonel. Seven other women were given direct commissions to assist in forming the MCWR, all assuming their duties without the benefit of the indoctrination training that was later provided to all other women awarded direct commissions. They were joined by 19 WAVES who had recently completed midshipmen's school at Smith and Mt. Holyoke colleges and were trading their navy commission for one in the marines.

The Marine Corps Women's Reserve was announced on February 13, 1943, and applications quickly exceeded places. Initially, enlisted women were sent to Hunter College to train with the WAVES, and officers and officer candidates trained with WAVES at the midshipmen's school at Smith and Mt. Holyoke colleges. The first class of 75 officer candidates commenced their training on March 13, 1943, and received commissions on May 4, 1943. The first group of 722 enlisted women marines arrived at Hunter College on March 26 and graduated a month later. In July 1943, training for both was shifted to the Women's Reserve Training Center at Camp Lejeune, New River, North Carolina.

After the MCWR and SPARS were separated from the WAVES for their basic training, they continued to take specialty training with the WAVES. Yeoman training took place at Oklahoma A & M College, Iowa State Teachers College, and Georgia State College for Women; radio operators were trained at Indiana University and Miami University; the Link trainer school was located at Georgia Tech; and other colleges plus various civilian organizations and naval stations were used as well. For example, the program to train women control tower operators produced 863 graduates including 632 WAVES, 215 women marines and 16 SPARS. The last class of WAVES aerographers (meteorologists) in 1945 included 139 women marines and 4 SPARS. The Link trainer program trained 260 women marines and 18 SPARS, along with 1,692 WAVES.

Prior to November 15, 1943, all officer candidates came directly from civilian life, including some who joined the Marine Reserves while in college. After that date, all but 41 of the 404 who earned commissions were recruited from the ranks of enlisted women. They continued throughout the war to be integrated with WAVES in specialty training.

Coast Guard

The Women's Reserve of the United States Coast Guard Reserve was created on November 23, 1942, and its members were known as SPARS (for the Coast Guard motto *Semper Paratus*, "always ready"). As with the WAVES, the SPARS acronym came first and the organization was always known by the acronym. At peak strength there were 918 officers and 8,911 enlisted SPARS. Beginning on November 24, 1942, SPARS officers were trained at Smith College with WAVES, but their training program was moved in June 1943 to the Coast Guard Academy at New London, Connecticut. Enlisted SPARS were initially trained with the WAVES at Hunter College, beginning February 17, 1943, when they consisted 20 percent of the initial class, but the training program was moved on June 12, 1943, to Palm Beach, Florida. As in the case of women marines, both enlisted women and officers of the SPARS took their specialty training with WAVES, and other programs and policies affecting the WAVES applied generally to SPARS as well.

The commander of the SPARS was Dorothy Stratton, a former dean of women at Purdue University who held a Ph.D. degree in student personnel administration from Teachers College, Columbia University. She was involved in three of the women's military services. In June 1942, while still dean at Purdue, she helped to select the original members of the WAAC. In August 1942, she joined the WAVES as a lieutenant and was the senior woman officer for the WAVES unit in training at the University of Wisconsin when she was picked to head the newly formed SPARS, with the rank of lieutenant commander (she later rose to captain). When the SPARS was formed, a dozen WAVES who had completed officer indoctrination or midshipmen's school at Northampton resigned their navy commissions and were appointed officers in the SPARS.

Women's Airforce Service Pilots

The WASP grew out of two organizations of women pilots created in the Army Air Forces at about the same time. Neither was initiated by the AAF; each was created as the result of efforts by women flyers. On September 10, 1942, the Women's Auxiliary Flying Squadron (WAFS) was established with headquarters at an army air base at Newcastle, Delaware, under the Air Transport Command. Its director was Nancy Harkness Love, a 28-year-old accomplished pilot and member of New

York society. The WAFS was organized to deliver airplanes, primarily from factories to air bases.

Among other requirements, women recruited to the WAFS were required to have had 1,000 hours of flying time; because gaining so much flying time involved considerable expense, most were from well-to-do families. After spending a few weeks in Delaware learning to fly "the army way," they were assigned to air bases in Michigan, Dallas, and Long Beach, California, which were near the aircraft factories whose planes the women would ferry.

As early as the fall of 1939, the celebrated flyer Jacqueline Cochran had discussed with First Lady Eleanor Roosevelt the possibility of women pilots serving in the Army Air Corps, and she continued to push the idea with her and with Air Corps officials throughout 1940 and 1941, to no avail. In early 1942, Cochran recruited a group of women pilots and took them to England where they joined the British Air Transport Auxiliary, a women's group engaged in ferrying planes for the Royal Air Force.

When Cochran heard in England of the formation of the WAFS she returned immediately to Washington and, according to Marianne Verges, confronted General H. H. Arnold, chief of the AAF, claiming that she had been promised that if women were accepted into the Army Air Forces, she would head the organization. In less than a week after the creation of the WAFS, the AAF created another women's flying organization called the Women's Flying Training Detachment (WFTD) to train women pilots for the WAFS, and Cochran was named director of it.

The WFTD began its training under contract with a private flight school at an airport near Houston, although Cochran maintained an office at the headquarters of the Flying Training Command in Fort Worth. (Cochran was married to wealthy businessman Floyd Odlum, who was then serving as a $1 a year man in Washington, but she was always known as Miss Cochran. Nancy Love was married to Col. Robert Love, a senior staff officer in the AAF headquarters in Washington, and was generally known as Mrs. Love.) In May 1943, the WFTD was moved to Avenger Army Air Field near the West Texas town of Sweetwater. A decision by the Air Forces Ferrying Command that only graduates of the WFTD would be accepted into WAFS brought a halt to direct recruitment for the latter organization. Further, it would have been difficult to find many additional women with 1,000 hours of flight time.

By the late spring of 1943, General Arnold decided that the WAFS and the WFTD should be combined. In August 1943, the two groups were merged into one organization to be known as Women's Airforce Service Pilots, with Cochran as director and Love in charge of the ferrying division. Like the WAVES and SPARS, the acronym WASP was selected before the full name of the organization was created.

There was no shortage of applicants for the WFTD or the WASP. Approximately 25,000 applied to join, of whom 1,830 were admitted; 1,070 of these successfully completed flight training. Initially the age range was 21 to 35, but later the minimum age was lowered to 18½; most were under 27 years of age. Other requirements for admission were that pilots be American citizens, high school graduates, and at least five feet tall; they also were required to have completed 200 hours of flying time and to pass a physical examination and an interview. Later, Cochran reduced the flying time required for acceptance to 100 hours, then to 75 hours and finally to 35 hours. This meant that women who were interested in flying but had never flown could quickly accumulate the 35 hours of flying time to join, as some did. Cochran recognized that the women had to be highly competent if the organization was to succeed, and as a result training standards were high. The failure rate was over 30 percent, in addition to voluntary withdrawals. Interestingly, the graduation rate for those 18–20 years of age was twice that of women 30–35.

The primary mission envisioned for the WASPs was to serve as ferry pilots, a term adopted from the British, so it was necessary that they be qualified to fly several different types of planes. Initially, they were allowed to fly only light planes such as Piper Cubs and BT-13s. Later, after completing the flight training program at Avenger Field, they went to advanced training to learn to fly various other aircraft. They were then allowed to fly any plane for which they could qualify, but they were occasionally required to fly planes in which they had little or no training. A WASP might, within a few weeks' time, fly a P-40, a P-38, a P-47, a C-47, and two or three different types of bombers. One WASP reported that she ferried a total of 32 different types of planes. When the organization closed WASPs had ferried a total of 77 different types of planes.

While the AAF planned that the principal job for the WASPs would be ferrying planes, they also flew planes towing targets for gunnery training, served as test pilots, and flew smoke laying, radar jamming and searchlight tracking missions. By August 1944, the number engaged in instruction and engineering flying and target towing exceeded the number assigned to ferrying planes. Thirty-eight WASPs lost their lives in flying accidents.

The WASP was disbanded on December 20, 1944. In mid–1944 the War Training Service, formerly the Civilian Pilot Training Program, was terminated, releasing several thousand civilian instructors who, together with combat pilots who had completed their missions and returned to the United States for assignments, served as ferry pilots and assumed other flying duties that had been performed by the WASPs.

From the beginning, Cochran and some of the senior officers in the AAF attempted to secure army commissions for WASPs, initially in the WAC and then in the Air Corps, but for legal and other reasons the effort did not succeed. The WASPs were members of the federal Civil Service and retained civilian status throughout the life of the organization. Since the WASP was a civilian organization, its members did not participate in veterans' benefits until 1979 when, with the support of Senator Barry Goldwater, an air force reserve major general, they were awarded veterans benefits retroactively.

Nurses

Nurses in the military services were highly regarded by all services during World War II. They went everywhere hospitals were established, including combat areas. Some were captured and interned for the duration, especially at the beginning of the war; for example, 68 were captured in the fall of Manila in early 1942.

The *American Journal of Nursing* reported that 43 percent of the registered nurses in active practice during the war volunteered for the army or navy. Most of them were single and 40 percent had some college education; college training was not required for licensing as nurses at that time. In early 1942, there were approximately 1,300 nurse training programs in the United States, of which only 75 were affiliated with colleges or universities; the remainder were operated by hospitals. Conscription of nurses was considered late in the war, but the anticipated shortage of military nurses was found to be overstated and it was not necessary to draft them. On the final day of the war, there were approximately 57,000 nurses on duty in the army and 11,000 in the navy.

Both army and navy nurses served overseas, including about 300 navy nurses who served aboard hospital ships. And both served as air evacuation nurses, flying the wounded from battle areas to hospitals. Navy nurses also served as instructors, training male sailors and WAVES as corpsmen, and army nurses served in a comparable role.

Prior to 1944, army and navy nurses did not hold commissioned rank, but instead held equivalent rank, with salaries and most benefits equal to those of commissioned officers. On February 26, 1944, however, President Roosevelt signed legislation (P.L. 238) awarding commissions to navy nurses, and on June 22, 1944, a law followed (P.L. 350) awarding commissions to army nurses. Also in 1944, legislation was enacted awarding commissioned rank to certain other health care personnel and to dietitians in both the army and navy.

Men and women in all kinds of noncombat jobs worked long hours and long weeks in World War II, but none more than nurses. As trained nurses left hospitals to join the army or navy, they could not all be replaced and their work had to be absorbed by those who remained. Federal law did not allow women to work more than six days a week during the war, but this restriction apparently was not enforced in the case of nurses, for whom overtime and long weeks became commonplace, leading many to exhaustion.

In the first year of the war, 30 percent of the registered nurses in the United States had entered the military services creating a nursing shortage so severe that many hospitals had to close wards, sections or floors. This shortage prompted Congress to pass legislation on June 15, 1943, establishing the Cadet Nurse Corps. The program began on July 1, 1943, and graduated its last student on June 30, 1948; during that period the government spent $161 million on the program. The program was operated by the U.S. Public Health Service, and, while it was not a military organization, the cadets were provided uniforms which most of them wore at all times, although they were not required to do so. The Cadet Nurse Corps attracted no little jealousy from members of the WAC, because the former not only wore more attractive uniforms but were paid larger stipends than privates in the WAC earned.

The act creating the program provided scholarships that covered students' tuition, fees, books, uniforms and maintenance plus a monthly stipend. Young women accepted into the Cadet Nurse program were required to agree to serve in either military or civilian nursing for the duration of the war upon completion of their training. Although those entering the program as beginning students in July 1943 did not complete their studies in time for wartime service in the military, many in the program were advanced students who did see wartime military service. Approximately 40 percent eventually saw military service. As of June 30, 1944, only 1,206 had graduated from the Cadet Nurse Corps program; in the 12 months ending June 30, 1945, some 15,248 were graduated; and 13,589 graduated in the year ending June 30, 1946.

About 87 percent of all nursing schools participated in the program, including virtually all of those affiliated with colleges and universities, and by the time the program ended, 132,000 young women ages 17 to 35 had been admitted. Between the initiation of the program in July 1943 and August 1945, 83 percent of the students enrolling in programs preparing nurses were cadet nurses. The act creating the program required that institutions accelerate nursing programs, reducing the completion time from 36 to 30 months or less. During their training, particularly in the clinical phase in civilian hospitals, cadet nurses often found themselves filling the roles of licensed nurses who had left for military service.

Volunteers

With patriotic fervor no less than that of young men who volunteered to fight, women who did not choose to work outside the home, particularly educated women, became involved in volunteer activities. As Mary Martha Thomas has noted, "Middle class women who had some college training were much more likely to volunteer than women from less privileged backgrounds. More educated women had experience with organized social activities outside the home and had learned the skills necessary to work effectively."

The Citizens Service Corps, which was developed under the auspices of the Office of Civilian Defense, sought women to conduct salvage campaigns (drives to collect used metal, paper, rubber, etc.), staff speaker's bureaus, serve as block captains, serve on a multitude of boards and committees, and perform other volunteer services. Civilian Defense Volunteer Offices, staffed largely by women, were established to coordinate the recruitment and placement of volunteers.

The Ground Observer corps, set up to spot incoming enemy planes, eventually involved some 600,000 observers of which women were the majority. The Civil Air Patrol (see Chapter VIII) admitted women pilots on the same basis as men, and women also served in the CAP as control tower operators, mechanics, ground school instructors, radio operators, and specialists in other non-flying capacities.

The Victory Speakers Bureau enlisted women volunteers who could fathom the complexities of the rationing system, and the Office of Price Administration sought out women to administer its regulations. Almost every city, and many smaller towns, had a USO (United Service Organization) center which served as a hospitality center for military personnel. Servicemen on leave or liberty knew the USO as a haven where they met other servicemen, were served refreshments, danced, and relaxed. All of the USO centers were staffed by volunteers, mostly women.

In Virginia, the Civilian Mobilization Program served as the state office of civilian defense and involved primarily women, who initiated a number of activities such as housing surveys, providing recreation centers for servicemen and promoting salvage collection and Victory Gardens. They also taught classes in nutrition and home nursing and provided information services for servicemen and their families at bus and train stations. In Newport News, Virginia, women of the Delta Kappa Gamma education society served as interpreters for German POWs arriving at the port there.

Members of the American Association of University Women were active in a large number of volunteer activities, including serving as nurse's aides, instructing first aid classes, and registering applicants for rationing and military service. Virtually all women's organizations contributed to the war effort, involving not only women with leisure time but working women as well. Members of the Business and Professional Women's Clubs of America, with chapters in most cities, helped in recruiting women for the military services, in conducting surveys, in organizing salvage drives, and in other activities, even though most of them were employed full-time. The club at Wilmington, Delaware, collected 1,000 keys in a scrap drive; in Covington, Louisiana, then a town of 4,000, the club set a goal of $25,000 in its war bond campaign and sold $86,000 worth of bonds. In Missoula, Montana, club members conducted a house-to-house survey for the local War Worker Recruiting Station to locate women who might be willing to accept war-related jobs.

The American Women's Volunteer Service was founded in January 1940 by a group of wealthy women and was modeled after a similar organization in Great Britain. Members served as air raid wardens, sold war bonds, served food to the needy, and ran many activities similar to those of the Red Cross. There were eventually some 400 chapters in the country with about 350,000 members. They contributed significantly to the effort of the various groups involved in volunteer work but were often not taken seriously because of their upper class status, culture and wealth.

Bundles for Britain clubs were organized in October 1940 to collect money and supplies for the British, with women providing most of the leadership. By the summer of 1941, a thousand chapters had been founded with a half million members. In Sheridan, Wyoming, for instance, the Bundles for Britain club sent 511 blankets and $16,000 in cash to England. In 1943, Bundles for Britain was integrated into Community Chest campaigns.

War relief agencies and activities were not the province solely of women, but women were in the large majority and provided much of the leadership. The number of war relief agencies ran into the dozens. For example, in Newport News, the Community Chest, later known as United Way, included among its beneficiaries the following organizations: Belgian War Relief, Greek War Relief, Polish War Relief, Refugee Relief Trustees, United China Relief, United Yugoslavian Relief, National American-Denmark Association, Philippine War Relief, American Relief for Italy and Holland, Friends of Luxembourg, Norwegian Relief, the Queen Wilhelmina Fund, Russian War Relief, United Czechoslovakian Relief, United Lithuanian Relief, British War Relief, and French War Relief.

Red Cross

The national headquarters of the Red Cross estimated that 3 million women served as Red Cross volunteers during the war, including members of the Canteen Corps, the Motor Corps, the Grey Ladies, and several other associated organizations devoted to aiding the war effort.

These were in addition to some 38,000 paid staff members, most of whom were women and some of whom served overseas near combat areas.

The American Red Cross was staffed largely by college educated women, both volunteers and paid staff, and it was not without some justification that the Red Cross was viewed as a haven for educated, upper class women with a "do-good" mentality. Lower middle class and lower class women, when questioned, indicated that they did not volunteer to serve in the Red Cross because they viewed it as an organization of elite women in which they would not fit. Most volunteer leaders of local Red Cross organizations were, in fact, generally socially motivated and intelligent women. In addition, they were more likely to have spare time to devote to volunteer activities than women of lower socioeconomic strata who were more likely to be employed.

Early in the war, it became apparent that commercial firms could not supply all of the surgical dressings needed by military hospitals, so women's volunteer groups were enlisted to prepare them. Volunteers throughout the country participated in the preparation of surgical dressings, with materials provided by the War Department, and the dressings were shipped to American military hospitals all over the world. In New York state the volunteers were known as the Red Cross Production Corps. By the time the need was met and the program closed in December 1944, women volunteers throughout the country had made more than a billion dressings.

Women volunteers also participated in a national program to knit and sew mufflers, sweaters, scarfs and other wearing apparel for servicemen. By mid-1944, women in Wyoming had sewed and knitted 50,557 such garments. In 1943, women in the Production Corps in Newport News, Virginia, devoted 229,028 hours to knitting 15,487 garments and sewing 30,000 others.

Women volunteers, under the sponsorship of the Red Cross, prepared thousands of kit bags which were sent overseas for soldiers and sailors who were hospitalized. A kit bag contained soap, playing cards, cigarettes, shoe polish cloths, razor blades, pencils, paper, chewing gum, a waterproof matchbox, buttons, needles, and thread. The name of the Red Cross chapter that prepared it was placed on the bag so that the soldier who received it would know its origin and be able to relate more personally to the donors.

FIFTY YEARS LATER, women were no longer merely serving in auxiliary positions in the American military services. They were filling most regular noncombat positions and many combat roles. Further, Congress and the military services were debating the question of allowing women to serve in all military positions occupied by men. In the civilian sector, women were found in virtually every profession and occupation. Women constituted a majority of enrollment in colleges and in some professional schools, such as law.

How much credit for these advances may be assigned to the new roles for women that emerged in World War II is an open question, but it seems reasonable to state that they were at least accelerated by American women's wartime experiences. And it is undeniable that women's contributions to the war effort were a crucial element in mobilizing the nation and keeping its troops supplied.

CHAPTER VIII

Civilian Defense

THE GERMAN INVASION of Western Europe in April and May 1940 caused more Americans to begin to think about the possibility of an attack on the U.S. mainland and led to the creation of a federal Office of Civilian Defense on May 20, 1941. Fiorello LaGuardia, mayor of New York, was named director, a post he held in addition to his mayoral duties. LaGuardia moved aggressively to set up a civilian defense organization throughout the country. By November 1941, all of the states and 5,935 towns and cities had defense councils, air raid wardens and civilian defense plans. They had little or no equipment at that time and about the only evidence of civil defense was the arm bands worn by CD volunteers. By June 1942, however, some 5,601,892 Americans were involved in civilian defense programs; 11,000 local defense councils were eventually established with 10 million volunteers on their rolls.

LaGuardia was an ebullient personality, given to dashing about the country urging states and cities to institute civilian defense measures or expand those already established. His aggressive promotion of civilian defense irritated many, including members of Congress. Many believed he emphasized minor cautions that inconvenienced people in a major way, that he was overly officious, and that he persisted in asking Congress for more money than was necessary to do the job. The appointment of First Lady Eleanor Roosevelt as assistant director of Civilian Defense led some of the president's political opponents, especially in Congress, to direct some of their antipathy for him toward the Office of Civilian Defense. Mrs. Roosevelt had appointed actor Melvyn Douglas to recruit dramatic talent for the war effort and a woman dance instructor to plan programs of exercise and dance for children. It was alleged that they were being paid high salaries, although Douglas was actually unpaid, and both became targets of congressional criticism. LaGuardia was replaced as head of Civilian Defense on February 10, 1942, and was succeeded by James M. Landis, dean of the law school at Harvard University.

Every state was organized to be prepared for possible invasion. Block or neighborhood leaders were responsible for keeping watch to see that lights were blacked out or dimmed when requested and to report unusual people or behavior. Virginia, for example, appointed 17,000 block and neighborhood leaders, who monitored an estimated 94 percent of the state's population. Blackouts became the norm on the East and West coasts and for a time in the interior as well. Well into the war period, all lights along the coasts were required to be extinguished or windows covered as protection against night bombing—a measure which seems unnecessary when viewed later but which seemed essential at the time. Strangely, New York City was not blacked out until April 1942, and it was not until the summer of 1942 that the entire East Coast was blacked out.

Air raid and civil defense wardens went about neighborhoods each evening to ensure that blackout rules were obeyed, and if a light was seen through the edges of curtains the warden would rap on the door and loudly remind residents to close curtains completely. Night baseball ended. Blackouts or dim-outs continued longer on the Eastern Seaboard, especially at Newport News, Virginia, and other East Coast cities where major war production factories were located. Once blackouts had become less common, the army periodically called dim-outs to ensure that the civilian population could readjust if needed. In dim-out drills, the top half of automobile headlights was covered. On April 12, 1942, a dim-out 30 miles into the interior was conducted on the East Coast. On August 12, 1942, the army ordered a test blackout of northern Illinois, southern Michigan and Wisconsin which affected 12 million people. In Hawaii the blackout was total until mid-1943.

Auxiliary police supplemented the work of local police, especially during holidays and in handling large crowds. Auxiliary fire departments and volunteer firemen assisted with fire control when there was a shortage of regular firemen.

Although some inland states were late in establishing civilian defense programs, those near the East Coast did not delay. In New York State, the Office of Civilian Protection was established early, appointing air raid wardens, auxiliary police and firemen, bomb reconnaissance units, demolition and clearance squads, emergency medical services, utility repair units and other civilian defense programs in preparation for a possible disaster. In fact, the state government in New York had established a block plan even before the federal Office of Civilian Defense was established, a plan later adopted across the country for reaching into every neighborhood in every state to ensure security and protection against domestic and foreign intruders.

New York City had established its auxiliary police corps on June 20, 1941, and it later added a corps of air raid wardens which, at its peak in

September 1943, had 290,000 volunteers. It was estimated that, with turnover, 400,000 volunteers served as air raid wardens in the city during the war.

The Illinois War Council (originally called the Illinois State Council of Defense) was created in April 1941 and built a large organizational structure which eventually had 16 standing committees, each with assignments for selected elements of defense, plus 30 advisory committees to back up standing committees. The council came alive after the Pearl Harbor attack, appointing retired General Frank Parker, a veteran of the Spanish-American War, as director, and under his leadership the council became one of the more active state civilian defense organizations. It created its own publication, *Illinois Mobilizes,* and formed a speaker's bureau whose members appeared before civic groups and service clubs all over the state to tell them what citizens could do to help in the prosecution of the war. With the state war council's leadership, 640 local councils of defense were formed, including one in the community of Mt. Vernon, which discovered $62.29 still in an inactive bank account from the Defense Council of World War I.

State defense councils were responsible for training volunteers, although the War Department sponsored three schools for the training of state leaders and instructors—at Edgewood Arsenal, Maryland; Purdue University and Texas A & M College. By February 1943, 150 graduates of these schools were providing leadership in Illinois, training defense volunteers, including block captains and other volunteers. In Chicago, Loyola, Northwestern, and DePaul universities and the University of Chicago all participated in training not only wardens, but teachers for defense volunteer groups elsewhere.

Within a few months after the attack on Pearl Harbor the fear of invasion by the Japanese or Germans began to subside and it became apparent that many of the precautions of the Office of Civilian Defense were unnecessary, if not a huge false alarm. Mayor LaGuardia's fussiness and intensity probably contributed to the feeling that the nation had gotten overly fearful of invasion. By the autumn of 1943 the prospect of invasion had disappeared and the number of workers in civilian defense was dwindling. The U.S. Office of Civilian Defense was placed on standby status in November 1944 and closed on June 30, 1945, almost two months before the end of the war. Blackout regulations had been lifted by the War Department following V-E Day.

Civil Air Patrol

On December 1, 1941, just a week before the attack on Pearl Harbor, the head of the U.S. Office of Civilian Defense created the Civil Air

Patrol. Having been a flyer himself in World War I, LaGuardia saw the need for an aerial observers corps that would patrol the eastern seacoast and spot enemy planes and ships.

Private pilots were recruited to search for incoming enemy planes and to look for submarines off the East and Gulf coasts. The CAP also trained high school juniors and seniors to become future aviation cadets and recruited flying cadets for the AAF. Pilots for the CAP wore the same uniforms as Army Air Corps officers, but with C.A.P. on the right shirt collar instead of officer rank. The members received no compensation, paid for their own uniforms and used their personal airplanes without compensation, except for operating expenses. At the program's peak, 40,000 CAP pilots were engaged in searching for enemy planes and submarines and 20,000 CAP cadets were in training.

In a few states, private plane owners had begun to organize before the attack on Pearl Harbor and were ready to serve as soon as the CAP was established. The Virginia Flying Corps, for example, became the Virginia Wing of the CAP and got under way immediately after the CAP was created. It flew missions as far out to sea as 60 miles, spotting German submarines and reporting to them to the Army Air Corps and the navy.

One of the largest divisions of the CAP was the New York State Wing, which numbered 4,800 pilots, observers, ground crew members and specialists. In addition to patrolling at sea in search of enemy submarines and surface vessels, they flew urgent missions to deliver materials between war production plants and towed targets for AAF gunnery practice.

The Illinois wing of the CAP had 3,000 members—pilots, ground crew, and other staff. Because of geography, it was not usually needed for patrols, so its members performed a variety of related duties including guarding airports, towing targets for gunnery practice, and providing courier service for war industries.

In 1943, the CAP was made an auxiliary of the Army Air Forces and operated under its direct control, particularly in searches for enemy vessels. The CAP functioned under this arrangement until August 1943 when the navy assumed responsibility for antisubmarine work. At that time the CAP was placed on a standby status.

Members of the CAP were a mixture of patriots who failed to meet physical requirements for military service, overage veterans of World War I, and civilians who simply liked flying and sought the opportunity the CAP provided to do what they enjoyed while contributing to the war effort. A few CAP members joined the AAF.

Ground Observer Corps

The Ground Observers Corps, a voluntary organization of civilians under the direction of the Army Air Forces Aircraft Warning service, was responsible for reporting planes that came within range of observers. The Ground Observer Corps established units all along the East Coast, especially in Virginia where there were several major shipbuilding installations; by July 25, 1941, 904 Aircraft Warning Posts had been established in Virginia. But the GOC functioned in states in the interior as well; in Illinois, for example, 11,000 observers were recruited to staff observation posts. Nationwide, the Aircraft Warning Service had organized a total of 6,000 ground observer posts.

Before the war was over, approximately 600,000 individuals had served in the Ground Observer Corps. It was cold, dull, boring duty, standing on a hilltop or on top of a building all alone with a pair of field glasses, searching the sky for planes. One rarely came into view, and when one did it invariably turned out to be friendly. Some viewed the massive effort of the Ground Observer Corps as a vast waste of human effort, since as it turned out, members were not really needed. Others have argued that if an invasion had occurred, the nation would have been eternally grateful for the Ground Observer Corps.

State Guard

Until the National Guard was called to active duty, federal legislation prohibited the establishment of any other type of state military force. This was changed in October 1940 when Congress passed a law allowing states to establish a state guard in the absence of their National Guard. In fact, when the National Guard in a state went to active duty, the War Department actively encouraged the state to create a state guard to replace it. The law authorized the War Department to furnish weapons to state guard organizations, but other expenses had to be borne by the states. By July 1941, 37 states had created state guards, which were known by such names as Defense Force, Reserve Militia, Reserve Military Force, Home Guard, Home Defense Force, Defense Guard, State Defense Guard, State Defense Corps, and Reserve Defense Corps.

Most officers of state guard units were retired officers and reserve officers who had gained their commission through ROTC and CMTC. In due course, the reserve officers, some of the retired officers and many of the enlisted men in state guard units were called to active duty for service in the army. Although a state guard was not under the direction of the state's cilivian defense office, there was close cooperation in every state.

The state guard was organized and functioned along the same general lines in each state, but there were some significant differences, as an examination of four states shows. The state of Virginia, recognizing that the Congress would likely pass legislation mobilizing the National Guard, on July 15, 1940, became the first state to move toward establishing its state guard to assume the duties for which the National Guard was normally responsible, such as quelling riots, suppressing disorders and meeting other domestic emergencies. It was called the Volunteer Protective Force until the summer of 1944, when the name was changed to Virginia State Guard to match more closely the names used in most other states.

To maintain their numbers, the maximum age for state guardsmen in Virginia was raised to 55 and the minimum lowered to 16. Young men, and some not so young, joined the state guard for patriotic reasons and in some cases for social reasons, particularly in Virginia where there was a strong tradition of military service. The Virginia State Guard wore blue and gray uniforms which were manufactured by the state penitentiary and paid for either by the guardsmen themselves or by city councils or other local governing bodies. Some 700 of the 3,400 enlisted men and most of the officers in the Virginia State Guard later went to active service in the army.

Other states were not far behind in establishing their state guards, usually within weeks after the state's National Guard had been called to active duty. When the 25,000-member National Guard in New York was called to active duty, the state moved quickly to establish a state guard. By October 25, 1940, the New York State Guard had been organized with at least one guard unit assigned to each of the 74 National Guard armories in the state. As in most other states, the New York State Guard was prepared for emergency service but was minimally needed during the war; it was called to active duty once to assist with recovery from a flood. The sabotage and other subversion that the public feared never occurred. At peak strength the New York State Guard numbered 16,700 members.

When the 33rd Division National Guard was mobilized in Illinois, the Illinois Reserve Militia was created, initially composed largely of veterans of World War I and known affectionately as "the Boys in Blue" because of their uniforms. It had between 6,000 and 7,000 members, although the number fluctuated because over a period of time approximately 5,000 members departed for active duty in the military services. As Mary Watters's comprehensive study of wartime in Illinois notes, 12 companies were mobilized in September 1942 to maintain peace during a strike at the Western Cartridge Company in Alton, and militia units were mobilized at various times for protection of bridges, airports, defense plants and other facilities. In 1943, Illinois experienced one of its worst floods ever and called on its state guard, the Civil Air Patrol, and regular service agencies to deal with it.

In Texas, promoters of the state guard also initiated action before federal authorization had been enacted, surveying veterans' organizations and seeking their assistance. Applications for guard units poured in from towns all across the state. On February 10, 1941, shortly after it met in biennial session, the legislature created the Texas Defense Guard, and by the autumn of that year 51 rifle battalions had been formed, one in each of 45 towns plus three each in Dallas and Houston. The battalions drilled at least once a week for two hours, some of them twice a week. The guard units were funded almost entirely locally. As in other states, the guard was rarely needed, although in June 1943 more than 1,500 of the guardsmen were called out to help quell a race riot in Beaumont.

In none of the states was the state guard as critical to domestic tranquility as some political leaders had expected, although they were called on occasionally for lesser threats, such as in Boston to deal with the excesses of the V-J Day celebration. Their presence on certain occasions provided a sense of security for the civilian population, and the knowledge that they existed and could be called in an emergency enhanced the ability of state governments to maintain order. In addition, guardsmen and their families found other ways to assist with the national emergency. In Texas, as in many other states, the guard became a social group, with wives of officers forming an organization to undertake activities to support the war effort.

On April 10, 1941, the War Department authorized the formation of a reserve militia as backup for the state guard, but it provided no assistance so the members supplied their own weapons (they were sometimes referred to as "shotgun soldiers"). Virginia was one of few states to create such a backup militia. In the early months of 1942, the United States suffered a number of devastating military defeats in the Pacific war, which stirred men to volunteer for service at home and made possible the rapid formation of the Virginia Reserve Militia, some of whose members were in their seventies.

Also known as Minute Men, they were not subject to performing such duties of the state guard as quelling riots and disorder; rather they served as observers, looking for sabotage and subversive activities in their communities while the state guard was otherwise occupied. Also, unlike the state guard they were not required to drill every week. The militia provided an outlet for military ardor with limited demands on its members. A horse-mounted unit was formed in Richmond which conducted parades and was involved in other activities normally identified with horse cavalry. The Virginia Reserve Militia eventually grew into 120 companies consisting of 7,790 officers and enlisted men, more than in the state guard.

Chapter IX

Patriotism

The attack on Pearl Harbor moved thousands of young men to volunteer for service in the army, navy and marines. On December 8, lines formed at recruiting stations all over the country. In New York City, a line of volunteers several blocks long was waiting to get into a single army recruiting center before it opened at 8:00 Monday morning. In Seattle, the Marine Corps Recruiting Office opened at 6:00 Sunday evening, and within 3 hours 78 men had enlisted, and the next morning both marine and navy recruiting offices opened at 6:00. In Boston, 41 men were lined up at the navy and marine recruiting office before 8:00 A.M., and in Norfolk, 60 men applied for enlistment in the army and 100 for the navy before noon Monday.

The rush to join the military services and fight the Japanese reached all segments of American society, including many who had been dedicated opponents of American involvement in the war. Representative Hamilton Fish of New York, a prominent isolationist, announced on December 8 that he would offer his services to a combat unit. With few exceptions, those who had opposed intervention in the European war changed their position immediately following the attack at Pearl Harbor and supported U.S. entry into the war. Even some prominent pacifists volunteered for military service, and others publicly announced that they regretfully endorsed the declaration of war. The rush to enlist was such that conscription was suspended for several weeks; volunteers for the navy, Marine Corps, Coast Guard and AAF were ample to meet needs up until December 1942 when voluntary enlistment was replaced by conscription of all services.

Selective Service

Although many people had been promoting the idea of conscription, Grenville Clark, a New York lawyer who had been an army officer in

World War I and had formed an organization called the Military Training Camps Association along with a group of friends, was credited with writing the plan and selling it to Congress. The country had never enacted a conscription law in peacetime and with the loud opposition then heard on campuses, in the Congress and among non-interventionists, the bill's chances of passage seemed slim. Clark called it Selective Service, but it was commonly referred to as "the draft."

The Selective Service Act was bitterly opposed by many organized groups in the country, including labor leaders who feared it would be used to destroy unions, college students, the Communist Party, the American Youth Congress, conservatives, clergymen, pacifists, American Nazis, anti-Semites, and mothers who feared for damage to their sons' morals. Many argued that it was a first step toward American entry into the European war.

Most of the press was editorially opposed to the act, although there were notable exceptions. The *New York Times* had editorialized against conscription, but following President Roosevelt's May 1940 speech, after Germany had invaded the low countries, the *Times* reversed editorially and called for conscription. The *New York Herald Tribune* was less restrained; it called for an immediate declaration of war against Germany.

Selective Service was not an administration bill. It had been introduced in late June 1940 in the House by Representative James W. Wadsworth, a Republican from upstate New York, and in the Senate by Senator Edward R. Burke, a Democrat from Nebraska, so it had bipartisan support. President Roosevelt supported the bill but was content to let the Congress take the heat without administration involvement. Following committee hearings, the bill was debated in the House and Senate during late July and August, during which time both members of the Congress and the president were besieged with pleas not to enact conscription.

The devastating defeat of the Dutch, Belgians, French and British in May and early June was clearly on everyone's mind and had much to do with pro-draft sentiment. In October of the previous year, only 39 percent of those polled approved of compulsory military service; by June 1940, a national poll showed that 50 percent approved of it; and when the poll was repeated in mid-August, 65 percent favored it. The bill was approved in the Senate on August 28 by a vote of 58 to 31 and in the House a few days later 263 to 149, a huge margin considering the vote on the extension of the bill to come a year later. President Roosevelt signed the bill on September 16 with registration for the draft to begin on October 16. The bill limited terms of service to one year, set a cap of 900,000 that could be inducted in the year, and carried an amendment that draftees could not serve outside the Western Hemisphere.

The first director of Selective Service was Dr. Clarence A. Dykstra, who had taken a leave of absence from the University of Wisconsin where he served as president; he served as director from October 15, 1940, to March 21, 1941. The deputy director was Lt. Col. Lewis B. Hershey, who succeeded Dykstra and served as director of Selective Service for 29 years—meantime rising to four-star general rank—until conscription was replaced by volunteer service in 1970 over his strong opposition.

Some 16,500,000 men registered on October 16, 1940, with 6,175 draft boards (there were eventually 6,443 boards) at 125,000 registration points, mostly situated in school buildings. Failure to register was punishable by a sentence of as much as five years in prison and a fine of up to $10,000. The selection of the first draftees to be inducted into the army was held in a formal ceremony in Washington on October 29 with speeches by Dykstra and President Roosevelt. Numbered slips of paper from 1 to 9,000 had been put into capsules and dropped into a large bowl; the secretary of war drew out one capsule and handed it to the president, who read the number aloud to those assembled in the auditorium and to millions who were glued to their radios all over the country. The reason for there being 9,000 numbered slips of paper was to exceed the largest number registered with any single draft board, which shortly before the lottery was 8,090 at Draft Board No. 5 in Baltimore County, Maryland. Selective Service set the number at 9,000 to be sure any late registrations were included.

The first capsule drawn was number 158, which meant that registrant number 158 in each of the 6,175 local draft boards had the dubious honor of being the first in his community to be drafted. The second capsule was number 192, and the third number 8,239. Additional capsules were drawn to determine the sequence in which individuals in each draft board were called for service. Thereafter, the selection of individuals to be drafted was the decision of local draft boards, within rules promulgated by the Selective Service Administration in Washington.

On December 20, 1941, legislation was passed requiring all males ages 18–65 to register, and making those aged 20–45 eligible for military service. The third registration occurred on February 16, 1942, when those aged 20–45 who had not already registered did so, and the remaining males 18–65 registered on March 19, 1942. No one in the 45–65 age group was ever inducted.

By the time the draftees began to be called in late November 1940, volunteers had exceeded anticipated numbers and it was not necessary to call as many right away as planned, thereby delaying induction of some draftees. The navy had received all of the volunteers it needed and continued to do so until December 1942 when volunteering was replaced by conscription for all services. By July 1, 1941, 606,615 selectees, as the draftees were called, had been inducted into the army. By the end of the war, 31 million men had registered for the draft, of whom just over 10 million were drafted.

On July 21, 1941, President Roosevelt asked Congress for legislation extending the terms of service of the National Guard, reservists and retired personnel of the regular army, and for authority to extend the Selective Service Law, lengthening the term of service to 30 months and removing the ban on troops serving outside the Western Hemisphere. The debate in Congress was heated. Roosevelt's opponents charged that he was trying to build a dictatorship and lead the nation into war without the approval of Congress. They denied that the threat to peace had increased and that the United States was in danger of attack. One member expressed the sentiment of many when he said, "I am convinced that unless we go out looking for trouble with a chip on our shoulder we need have no immediate fear of being attacked or involved in war."

Members of Congress had heard from families of young men who were already drafted or who would be drafted, and the pressure not to extend the period of service was enormous. Further, the army was not yet properly equipped; some draftees used wooden sticks as rifles and on maneuvers trucks were used to simulate tanks, which gave an artificial atmosphere to the training. The morale of draftees plummeted. They complained bitterly that the government had deceived them, and they threatened to desert when their year was up if the law was extended. (The desertion idea was referred to by the draftees as O.H.I.O.—Over the Hill in October.) They also complained about the income differential they suffered in comparison to friends who had managed to avoid the draft and were earning large incomes in defense industries. At that time, an army private earned $21 a month, increasing to $30 after a four-month probationary period, while many of his contemporaries working in defense industries were earning six or seven times that amount. (The base pay of privates was increased to $50 per month in June 1942.)

Army Chief of Staff Marshall told Congress that rejection of the act would result in a loss of two-thirds of the enlisted personnel and three-fourths of the officer corps and would lead to disintegration of the army. New draftees could be brought into the army, but who would train them? The 18 mobilized divisions of the National Guard would have to be released with none to replace them, and reserve officers would also depart. By this time, Marshall's credibility with Congress was already established. As the war progressed, Marshall increasingly enjoyed the confidence of congressional committees before which he testified because of his honesty, candor, sound judgment and nonpolitical stance. His support in the Congress was due in part to the fact that his recommendations prior to the war proved sound and did much to bring the army to the level of preparedness that existed at the time of the Pearl Harbor attack.

The *New York Times* editorialized on July 22, 1941, regarding extension of the Selective Service Act, that "An immediate endorsement of the President's recommendation by overwhelming majorities in both branches of Congress would be worth ten battleships. It would warn Japan, shake Germany, cheer Britain, and give fresh impetus to democracy in every corner of the world." But there was no chance of overwhelming support for the legislation. A national poll showed that only 51 percent of the public favored extending the length of service, although the bill garnered greater support among newspaper editorial writers, especially if it included the prohibition against overseas service. One of the major factors in the passage of the bill was the assiduous work of the American Legion, then a highly influential lobby in Washington, on behalf of extending selective service.

The bill passed the Senate by a margin of three to two—45 to 30—but it passed the House of Representatives by only a one-vote margin—203 to 202. Without heavy lobbying by the American Legion, it almost certainly would have failed. The narrowness of its passage on August 12, just as the meeting of Churchill and Roosevelt off the coast of Newfoundland was ending, shocked not only the British but the Americans as well. More than anything else, the slim margin revealed the desire of the American people to avoid war and indeed the actual hope at that late date that it was possible to do so. The vote prompted the British prime minister to send Lord Beaverbrook, who was then British Minister of Supply and a confidant of Churchill, to Washington in late August especially to assess the American attitude toward entering the war. Beaverbrook reported to Churchill that there was not the slightest chance of America entering the war until the enemy was on its shores, and that probably meant after the defeat of Russia and Britain.

After the attack on Pearl Harbor voluntary enlistment boomed, meeting most of the military's needs without the draft. But the country was now faced with building an army and navy quickly, and soon men were being drafted by the thousands. Although the draft age was lowered to 20, for several months it was irrelevant, because men were enlisting voluntarily in numbers sufficient to meet most of the needs of the military services. By the fall of 1942, however, the supply of draftees was declining, and in November 1942 the draft age was lowered to 18.

On December 5, 1942, the president issued an order ending voluntary enlistment in the military services and transferring the Selective Service Office to the War Manpower Commission. Voluntary enlistment had created a number of problems, most importantly the maldistribution of able personnel among the services and unbalanced competition in recruiting. While the army had to rely largely on draftees—except for a short time immediately after the attack on Pearl Harbor—the other services had been able to rely solely on volunteers. The army, especially the infantry, was seen by most young men as the last choice. As a young man's draft number came up, he was likely to volunteer for the Air Corps, the navy or Coast Guard, and consequently these services were enlisting more of the talented young men, thereby creating a problem for the army. In addition, the draft was calling some men who were needed in essential industries or other civilian service.

Thereafter, inductees were assigned to each service in proportion to its quota for the month. Notwithstanding the change, draftees were often able to choose the service they would enter, provided vacancies existed. The Marine Corps was even able to secure delays for selected draftees until new quotas were issued, usually a month later. The Marine Corps had always prided itself on being composed of volunteers only and tended to believe there was a stigma attached to being a draftee, so the new procedure caused problems. The recruiting service handled the matter by allowing inductees to be discharged and immediately enlist, but about one-third of the inducted Marines did not choose this option. After the rush to enlist that followed the outbreak of war, the Selective Service Administration was often unable to meet the army's demand for draftees because its monthly quota exceeded the number of men called, and that continued to be the case throughout most of the war. The Marine Corps and navy responded by accepting 17-year-old volunteers, but the army and AAF continued to adhere to the minimum age of 18 for enlistment.

Throughout World War II the Selective Service Administration frequently changed regulations concerning who would be drafted. At various times, exemptions or deferments were allowed fathers with varying numbers of children, sons of widowed mothers, and individuals faced with hardship situations; they were also granted for a multitude of occupational reasons and because of age. In reviewing the selective service experience after the war, General Hershey said, "In 1940 we began to induct men between 21 and 35. Before the first year of operation was out, we had changed the terminal age to 28. When a few more months had passed and Pearl Harbor was upon us, we moved up to 45; then we moved back to 40, to 38, to 27, to 26, and again to 30 when the [Battle of the] Bulge came."

Although the draft briefly took men up to age 45, the majority of those over 40 were unable to meet physical requirements, and on December 5, 1942, the top draft age was lowered to 38. Further, farmers and fathers were initially deferred. The Tydings Amendment to the Selective Service Act in 1942 deferred fathers engaged in agriculture, and by

September 1, 1943, more than 1.4 million agricultural workers had been deferred by reason of occupation compared to 1.2 million in all other industries. Some young men remained in farming who might not otherwise have done so, and some industrial workers sought work on farms to avoid military service. This shift deprived industry of workers while labor was plentiful on nearby farms which, in some cases, were producing little or nothing in short supply nationally.

By early 1943, a scarcity of men eligible for induction had developed, and draft boards began to consider men who had previously been deferred. In February 1944, having begun to routinely fail to deliver the quotas set by the military services, the Selective Service Administration instructed state and local draft boards to review again those individuals aged 18–37 who had been deferred for occupational reasons, including farmers. From then until the end of the war, the Selective Service Administration constantly struggled to find young men to draft. By the fall of 1944, the shortage of draftees was serious, with draft boards failing to meet their quotas almost every month. This shortfall led the Selective Service System, with the approval of the OWM, to direct local draft boards to draft more young men from farms. The decision provoked protest from the farm bloc in Congress, but President Roosevelt supported the Selective Service Administration, and the policy stuck. In January 1945, an article in the *New York Times* expressed the frustration of men whose deferments had been canceled, pointing out that there were 667 civilian automobiles in Washington, D.C., driven by male chauffeurs, some of whom were eligible for the draft.

Early in the war, the army rejected almost half of those called for examination due to physical or educational deficiencies. Author William Manchester contends that the high incidence of physical deficiencies was a direct result of inadequate nutrition during the Depression years. The army's physical exams also found a high incidence of communicable diseases among draftees, particularly including tuberculosis and venereal diseases. Louis Lautere reported that 2.3 percent of the white men and 27.2 percent of the black men who took the army induction exam had syphilis. Later, as the pool of draftees dwindled, the army inducted men who had been rejected earlier, including men with one blind eye. In the early days of the draft, a shocking number of draftees were rejected because they were illiterate; later, the army inducted some of them and taught them to read and write.

Sentiment against drafting fathers was especially strong among local draft boards, leading them to call some categories of occupationally deferred workers before finally turning to fathers. Although social pressure was heavy on young men to join the service and fight for their country, there was at the same time widespread opposition in the country to drafting men with children.

In an effort to avoid calling fathers, draft boards began in early 1944 to cancel occupational deferments of many young men under 26, some of whom were in fact in essential jobs in government and war industries. The manpower situation eased temporarily in April 1944 when 100,000 members of the Army Specialized Training Program on college campuses and 30,000 air cadets were transferred to troop duty, primarily infantry divisions.

At various times Selective Service was used as a weapon or threat against strikers, even before the Pearl Harbor attack. When workers at the North American Aviation plant in Los Angeles struck in June 1941, local draft boards began to reclassify the strikers. And when coal miners in mines that had been seized by the government went on strike in the fall of 1943, plans were made to draft them and put them back in the mines in uniform. In several other cases, individuals who had left their war production jobs, including strikers, were drafted, but it was not a widespread practice. Drafting was used more often as a threat, such as in the Philadelphia transit strike in 1944, to force strikers back to work.

Several times during the war, efforts were made to establish national service legislation similar to that in Britain. A leader in this effort was Grenville Clark, the New York attorney who organized the effort to pass the Selective Service Act in 1940. The labor movement strongly opposed the measure, with the exception of unions that were generally considered to be controlled by or sympathetic to the Communist Party, such as the National Maritime Union. Predictably, the military supported it. The idea began to gain popularity in the summer of 1942, and legislation was introduced in both houses of Congress in 1943 which would make all men ages 18 to 65 and all women 18 to 50 subject to national service. Hearings were held, but the bill never got out of committee.

With the spread of strikes in 1943, a push was made to revive the national service idea, and indeed President Roosevelt—who had previously been ambivalent about the idea—called for such a bill in January 1944, arguing that there should no difference between the men and women on the battlefront and those producing war materials. Sympathy for the idea grew among the public, primarily in reaction to strikes in war production plants. The fact that Great Britain required all men and women to register and be engaged in work important to national needs was used as an argument for enacting similar legislation in the United States. Opponents argued that Britain faced invasion and that its situation was therefore unlike that in America.

By the autumn of 1944, some workers in war plants were resigning to take jobs in businesses serving the civilian market. The perception was growing that after the war unemployment would become rampant, and they wanted to get civilian jobs first so they could build up seniority and job security. As a result war plants in several areas experienced a serious labor shortage.

The Battle of the Bulge in Belgium in December 1944 alarmed the public which, when combined with labor shortages and a perception of growing laxity among some workers in defense industries, resulted in renewed calls for national service legislation, especially among the military leadership. In his state of the union address in January 1945, President Roosevelt urged Congress to enact national service legislation which would freeze male workers in their jobs unless a transfer was approved by the government, would include a "work or fight" clause, and would include women. A considerably weakened bill, which included only males 18–45 and lacked enforcement provisions, was approved in the House. But with the war virtually over, a similar bill in the Senate, which was also disappointing to the military, failed by a vote of 46 to 29.

Polls showed that the public strongly favored "work or fight" legislation (a requirement that men eligible for the draft either accept work in essential war production or be drafted), especially during periods when strikes were making newspaper headlines. The idea was considered in Congress and the administration several times during the war but was bitterly opposed by union leaders, and never gained enough support in Congress to secure enactment. However, action tantamount to work or fight became a reality in 1944, precipitated by the serious labor shortage on the West Coast. The director of the Office of War Mobilization, after discussion with the War Manpower Commission, Selective Service and other concerned agencies, issued a directive to draft boards in December 1944 that all men between 18 and 38 years of age who were not engaged in war work should be reclassified and inducted into the military, unless they were deferred or exempted on some other basis. Fairchild and Grossman estimated that this policy brought a net gain of 1.7 million workers back into war plants in January and February 1945.

Draft Boards

Service on a draft board was generally an unpopular job since inevitably some individuals would be drafted while others who appeared equally eligible were deferred or for some other reason not drafted. In one community after another animosity developed between old friends when a member of a draft board refused to intervene on behalf of the son of a friend, and board members often suffered social ostracism. Despite their efforts to be fair, board members inevitably incurred the disapproval of many in the community, as did citizens serving on rationing and price administration boards.

There was uncertainty from time to time in the Washington office of the Selective Service Administration which led to confusion in state headquarters and even more confusion among local boards. Often when local boards were asked to be prepared to send a given number of draftees, the men they alerted would prepare to leave for service only to wait weeks or even months to be called. Meantime, the draftees might have left school, resigned civilian jobs, sold property, made arrangements for others to oversee their businesses, or even bade loved ones goodbye; thus, a wait of several weeks understandably provoked frustration and criticism of the local board.

Each draft board was composed of at least three persons (more in some cases) drawn from the community where it was located. Members were usually community leaders, individuals whose judgment and fairness were respected, who served without compensation. There was at least one draft board in every county in the country and in some there were several, averaging one board for every 30,000 population. In New York City alone there were more than 200 draft boards. According to Spencer King, a survey in North Carolina—which had 155 draft boards—found the following occupations among board members: 121 farmers, 33 lawyers, 23 manufacturing executives, 19 educators, 19 in the insurance field, 17 professionals, 14 bankers, 14 physicians and dentists, 11 public officials, 8 craftsmen, 8 salesmen, 6 brokers, 5 clerks and several in categories with fewer than 5 each. An advisory board was created for every ten local boards to render expert opinions in doubtful cases. In addition, there were boards to consider cases that were appealed for any reason; as of November 1942 there were 274 of them.

Conscientious Objectors

In his research on pacifists and the peace movement, historian Lawrence Wittner found that of 10,022,367 individuals ordered to report for induction through the Selective Service System during World War II, 42,973 declared themselves to be conscientious objectors; of that number 11,887 were classified IV-E (alternative service) and 6,086 refused induction and were sent to prison. Approximately 25,000 were classified I-A-O (noncombatant) and inducted into the military where they worked in service roles, primarily the Medical Corps. Wittner extrapolated these numbers to the entire population of 130 million and concluded that, including all ages, there were more than a half million who were philosophically conscientious objectors during World War II.

In their book *Conscription of Conscience,* Mulford Q. Sibley and

Philip E. Jacob estimate that there were at least 100,000 conscientious objectors subject to military service in World War II, of whom 20,000 avoided military service on conventional grounds, such as physical and mental deficiencies, or were deferred because of family obligations or critical defense work. They concluded that the exact number of conscientious objectors cannot be calculated since local draft boards did not always report to Washington complete statistics on COs, especially those who accepted noncombatant military service (although this category was reported to number 25,000 it may actually have reached 50,000). The Selective Service Administration did not allow a draftee to claim CO status until he had been declared to be 1-A, readly for induction; thus many COs were exempted on a variety of other grounds.

The Selective Service Act provided that individuals who could not serve in combat because of religious conviction were allowed to enter alternative service; Civilian Public Service camps were established to accommodate them. The Civilian Public Service camps grew out of efforts by the National Service Board of Religious Objectors, an arm of Historic Peace Churches. Immediately after passage of the Selective Service Act, the group had begun negotiations with the government concerning the fate of conscientious objectors. In late 1940 when it appeared that the Civilian Public Service camps were about to be placed under the army, the Board of Religious Objectors acted to provide financial support, eventually spending some $7 million to operate a number of camps, and served as the agency for enlisting other organizations to support and operate CPS units.

The Civilian Public Service camps were operated through agreements with the Selective Service Administration by about a dozen different groups—including most prominently the Friends Service Committee, the Mennonite Central Committee, the Disciples of Christ, the Church of the Brethren, the Board of Religious Objectors and the Selective Service System itself—each of which provided or arranged for funding of operating costs. Most of the so-called "regular CPS camps" took over former Civilian Conservation Corps camps, and the men worked in soil conservation, park maintenance and forestry development. On the West Coast and in the Mountain states they also served as smoke jumpers for the Forestry Service. Although most of the camps were operated by pacifist groups, each camp or unit had a technical manager to direct the work of the COs. Of the regular camps the Forest Service served as technical manager for 30; the Soil Conservation Service ran 19; the Park Service 9; the Bureau of Reclamation 4; the Farm Security Administration 2; the Fish and Wildlife Service 2; and the General Land Office 1.

In addition to the regular camps, more than half of the units worked on special projects at the following types of facilities: 40 state mental hospitals, including 17 schools for the mentally deficient, in which 2,000 COs served as attendants and in other service jobs; 34 county dairy farms; 17 state dairy testing herds; and 9 state agricultural experiment stations. The largest number of the special project units were operated by 32 universities, mostly medical schools, through contracts with the federal Office of Scientific Research and Development. Some 500 conscientious objectors volunteered to serve as human guinea pigs for medical experiments, submitting themselves to tests of drugs for malaria, typhus, infectious hepatitis, and pneumonia plus altitude tests, starvation and dietary research, and psychological studies. In addition, in nine units operated by the Office of the Surgeon General COs volunteered to serve as guinea pigs for medical experiments. Over the course of the war a total of 151 Civilian Public Service camps and other units for conscientious objectors existed, not all at the same time.

The incidence of conscientious objection to military service on religious grounds was concentrated in a small number of religious denominations and sects such as Hutterites, Mennonites, Church of the Brethren and Jehovah's Witnesses, though not all members of those denominations claimed exemption from military service.

The largest group of conscientious objectors were Jehovah's Witnesses who claimed exemption on the basis that all members of that religious group were ministers, but their claim was denied by the Selective Service Administration and rejected by the public at large. The public stance of the Jehovah's Witnesses evoked strong reaction; members suffered harassment, lost their jobs, and in Little Rock, Arkansas, were actually beaten up on the streets. Of approximately 6,000 conscientious objectors who were sent to prison, three-fourths were Jehovah's Witnesses, including 1,624 who failed to report to Civilian Public Service camps. Some Jehovah's Witnesses did accept noncombat service.

About three out of four Quakers accepted conventional military service and most of the remainder accepted noncombat service, as did 1,382 members of the Church of the Brethren. In fact, less than one in eight members of the Church of the Brethren refused to accept military service when called for induction. And 62 percent of the Brethren churches dropped the convenant against military service as a condition of church membership. The largest group of conscientious objectors serving in noncombat roles in the armed forces consisted of some 12,000 Seventh Day Adventists—all of whom, after January 1943, were serving in the Medical Corps.

Conscientious objectors were a mixed lot educationally. Among those who objected to military service on grounds other than religious conviction and ended up in federal prison, the educational level was disproportionately high. The educational level of those in CO camps was lower than the national average, but college men were well represented in alternative service.

Conscientious objectors were not alone in refusing military service during the war, but there was no way to determine accurately how many of those who based their refusal on religious grounds were, in fact, religious pacifists. It was widely suspected that some who claimed exemption on religious grounds were not actually religious persons. Certainly not all so-called "draft dodgers" were religious pacifists; some were agnostics or atheists. Local draft boards were sympathetic to those who refused to fight for religious reasons—the Selective Service Act recognized religious grounds as the only basis for refusing military service—but not to members of the Moral Rearmament Movement. Members of this group, which had grown out of the Oxford antiwar movement of the early 1930s, were philosophically opposed to war but professed no religious grounds for their opposition.

In addition, significant numbers of men refused to register or when called for induction failed to report because of cowardice, fear, and personal reasons not based on religious or philosophical opposition to war or to military service. There were thousands who managed to avoid military service by finding jobs in the defense industry, on farms, or in the government, by studying specialized subjects in college, and in a few cases by inflicting wounds on themselves.

Victory Corps

In September 1942, the U.S. Office of Education (later renamed the Department of Education) created the High School Victory Corps, in the belief that high school pupils should be involved in the war effort. Pupils who joined could choose one of five divisions: air, land, sea, production, or community service. The air division was the most popular but was open only to boys in the last two years of high school who had studied or were enrolled in at least three of the following subjects: mathematics, physics, aeronautics, radio, electricity, aircraft repair, and military drill. The military services supported the Victory Corps, particularly the AAF which saw it as a means of preparing boys for enlistment. In fact, *Scholastic*, a weekly paper for high school pupils, ran a regular column on matters of interest to the Air Service Division of the High School Victory Corps.

The Victory Corps became popular immediately. There was broad public support for the program, as evidence by a survey showing that 93 percent of those polled thought it a good idea. Within two months, more than half of the high schools in the country were participating, and a year later 70 percent had established Victory Corps units. Pacifists opposed the Victory Corps, arguing that it promoted militarism and the love of war, but in a nation dedicated to winning a war it was difficult to build a case against anything that included the term "victory."

Those who joined the Victory Corps wore a badge and a kind of uniform, which for boys consisted of a white shirt and dark trousers and for girls a white blouse and dark skirt. In addition to studies related to their chosen specialty, they participated in salvage drives, bond sales, parades, public assemblies to support war activities, and a strenuous physical education program. The curriculum for all high school students focused more heavily on mathematics and science, and added instruction in map reading, navigation, seamanship, aeronautics, and close order drill. Teachers of traditional courses in English, mathematics, history and other subjects injected material of wartime relevance, using examples from the military, war production and nationalism.

School leaders viewed the Victory Corps as a means to bring about curriculum change, to inject more vocational and practical training into high school preparation. Most observers agreed after the war that the Victory Corps gave pupils the satisfaction of participating in the war effort and may have taught them some useful vocational skills.

Books for Servicemen

Early in the war, the American Library Association established the Victory Book Campaign, through which it collected 4 million books from Americans to send to soldiers, but as with any drive to collect voluntary donations of books, most of the titles were not what soldiers wanted to read. Although information and education officers in the army and navy were grateful for the books, it was apparent that these books would not fully satisfy the reading interests of servicemen.

Earlier, the leading publishing houses had organized the Council on Books in Wartime to promote the idea that books could contribute to the war effort. In mid-1943, the army approached the Council on Books in Wartime about providing large numbers of books which the army and navy could give to servicemen for recreational reading. The council agreed to provide the books at the lowest price possible and established Armed Services, Inc., with an experienced publisher as its director to manage the enterprise, including the printing of the books.

In September 1943, the first paperback of the Armed Services Edition series rolled off the press. Three years later, John Jamieson writes, the council had published 122 million copies of 1,080 titles at an average cost to the army and navy of 6.09 cents apiece, of which the author and the publisher holding the copyright received one-half cent each. The council was able to keep the price low by publishing in such large volume and on cheap paper with paper covers. The council, assisted by critics, librarians and booksellers, chose 30 titles a month (later 40) ranging from classics to spy stories to westerns, including best-selling fiction, based on the best estimate of what soldiers and sailors would like to read. As a result, soldiers and sailors on the most remote islands were able to read best-sellers almost as soon as the civilian public.

In the last year of the war, it was common to see soldiers in combat with paperbacks in their back pocket, and when there was a lull in battle or rest stops on long marches, soldiers could be seen reading their hip pocket paperbacks. In passing them out overseas the army asked soldiers not to bring them back to the States, but instead to pass the books on to someone else when they finished a book. Thus, each paperback went through many hands and was read by untold members of soldiers and sailors before it was worn out from handling.

Morale

Early in the war many civilians—not only those holding non-defense jobs but some who worked in war plants—were bothered by a guilty feeling that they were not contributing substantively to the war effort. The Office of War Information recognized their discontent and mounted a campaign to build civilian morale with such slogans as "the Man Behind the Man Behind the Gun."

Citizens from all walks of life besieged government agencies to offer their services in the war effort. Corporate executives went to Washington to work in war agencies for $1 a year, with most of them continuing to draw salaries from their civilian employers. Most were men, but Oveta Culp Hobby, who went first to the War Department and was later named head of the WAAC, was an example of a female $1-a-year volunteer.

Blood for shipment to combat areas was in constant demand, and blood drives were a recurring activity; 5 million pints were donated in 1944 alone. Copper pennies disappeared, going to defense needs, and were replaced by lead coins, and the nickel in the five cent piece disappeared. Dozens of other substitutions occurred in standard products and services. On "Your Hit Parade," a weekly radio program of top songs of the day, the American Tobacco Company (which sponsored the show) advertised its Lucky Strike cigarettes with the theme "Lucky Strike Green Has Gone to War" to explain the change from green to white on its cigarette package cover. The rationale for the color change remained vague, but it seemed like a patriotic sacrifice on behalf of the war effort.

The "V for Victory" sign became a major factor in maintaining morale. The opening strains of Beethoven's Fifth Symphony—the first four notes of which corresponded to the dot-dot-dot-dash or V of the Morse code—was used by some radio stations to sign onto the air. Sociologist Edgar A. Schuler traced the origin of the V sign and found that it started in Belgium. After Hitler's invasion of Western Europe, the letters RAF were found scrawled on bridges, buildings, and other public places, indicating Belgium's support for the Royal Air Force. Belgian lawyer Victor de Lavelaye thought the single letter V would be more effective and suggested it to the British Broadcasting Corporation, which, in its broadcast to the Continent on January 14, 1940, suggested the V to its listeners. It caught on immediately and spread all over Western Europe. Then J. B. Priestley, the English writer, introduced the V campaign to shortwave listeners in North America in a broadcast over the BBC on July 16, 1940. Bundles for Britain adopted the V and provided buttons for American donors and workers to wear to help publicize the effort. The V campaign gained wide publicity from Winston Churchill, who made it famous by raising the index and middle fingers of one hand to form a V in a kind of salute or greeting, seemingly every time a news camera appeared.

In America there was widespread trust of public leaders throughout the war. President Roosevelt enjoyed strong support, even hero worship, among a vast portion of the population, based in part on his leadership during the Depression. Any other president probably would have had to forego a try for a then legal but precedent-breaking third term in 1940; Roosevelt, however, not only ran but won by a comfortable margin. He also prevailed in 1944, although it should be noted that much of Roosevelt's margin in the 1944 election was owed to legislation allowing military personnel to vote wherever they might be, rather than requiring them to cast absentee ballots in their home districts. Of the 3 million military personnel who voted, most voted for Roosevelt.

General Marshall was universally viewed as a what historian John Morton Blum has called "a pillar of integrity." General Dwight D. Eisenhower, as commander of Allied forces in North Africa and the invasion of Europe, enjoyed astonishing support by virtually all Americans throughout the war, strong enough to bring him the presidency in two elections. Whether he was a superior battle strategist is perhaps debatable, but he was a superb manager and master at human relations and was wise enough to surround himself with capable strategists whom he trusted and heeded.

George S. Patton, the most aggressive field commander in the

American army, came close to losing his career when it was revealed in late 1943 that he had slapped a battle fatigued soldier in a hospital in Italy, accusing him of cowardice. But his superb leadership in Europe in the latter half of 1944 and early 1945, in which his Third Army raced across Europe, redeemed him with the American public. After the war he would again draw sharp criticism, this time as occupation commander in Bavaria for appointing former Nazi party members to civil government posts, under the rationale that they were the only ones who knew how to do the job and that most of them had been only nominally party members as was required to hold their jobs during the Hitler era. Patton may have been right, but at that time the American public was in no mood to listen to excuses by former Nazis.

As the war progressed, the American people not only supported but genuinely admired and liked the people of Great Britain, Canada and Australia. Admiration for the Soviets was mixed; after all, just a short time earlier the Soviet Union had been supplying Germany with vast amounts of war matériel, and there had been widespread distrust of the USSR in America from the Bolshevik revolution onwards. But many Americans agreed with Churchill that "the enemy of my enemy is my friend," although Churchill did not trust the Soviets.

This is not to suggest that there was no grumbling during the war. When steel workers were granted a 15 percent wage hike without comparable increases for some others, underpaid clerks resented it. Wage rates did not rise as much as the cost of living, but total incomes rose sharply thanks to six- and seven-day work weeks and sometimes ten-hour days. Although price controls did not always work, control of wages was generally effective. The OPA even put a cap of $25,000 a year on salaries, a level that affected only a handful of corporate executives—notably movie mogul Louis B. Mayer, whose 1941 pay was $949,766—but served an important symbolic purpose. The cap was soon canceled by Congress.

Most of the union leadership strongly supported government drives—war bonds, blood banks, salvage, and other patriotic activities—as a means of building of a common bond to do everything possible toward winning the war. Labor unions were especially helpful in promoting the sale of war bonds, which were important not only in paying for the war but in building public support for it.

The government cautioned constantly about the need for secrecy. In every bar in port cities and near military bases hung a large sign reminding patrons that "Loose Lips Sink Ships." To what extent loose talk by merchant seamen about sailing schedules of ships got to the enemy and resulted in ship sinkings is unknown, but it was widely believed that such leaks did occur. Army and navy men were cautioned constantly to avoid speaking of troop movements, numbers of troops in any given location, the state of readiness of a particular unit, or particularly the overseas destination of units.

During the first year of the war, losses on island after island in the Pacific and unsuccessful naval battles made people begin to wonder whether America could prevail. The American victories at Midway and the Coral Sea in June 1942 bolstered public confidence, as did the Doolittle raid on Japan in April, yet Japan continued to occupy territories and defeat American forces in battle. Had not the news media voluntarily withheld much of the worst news about losses, morale would have undoubtedly suffered even more. But when American forces landed successfully in North Africa in November 1942 and progress was made in the battle of Guadalcanal, the tide of confidence began to shift.

War Bonds

One of the major successes of the war on the home front was the sale of war bonds. All of the bonds could have been sold in the commercial market, as evidenced by the fact that all eight war loan campaigns were oversubscribed by banks, insurance companies and other organizations with large amounts of cash to invest. But the secretary of the treasury decided that it was good national policy to ask ordinary people who did not have much money to help finance the war. It had the virtue of redirecting some of their earnings away from consumption purchases, thereby reducing demand for consumer goods and helping to control inflation, but his primary reason was that he wanted everyone to buy into the cost of the war. People were asking how they could help; the secretary wanted to give them an opportunity to help finance the war if only a small way.

The Treasury Department sold war bonds in denominations as small as $25, known as the E bond. The E bond, which cost $18.75 and was worth $25 when it matured in 10 years, was the mechanism through which ordinary people bought war bonds. Those who could not afford to buy a bond could buy war stamps which were available in denominations as small as 10 cents; a book of war stamps, when filled, could be exchanged for a $25 war bond. Even though the E bond could be redeemed after 60 days, only about $7 billion worth, or about 20 percent of the total sold, had been turned in by the end of the war.

War bonds and stamps were sold in post offices, grocery stores, bars, restaurants, theaters, sports arenas, department stores, and many other public and private establishments. Children joined in the war bond campaigns, selling $2 billion of war stamps. Members of American Women Voluntary Services and other women's organizations staffed tables that were set up in stores or public buildings to sell war bonds.

People could buy war bonds and stamps because they had money to save and were disposed to do so. The lack of durable goods to buy, coupled with the fact that most people had no money to save throughout the Depression, led to phenomenal saving during the war even though interest rates were low. A war bond's interest rate was lower in the first few years of the life of the bond, but as it grew toward maturity the rate accelerated, a measure to encourage holders not to cash the bonds in before they matured. The public was encouraged to buy war bonds and stamps regularly through payroll savings plans, and millions did so. At Phillips Academy in Massachusetts, 99.2 percent of the pupils signed a pledge to buy war stamps regularly. By one estimate, 85 million individuals bought war bonds and war stamps during the war.

The press, radio and other communications media adopted the war bond program and promoted it enthusiastically. Employees of businesses and industries and servicemen in the armed forces were urged to sign up for regular payroll deductions to purchase war bonds. War loan drives were frequent, often incorporated into or serving as an excuse for a social occasion such as a charity ball. Movie stars entertained without compensation at events staged to sell war bonds. Actresses auctioned off personal items such as nylon hose and scarce items like tickets to Broadway shows. Special trains were arranged for movie stars to crisscross the country, stopping at towns and cities along the way, often performing from the back of the train or on a stage set up next to the tracks. People turned out to see their favorite movie stars in the flesh and ended up buying bonds.

Appeals were made to owners of binoculars to lend them to the navy, with the promise that they would be returned after the war. Those who loaned binoculars were rewarded with $1 in war stamps. The Signal Corps asked the public to donate radios that repairmen could practice on, for which donors were given $1 each in war stamps.

Appeals to patriotism were central to war bond advertising and propaganda, which even suggested that if people did not buy bonds, fighting men would suffer. In fact, the main motivation of most people who bought war bonds was thrift, the desire to save for the postwar years when income might decrease and funds might be needed. After all, people had endured almost a decade of depression, so it was natural to assume that the large wartime incomes would end when the war ended. The kind of government cushions for the unemployed that were available a half century later did not exist then. By one estimate, the American people saved more than $90 billion during the war, and many families were accumulating the first savings they had ever known. It was this reservoir of savings that fueled a postwar buying spree and helped to stave off the depression that many economists had predicted.

Salvage

Scrap drives were mounted continually during the war, for two reasons: the country needed the materials for the war production manufacturing, and the drives represented a way to involve citizens in the war effort who otherwise might not have a role. In 1942, the War Production Board called for a drive to collect 4 million tons of scrap metal in two months, and the country swung into action with fervor; within three weeks, more than 5 million tons had been collected.

Elementary and secondary school pupils competed in scrap drives, with the winners receiving prizes and recognition. In June 1942, Interior Secretary Harold Ickes, responding to President Roosevelt's fear of a serious rubber shortage, mounted a campaign to collect all of the surplus rubber he could find and to marshal every American in his campaign. As a result, millions of Americans scoured their attics and basements for discarded hot water bottles, rubber boots, inner tubes, bathing camps, jar rings, overshoes, garden hose, rubber shoe heels and soles, and anything else containing rubber. Ickes even filched rubber floormats from the Department of the Interior building. In Virginia, some 15 million pounds of used rubber were collected.

Managers of scrap drives advertised that one discarded lawnmower would make six 3-inch shells, one small heater would make seventeen 30-caliber shells, one set of golf clubs would make one 30-caliber machine gun, and one large garbage can would make two steel helmets. The appeal for aluminum pointed out that 10,000 tons of pots and pans would provide the aluminum necessary to build 740 bombers or 4,000 fighters. When the final tally was made, the American people had gathered and contributed 70,000 tons of aluminum scrap. Unfortunately, it was discovered that recycled aluminum was not strong enough to use in airplane construction, and while some of the aluminum was used for other military purposes, much of it was melted down and used to make new kitchen utensils.

The recycling of metal for environmental reasons was virtually unheard of in the 1940s, but homemakers were urged to save every can. Both ends of a can were cut out, then the remaining can was crushed with a foot and turned in to a salvage center. Throughout the war homemakers saved fats and turned them in to their local butcher, from whom they were collected and used in the manufacture of explosives.

The collection of scrap involved nearly every civilian in the country. Scrap collection became the center of social occasions, a mission. Full-page newspaper ads appeared: "Whose Boy Will Die Because You Failed [to give scrap]?" From March 1942, when the War Production Board initiated its first drive for scrap iron and steel, until the end of that year, the state of Ohio shipped 457 pounds per capita and Michigan 432 pounds.

In Warrenton, Virginia, the scrap heap collected a 1913 Pierce Arrow automobile and a 1911 Rolls-Royce; another town found a discarded railroad locomotive to donate; and a third dismantled an abandoned railroad bridge. The Mariners Museum in Newport News, Virginia, donated an eighteenth century cannon.

Drives to collect paper soon met the demand for recyclable paper; junk dealers were swamped with paper, and reduced the price paid from 60 to 20 cents per hundred pounds. The abundance of paper was due in part to the zeal of the Boy Scouts, Girl Scouts, 4-H Clubs, Future Farmers of America, Grange Juniors and other youth groups which did most of the collecting of scrap paper. In 1944, they collected 634,000 tons of waste paper.

The Boy Scouts deserve special mention as salvage collectors. They served as collectors in many drives, including some planned and directed by other groups. For example, in the American Library Association book drive the Boy Scouts did the actual collecting of 3 million books. They collected 109 million pounds of rubber, more than 23 million pounds of tin, and more than 370 million pounds of other scrap metal.

By 1944 the enthusiasm for drives had begun to abate; the public was tired of the constant exhortations in newspapers, on radio and billboards urging people to contribute to scrap drives, to buy war bonds, and participate in dozens of other activities to support the war. The Office of War Information continued to fill newspapers, magazines and radio with appeals for citizens to do the patriotic thing, but it was intended as much to maintain the patriotic spirit as to keep the salvage movement alive.

Chapter X

The Home Front

When a nation goes to war it needs the support of its citizens in order for the war effort to be most effective. Its people must be intellectually convinced that it is necessary to go to war, but that is not enough. They must become emotionally committed to the cause, persuaded that their country has been or is about to be mistreated by another or that the cause is of such profound moral import as to demand the country's intervention. Intense emotional fervor is indispensable to success, particularly in a democracy.

Before and during World War II, Germany and Japan built high levels of citizen support through well organized and effective government propaganda agencies. In Italy the propaganda agency was never able to enlist comparable zeal for the war, and the results were reflected in the performance of its soldiers.

The U.S. government established a vigorous propaganda program during World War II which undoubtedly influenced public attitudes toward the war, but the attack on Pearl Harbor united the country in support of the war to an extent that would not have been possible through propaganda alone. People were infuriated over Japan's "sneak" attack while the emperor's emissaries in Washington were still ostensibly negotiating for peace. When Congress approved the declaration of war on Japan on December 8, 1941, its vote reflected almost a profile of American public opinion. With the exception of a small number of first generation Japanese, Italians, and Germans who remained loyal to the country of their birth, virtually the entire nation was of one opinion, including recent antiwar activists, isolationist members of Congress, and even many pacifists.

A population's emotional commitment to a war is essential if the people are to bear wartime shortages, deprivations and inconveniences; the absence of loved ones, and especially the specter of death hanging over those serving in the military; and finally the actual death of husbands, sons, other relatives, and close friends. Americans not only were convinced that declaring war on all three countries was necessary but were virtually unanimous in the belief that the country was on a campaign for a moral cause. They knew that their government sought no land or material benefit from any other nation. Years of reading about the unjustified invasion of peaceful countries by Germany, Italy, and Japan and the brutal treatment of people in captured countries had already persuaded Americans that all three countries were pursuing evil objectives. While Germany's abuse of Jews within its own borders and in occupied countries was not then fully understood, Americans knew enough about what was taking place to be revolted.

In order to put wartime America into context, it is useful to review how Americans lived in the years immediately preceding the attack on Pearl Harbor, for their prewar lives significantly shaped the way they lived and behaved during the war. Studying this background aids in understanding how the American civilian population mobilized for war, the support they provided the military forces and the government, the adjustments they were forced to make in the interest of the national emergency, the privations they experienced and the ways various sectors of society responded to the war.

The Way It Was: Prewar America

The 1920s had been a gaudy, madcap time, popularly characterized by hedonistic living. During the 1930s and the early war years, when unemployment and poverty shaped the general condition, one might expect people to have been somber, even grim. Many were to be sure, but at the same time there was still frivolity. Practical jokes abounded, to an extent that seems strange if not childish today, and slapstick comedy was immensely popular. Songs of the period included "Three Little Fishes," "A-Tisket, A-Tasket," and the nonsensical "Hut Sut Song."

Social observers have characterized the years immediately preceding World War II as a time of innocence. The majority of the American population had limited access to information about current events. Educated persons living in cities read newspapers and news magazines, and some of them had a good understanding of national and international affairs, but most of the population lived in rural areas, on farms and in small towns, and were not well educated. Some listened to radio news, but it was at best incomplete, and listeners often did not have the background to understand the complexities of news they heard. The Rural Electrification Administration had brought electricity to most of rural America by 1940, but there were still large areas that had not received electricity and thus still did not have radios (except for the few who had battery-powered sets) or any of the other benefits of electricity that many already took for granted.

The daily newspaper, now taken for granted by an affluent society, was not so common in rural America in the days immediately preceding World War II. Many rural homes received no newspaper at all or merely a county weekly paper that reported only local news, perhaps with a smattering of state news. As one views the transformation of American society in the last half of the twentieth century, nothing has had more impact on how people view the world and themselves than the communications industry. Even allowing for distortions and biases in the media, access to information has made it possible for most people to make decisions that result in a better quality of life than could have been imagined as America approached World War II.

Until shortly before the war, poverty was the norm for many young people; indeed they had not known anything else. Many had never had a full-time job and lived in homes where the breadwinner worked only occasionally or not at all. Half of the children in America were found in families that earned less than $1,500 a year.

The so-called privileged class was not immune to unemployment. Many physicians and lawyers were out of work or working for substandard salaries; some were digging ditches or working for the WPA. Between 1930 and 1936, 86 percent of the colleges and universities reduced professors' salaries at least once; a significant number cut them twice, and a few even cut them three times. The example of a full professor at the University of Tennessee whose salary in 1938 was $1,800 was not unusual.

As World War II approached, the crushing poverty of the 1930s was beginning to ease, thanks in large measure to the development of new defense industries. People were living a little better, and there was hope that life in the future would be much better. Hope had been so elusive for so long that the mere anticipation of a better life improved morale. To be sure, the Depression was not over; as 1940 began, 8.1 million were still unemployed, or 14.6 percent of the labor force of 55.7 million. As many observers have noted, it was World War II that ended the Depression in the United States.

Wages were low but were far better than just a few years earlier, and more people had jobs. The average factory wage was 66 cents an hour, although the federally legislated minimum wage was 30 cents an hour and would remain so until the end of the war. The average daily wage of working men was $6.00, and take-home pay averaged $25.20 a week, which at the time could support what was considered a passable, if not luxurious, standard of living.

In New York and other major cities, a loaf of bread cost 8 cents, a man's haircut 50 cents, round steak at the butcher shop 30 cents a pound, butter 35 cents a pound, milk 13 cents a quart, coffee 5 cents a cup and a good suit of clothes $40. In a small town in the South, prices were even lower: T-bone steak 20 cents a pound, a man's haircut 25 cents, and a man's suit at OPO Mayo, a national discount men's clothing store, $15. A new Chevrolet with all accessories cost less than $1,000. The national budget for 1939-1940 was $9.1 billion, and the typical federal income tax was 4.09 percent. A hardback novel sold for $2.50, and the 25 cent paperback book introduced by Pocket Books in 1939 was a booming business a year later. The New York Stock Exchange traded fewer than 500,000 shares a day, compared with the mid–1990s when daily volume frequently topped 300 million shares. The gross national product in 1939 was less than $100 billion, compared to $103 billion in 1929, then $56 billion in 1933 in the depths of the Depression, and more than $6 trillion in 1994.

Fear and apprehension about the war afflicted almost everyone, but the impact was less than it might have been. The country had lived through a decade of depression that saw 10,000 banks close without insurance, resulting in the loss of lifetime savings for millions of people, so the country had become accustomed to adversity. With growing employment, people had money to spend and they began to spend it, purchasing goods and services whose production and distribution created more jobs. With the growth of purchasing power, more luxury items appeared on store shelves. In 1941, cigarette smoking increased 12 percent over the previous year, although in some circles it was still considered unseemly for women to smoke in public. People spent more for entertainment and luxuries, as well as for necessities. Liquor consumption rose and nightclubs flourished.

The 1939 New York World's Fair had displayed hundreds of gadgets and new products that would be available in the future, and people were fascinated with what they saw. Something called television was displayed, and onlookers were assured that before long every American home could have one and see performers as well as hear them, but radio continued to be the main medium of home entertainment. Radios were found in most American homes.

Frederick Lewis Allen, editor of *Harper's*, observed that a 1920s cocktail party in New York City would find the literati ridiculing the common man and espousing clichés of the elite, either unaware of or insensitive to the problems of society. By the mid–1930s this attitude had disappeared; the conversation at such a party focused on societal ills and how to solve them, and would remain so up until World War II. Values had shifted to the left, and the literati who did not join the Communist Party were likely to be sympathetic with many of its goals and rhetoric. The

Depression had made everyone aware of the plight of the poor; even well-to-do people who might have been little inconvenienced themselves were conscious of the widespread poverty that afflicted the country.

But along with the development of social consciousness was a lot of frivolity and foolishness. Flagpole sitting, which began in the 1920s, remained popular. Unemployed men or people with a cause or extroverts who simply wanted to attract attention to themselves would anchor a flat surface to the top of a flagpole and sit for days or weeks, usually trying to set a record for sitting. Predictably, the event was covered by newspapers and news cameras and was shown in movie houses. The last flagpole sitter was Shipwreck Kelly; after sitting on a flagpole for days in Palisades Park, New Jersey, in 1942, fell off and had to be hospitalized.

Marathon dance contests were popular. An entrepreneur would offer a large prize to the couple, out of 50 or so contestants, who could dance the longest. Except for brief hourly stops for toilet visits and food, they danced for days; at the end they would barely be on their feet and one of the dancers would be supporting the other to keep him or her from going to sleep. The movie camera recorded the ordeal at critical stages, especially near the end, and the film was shown in movie houses all over the country.

Wartime

Lifestyles changed markedly during the war, introducing ways of living and doing business that persisted after the war ended. For example, before the war it was common in small towns for homemakers to order groceries by telephone and have them delivered to the kitchen door; with the shortage of labor, this practice became rare during the war and virtually disappeared afterwards. Although the customer was still served individually in most stores, self service in grocery stores became more common during the war, resulting in a major change in marketing after the war.

In addition, many who had long relied on servants found themselves doing without, for the servants had gone to work in defense industries. Cooks, maids, store clerks, and other personnel employed in restaurants, hotels, shops and assorted service businesses became scarce as they departed for wartime industries that paid higher wages. Affluent homemakers who were accustomed to maids and other assistance had to learn to do their own laundry and clean their own houses.

Long before the Japanese attacked Pearl Harbor, the effects of defense preparation began to be felt, and as soon as war was declared they became pervasive, not only in increased employment and income but in the appearance of restrictions and shortages. When war was declared, the army and navy needed many items which industry could not produce in sufficient quantity quickly enough. They called on civilians to sell, lease or give a variety of items to the army, navy and other government agencies. Work boats, private yachts and other pleasure craft were "called to active duty" by the Coast Guard, navy, and army, and the AAF requisitioned private airplanes for training.

With the rapid growth in government employment in Washington and the lack of typewriter production, civilians were urged to sell their typewriters to the government. The Carnegie foundations estimated that 25 percent of its typewriters were turned in to the government. The navy also called for typewriters; it said 59 typewriters were needed on every battleship and only slightly smaller numbers on smaller vessels.

Scarcity and Rationing

By the end of 1941 the Japanese had captured much of southeast Asia and were in command of most of the Pacific Ocean, ending shipping from Asia to America. Spices from Indonesia disappeared, as did imports of tea, silk, rubber and other commodities from Asia.

Fuel for heating was scarce throughout the war, and the government urged that homes, offices and industries make every effort to conserve energy. Early in the war, Secretary of the Interior Harold Ickes announced that there would be a shortage of fuel for home heating in New England and the East Coast, not because of a lack of domestic oil production but because there were not enough tankers to move it from Texas and Louisiana to the East Coast. Ickes, a highly controversial figure who served in his position throughout the FDR presidency, was labeled an alarmist by newspaper editors who looked at production figures and thought he was lying. In October 1942, the government announced a decline of 25 percent in the supply of heating oil and instituted rationing in 17 Eastern and 13 Midwestern states. When the shortage occurred, Ickes delighted in telling the press, "I told you so."

In spite of the large amounts of petroleum shipped to Great Britain, the shortage of heating oil was eased when construction of pipelines from Texas to the East Coast was completed in 1943. Yet fuel remained in short supply. By January 1945, the situation had grown so serious that the government asked all public agencies to keep room temperatures below 69 degrees in the winter.

In the spring of 1942, the War Production Board prohibited the use of metal to manufacture hair curlers, corn poppers, cocktail shakers, spittons, beer mugs, and dozens of other nonessential items. The manufacture of radios, typewriters, toasters, musical instruments, bicycles, golf clubs and many other metal items was halted as those factories shifted to the manufacture of war materials. On May 5, 1942, the WPB announced that some 400 household and consumer products could no longer be manufactured. Virtually all household items made of metal, such as hot water heaters, refrigerators and stoves, became scarce. Cameras, field glasses, hairpins, cosmetics, cheap clothes, leather goods, kitchen utensils and paper became either scarce or unavailable. By Christmas 1943, ladies' handbags and gloves were rarely found in stores and children's toys were limited largely to those made without metal, as most toy manufacturers were busy making war materials.

With the manufacture of essentially all household appliances suspended for the duration of the war, families had to make do with the old toaster or other appliance until it could no longer be repaired, then do without. The government released the results of a survey in 1944 in which it found that the main appliances people missed most and planned to buy as soon after the war as possible were, in order of priority, washing machines, electric irons, refrigerators, stoves, toasters, radios, vacuum cleaners, electric fans and water heaters.

The government took the position that consumers could make do with the durable goods that they had. But it was recognized that in the cases of essential items that were already scarce or would become scarce, especially food, the only way to assure fair allocation of the available supply was to ration it.

Rationing covered a wide range of foods and other materials and caused the civilian populace no little inconvenience and irritation, and some real deprivation. The extent of the rationing was not nearly as draconian, however, as in Britain and the occupied countries of Europe, not to mention Germany, Italy, Russia and Japan. Rubber tires and tubes were rationed beginning December 30, 1941, and automobiles and recapped tires were placed on the approval list on February 12, 1942.

A sugar shortage developed early in the war. The United States had been stretching its supply by shipping sugar to Britain and Russia, so the loss of the Philippines—a major source—in the spring of 1942 created an immediate problem. Sugar rationing went into effect May 4, 1942, but it had been announced in late January, and as a consequence sugar disappeared from store shelves before rationing began. Many people found that they could get along quite well with less sugar than they were accustomed to; some discovered, for instance, that they could eliminate sugar from their tea and coffee entirely and still enjoy it.

Coffee rationing began on November 11, 1942—one pound per person over the age of 16 every five weeks—but within a few months it was discovered that the supply was adequate, and coffee was removed from the ration list in July 1943. An array of foods was added to the rationed list in March 1943—edible fats and oils, cheese, canned milk, canned fish, meat, butter, margarine, soups, canned fruits and vegetables, fruit juices, and briefly dried peas and beans.

The rationing system involved a combination of classes, with allocation for varying amounts based on need and justification. Red stamps were for meat, butter, and fats; blue stamps were for processed foods. Then there were varieties of red and blue stamps—A, B, C, and D. It was a constant struggle for most people to meet the family's food needs, not only because of rationing but especially because of the confusing and ever-changing rules and regulations.

Initially rationing did not affect restaurants, but so many people began to eat in restaurants to save meat coupons that rationing was applied to restaurants, some of which exhausted their ration by the middle of the month and closed until the next ration period began. Others closed one day a week at first, then two days a week, and finally operated only three or four days a week.

Meat soon became scarce and was put on the list of rationed items on March 29, 1943. In November 1942, prior to the institution of meat rationing, the Office of Price Administration had promoted voluntary meat rationing, urging people to eat cheese, fish and other dishes instead. At the request of the OPA, the Office of War Information launched a national campaign asking that meat not be served on Tuesdays, and throughout the country "meatless Tuesday" became standard fare. Restaurants, like almost everyone else, abided by meatless Tuesday, and in Philadelphia hotels agreed in the fall of 1942 not to serve meat on Tuesday or Friday.

Meat counters soon became bare, and some food markets, particularly specialized butcher shops, closed either until the next ration date or permanently. Meat inspired more black market activity than any other rationed item during the war. Dishonest butchers sold it at exorbitant prices and honest butchers saved portions for their longtime customers. The *Journal of Commerce* reported that by the summer of 1944 as much as 40 percent of the meat supply was sold on the black market. Yet many people who paid black market prices did so without knowing it, and much that was technically black marketing was not considered so by customers and merchants.

In prewar America it was common for consumers to shop regularly at a single grocery store and butcher shop and to develop a personal relationship with the butcher. At that time, before meat markets cut and prewrapped meat for self service, the butcher cut each order according to the customer's request. Often butchers came to know customers' individual preferences and would sometimes place aside a special cut of beef for a particular customer to build loyalty. Thus, when a shortage of meat developed, butchers who considered themselves honest and patriotic saw nothing unusual or illegal in saving meat for their regular customers, while carefully obeying price limits and limiting the portion to what the customer's ration coupons permitted.

Soldiers and sailors enjoyed an ample supply of nearly all kinds of food, at least in the States and in some overseas areas where supplies could be transported readily. At its peak the military accounted for only about 10 percent of the national population, but 30 percent of the meat supply went to the armed services.

Many farmers and ranchers slaughtered their own meat supply, some without knowing that rationing rules limited them to the same amount of meat as city dwellers. Farmers who canned their own fruits and vegetables felt deprivations least. Actually, glass jars were used, due to the shortage of steel and aluminum for cans. Beer, including that sent overseas, was sold in glass bottles for the same reason.

As clothing manufacturers shifted to the manufacture of military uniforms, clothing for men and women became scarce or in some cases impossible to find, so rationing was eventually implemented. In March 1942 the War Production Board, in anticipation of a shortage of wool, ordered clothing manufacturers to end the practice of providing a second pair of trousers with men's suits, omit cuffs on trousers, eliminate patch pockets, and switch from double breasted to single breasted suit jackets. As with many involuntary changes, men complained but eventually found that they liked trousers without cuffs. Imports of Australian wool eased the shortage in early 1943, and short men were then able to secure trousers with cuffs.

With the emphasis on saving cloth, the two-piece women's bathing suit replaced the one-piece model. Women's skirts rose, ostensibly to save fabric; later, social theorists said that it was simply a manifestation of the fact that women's skirts always rise in time of war. Women began to wear slacks on the street and in the workplace, a safety measure for women employed in factories but a convention that previously had been condemned as improper in some circles. The manufacture of nylon hose, which had been introduced on May 15, 1940, was terminated in early 1942, with manufacturing facilities diverted to making parachutes. Many women, however, had stocked up when it was announced that production of nylon hose would be halted. So did merchants, and prices rose predictably as nylons became more scarce. On November 28, 1942, the OPA set the ceiling price of nylons at $1.55 to $2.50 a pair; the prevailing price had been $2.50–2.95 a pair. Later, nylons disappeared from store shelves and could be found only on the black market.

Shoe rationing began in February 1943 and initially limited each person to three pairs per year, which was not particularly a hardship since the average person did not buy more than three pairs a year. Later in the war many of the shoes had composition soles which looked like cardboard and wore out quickly. By 1944, the ration was reduced to two pairs per year, again not severe compared to European countries where the ration was typically one pair a year.

Gasoline rationing began on the East Coast in May 1942, initially affecting service stations only. When gasoline supplies to the East Coast first declined, deliveries to dealers were reduced to 80 percent of 1941 deliveries, then to two-thirds and then to half. Service station operators rationed gasoline to customers, but this informal approach did not work equitably, and government-controlled rationing was instituted. Initially, the shortage on the East Coast was due to lack of transportation, the result of German submarines sinking tankers bringing fuel from the Gulf Coast. Then, in mid–1942, it became apparent that the only way to conserve rubber was to limit automobile travel, and the decision was made to ration gasoline nationally, beginning in the East and moving incrementally westward until the whole country was under rationing by December 1942. A voluntary ban on pleasure driving went into effect in December 1942, but it was routinely violated, resulting in loud protestations from those who complied, and in March 1943 it was lifted. While the gasoline shortage was real, the most serious aspect of unnecessary driving was the rubber shortage. A shortage of containers prevented most people from stocking up when gasoline rationing was instituted, even though they had anticipated it. Nonetheless a few cases were reported in which individuals stored large quantities of gasoline in the attic or basement and were discovered by fire wardens or others on official inspection.

The standard "A" ration allowed four gallons per vehicle a week until October 1943, when it was reduced to three gallons a week; it was further cut to two gallons a week in March 1944, but returned to three gallons a week in June 1945. Vehicles that served special purposes, including transporting multiple riders to work, were granted B stickers for the windshields; C stickers were for physicians, taxis, government agencies and others engaged in essential travel; and T stickers were for trucks. Servicemen home on furlough were given a total ration of five gallons, but men in the mountain states complained that this was not enough where distances to drive were much greater, and the OPA changed the ration in August 1944 to one gallon per day of furlough, up to a maximum of 30 gallons.

Automobile owners were limited to five tires per vehicle and were required to register the five tires by tire number with their local rationing board. Any tires in excess of five per vehicle had to be turned in to the government.

Despite efforts to distribute rationed food fairly, inequities were fairly common. Allocations of food and clothing were based on population figures from the 1940 census, which caused problems in towns and cities like Mobile, Alabama, whose population had grown significantly as factories for defense production were established and the population swelled.

Rationing stimulated a great deal of predictable but irrational behavior. When people saw a line at a grocery store, for example, many got into it without even knowing what the line was for, assuming that something in short supply like toilet paper was being sold. And when coffee rationing was eliminated in 1943, the price actually dropped, indicating that when something was believed to be scarce it became dear. In late 1943 there was discussion of reinstituting coffee rationing in response to reduced shipments from South America, and the mere mention of new rationing was enough to create a black market for coffee.

Rationing inevitably led to hoarding, a major problem throughout the war. Immediately after Britain and France declared war on Germany, American homemakers, remembering the shortages of World War I, stocked up on foods that might become scarce, emptying grocery store shelves of certain commodities in a single day. President Roosevelt made a nationwide radio address on September 7, 1939, to assure the country that there were ample supplies of food and that it was unnecessary to stock up. After the attack on Pearl Harbor, hoarding became worse, and grocery stores were again virtually depleted of certain foodstuffs, soap, and other items likely to be in short supply.

When a rumor spread that a particular commodity was destined to be added to the list of rationed items, people rushed out to stock up on it "before the hoarders got there." As a consequence, the item was in short supply immediately, sometimes forcing rationing before it should have been needed. The comedian W. C. Fields filled a spare bedroom with cases of canned vegetables in preparation for the anticipated shortage, notwithstanding the fact that he rarely ate vegetables. Some people accumulated extraordinarily large amounts of rationed commodities, sometimes more than they could use in a year. But the urge to boast about their hoarding got some of them in trouble, as for instance when one first grade pupil blurted out that her mother had 100 pounds of sugar in the attic.

In every community there was at least one War Price and Rationing Board composed of local citizens who served without compensation and whose unhappy task it was to determine who, among the many petitioners, was justified to receive more than their rationed shares. Boards at first consisted of between 3 and 12 persons, but before the war ended some boards had 50 or more members. The plan called for one rationing board for not more than 50,000 inhabitants. New York, then the most populous state, established rationing boards on December 22, 1941, and was probably the best organized state in the country when rationing was invoked on large numbers of items. It eventually created 220 rationing boards.

One of the jobs of the local board was to try to restrict black market operations. As soon as a commodity or item was placed on a rationing or restricted list, the black market would make it available—for a price. Sugar, fats, meat and other foods were always available "under the counter."

As noted earlier, practices that the government regarded as violating rationing or price control regulations were not viewed in the same way by a great many consumers. For example, tie-in sales had been a practice for many years and continued during the war, only now involving goods subject to rationing and price controls. In a tie-in sale, the purchase of a particular item was conditional on buying another, less desired item. Although customers may have paid only the OPA price for each item, they were forced to purchase something they may not have needed. In addition, the offering of discounts and rebates to favored customers was a normal business practice.

Cigarettes were not rationed, but they became scarce in 1944. While civilians often had to do without cigarettes or roll their own, servicemen had abundant supplies. The OPA did not put liquor on the rationed list (although some states with monopoly liquor stores such as Virginia and the Territory of Hawaii did so) but it too became scarce. The better brands of whiskey were rarely to be found in liquor stores; instead, brands that few had heard of began to appear on store shelves. When liquor and cigarettes became scarce, a black market predictably developed for both. The War Production Board required producers of bourbon, gin and other spirits to shift their production to war-related purposes. People who could travel to Mexican border towns found whiskey in ample supply, but often it bore a strange label. If it bore a familiar label the taste differed from what was expected, leading one to suspect adulteration or substitution, such as blended scotch that had been blended with tequila.

Rum, which was available in ample quantities from Latin America and the Caribbean, filled the void when American distilleries switched to war production or cut their output, and in some locales replaced bourbon as the number one seller in liquor stores. Sales of rum increased when the Andrews sisters recorded "Rum and Coca-Cola," which became one of the most popular records on radio stations all over the country until it was banned as naughty (for a subtle reference to prostitution) by a radio station in Tulsa, then by stations elsewhere. Beer did not become scarce until the middle of 1944, but even before then customers could often find only brands they had never heard of, some of which were of dubious quality.

The *Wall Street Journal* reported on August 23, 1943, that nylon hose could still be obtained for the exorbitant price of $5.00 a pair and that Haig and Haig Scotch was available for $7.50 a fifth and Three Feathers whiskey for $2.95 a fifth. The ceiling price of gasoline was 21 cents a gallon, but it could be found at twice the price without coupons. Ham, for which the ceiling price was 69 cents a pound, sold for $1.25 on the black market. More than 1,000 service station operators went to jail for selling gasoline illegally—either above the controlled price, without collecting coupons, or both. While this was 1,000 too many, it should be remembered that this number constituted only a small fraction of all gasoline retailers.

The innate tendency of Americans to resent government interference with their lives led them to actions that supported the black market, indirectly if not directly. Their irritation was stoked by servicemen's stories of military mess halls wasting many foodstuffs that were rationed or in short supply to civilians. Some probably never thought about the moral implications of their actions, while many rationalized them in a variety of ways. Frequently they knew that a particular commodity was not scarce, at least not in their community, and saw nothing wrong in black market purchases. Consumers considered the OPA inept at best and more often unnecessarily punitive, believing it used rationing to build support for the war even when there was no need for it. If the shortage of food supplies had become as acute as in some other countries, for example Great Britain, perhaps Americans would have become more sensitive to the need for adhering closely to rationing regulations.

Rationing and price control boards sometimes tried to prosecute black marketers, but most of the time they did not because they had too much to do, it was too much trouble, and there were not enough police and prosecutors. The publicity might have led people to believe that almost everyone participated in the black market, but in fact most people disapproved of black markets. A Gallup Poll in May 1945 found that 77 percent of the women and 71 percent of the men said buying at black market prices was never justified.

Despite shortages and rationing, no one went hungry due to food shortages. To be sure, consumers suffered considerable inconvenience and irritation, and had to do without certain foods to which they had become accustomed, but on the whole the food supply was adequate, for two principal reasons. Farm production during the 1930s had greatly exceeded demand, leading the government to purchase huge quantities of food and fiber which were in storage when war began. This surplus, along with large increases in farm production during the war, not only provided minimum requirements for Americans but accounted for much of the food consumed in Britain and Russia. Louis Bromfield, the Pulitzer Prize winning novelist and sometime Ohio farmer, predicted the United States would run out of food, but it never did.

The OPA invaded the lives of all Americans and irritated almost everyone. Many of its regulations seemed not only useless but silly to the average citizen. Not only did its mere existence irritate homemakers, but it frequently changed the rules for rationing items like bread, canned fruit and vegetables, meat, sugar, gasoline, tires, butter and dozens more foodstuffs and apparel.

On a conscious level, people knew they had to tolerate such nuisances, but it still rankled them. After all, they had borne ten years of deprivation during the Depression, and just as family incomes began to rise to the point where they could begin to buy things and enjoy life, rationing clamped down and faced them with further deprivation. Nonetheless surveys found that the large majority of civilians thought the point system of rationing was fair.

In spite of rationing and shortages, people went on a buying spree for food, recreation, amenities, and entertainment that they could find but that they had not previously been able to afford. Who knew what the postwar situation would be! Within two years after America entered the war, the sales of women's clothing had doubled, although part of the increase was due to the disappearance of low-cost clothing which had been replaced by higher quality materials with a higher profit margin.

Wages had shot up from 35 cents an hour to 80 cents an hour in many lines of work before wage controls came in, and jobs were plentiful. If one lost a job, it was easy to find another, particularly in towns with war production plants where turnover of workers remained high throughout the war. As a result of wage rises, increased employment and longer hours of work, the annual per capita income in the United States rose from $539 in 1939 to $1,192 in 1945. Not only was the breadwinner employed and bringing home an increasingly healthy paycheck, but in many homes there was now a second income, with 5 million more women working by the end of 1943 than in 1941. And by 1944 high school students could earn 55 to 65 cents an hour clerking in department stores. As a result, many families that for years had lived in poverty now found themselves with a large increase in family income and a substantially improved standard of living, despite the scarcity of many necessary items and the unavailability of many luxuries.

As soon as the war ended, gasoline, processed foods, cheese, and lower grades of beef were removed from the ration list. Automobiles and shoes were removed in October 1945 and meat in November, leaving sugar the only commodity rationed. The last of the local rationing boards closed in October 1946, and supplies soon returned to normal, in contrast to Britain where rationing remained in effect until the early 1950s.

Price Controls and Inflation

When Hitler invaded Poland in September 1939, prices of wheat, lard and rubber jumped 30 percent in the United States, giving government officials and consumers a fright, but within a few months prices had calmed down considerably. Then, as war production began to increase in 1940 and employment improved, demand for consumer goods grew and prices began to rise.

Memories of inflation in World War I were still fresh in the minds of government officials concerned about the national economy. In the 20 months the United States was in World War I, the consumer price index rose 63 percent. Galloping inflation had been the norm in most wars, and the government recognized that without some control, it would return in World War II.

As soon as war was declared, most people assumed that rationing and price controls would be instituted, and indeed they were not long in coming. In April 1942 the Office of Price Administration announced that price controls would go into effect in May at prices that existed in March of that year. The list included almost everything people wore and at least 60 percent of what they ate. In October of that year other foods were placed on the price controlled list. Although little humor was associated with price control, some people were amused by the fact that the OPA insisted that bootleggers in Oklahoma—a "dry" state—post their prices to assure that they did not exceed the ceiling prices for whiskey.

Inflation occurred in spite of price controls, but not at nearly the rate that might have occurred without controls. According to the Bureau of Labor Statistics, with the 1935–39 period as a base of 100, the cost of living index in 1940 was 100.2; in 1941, 105.2; 1942, 116.5; 1943, 123.6; 1944, 125.5; and 1945, 128.4. As these figures show, most of the inflation occurred in the first two years of the war; after 1943, prices remained fairly stable. But this can be misleading, since official cost of living indexes do not reflect the disappearance of low-cost, low-profit items from store shelves, the substitution of items of lower quality, and prices on the black market. Further, averages do not tell the full story, since many items rose more sharply than the average.

Wholesale prices increased during the war years much more than retail prices, and wholesale prices of farm products outran everything else. The prices of agricultural commodities rose three or four times as much as manufactured goods, and net farm income doubled. On the other hand, wholesale price increases of many items were well below the average. Prices of gas and electricity actually declined.

In general, the price increases during the war years were above average for food, clothing, and home furniture, and below average for fuel, rent and most other items. Yet, the price of sugar remained stable at around 7 cents per pound, far below the World War I price of 23 cents per pound.

Increases in wholesale prices between September 1939 and December 1945 are illustrated by the following examples: grains, 104 percent; fruit and vegetables, 108 percent; oils and fats, 111 percent; pharmaceuticals, 44 percent; and meat, 40 percent. Much of the increase was in farm produce, on which the government allowed prices to rise in order to compensate for low prices in the past and to provide incentive for production. But the inflation of the price of meat is deceiving since so much meat, both wholesale and retail, was sold on the black market.

In January 1942, in order to stimulate farm production, Congress raised price supports for farm commodities to 110 percent of parity (the average price during a previous period, in this case 1910–1914), although they were scaled back in October 1942 to 90 percent of parity, which was of little consequence since on average the prices of farm products exceeded 100 percent of parity after 1942. Farm products had declined sharply during the Depression. In March 1929, the *Wall Street Journal* reported that wheat was selling for $1.20 per bushel on the Chicago exchange, but by October 1934 it was selling for 52 cents per bushel. Cotton sold for 20 cents a pound on the New Orleans exchange in April 1929, but for only 7 cents a pound in October 1934, with farmers in small markets in the deep South receiving as little as 5 cents a pound. As soon as war was declared, prices turned up; by June 1944, wheat had risen to $1.71 per bushel and cotton to 20 cents a pound.

Price control was the key to the relative stabilization of prices and control of inflation, but low inflation was also due in part to measures to keep interest rates down. Rates actually reached an all-time low during World War II. The interest rate on one-year treasury bills sold on June 20, 1943, was 0.75 percent, and the annualized interest rate on short term commercial paper was only 0.5 percent. Although spending for luxuries and entertainment increased, farmers and factory workers used part of their income to pay off mortgages and debts. Doing so kept part of their earnings out of the consumer market and thus reduced inflation. There was no better evidence of the effect of price controls than the fact that when they were lifted in the spring of 1946, the Bureau of Labor Statistics recorded a 5 percent jump in inflation in one month, 15 percent jump by the end of the year and a continuing upward trend.

Housing

Of all the critical scarcities, housing probably topped the list. Shortages of housing occurred everywhere, most acutely in towns with swollen populations of defense workers or families of servicemen near newly established or expanded military bases. Almost every town and city in the country felt the housing shortage, however.

War plant workers lived in garages, converted chicken shacks, and lean-to sheds. Marilynn S. Johnson describes a particularly dismal housing situation on the West Coast. In the summer of 1942, hotels in the San Francisco area set up cots in their lobbies for war workers, and hundreds of war plant workers slept on park benches in Oakland. Discarded cars from the Third Avenue elevated railway in New York City were shipped to Oakland and converted to housing for war plant workers. Managers of war production plants pleaded with the government to build housing near their plants because they were losing workers who could not find housing for their families. Parks of tiny trailers—not at all like the luxurious mobile homes of later years—sprang up near defense plants.

In spite of the government's efforts to build plants all over the country close to pools of labor, in part to avoid uprooting of people, there was massive migration—particularly from the South, from rural Appalachia, and from rural areas in the Midwest—to defense plants on the West Coast and Detroit, Cleveland, Chicago, and other major industrial cities in the Midwest.

Towns and cities with defense industries were flooded with immigrants for whom there was no housing. Some sense of the housing problem can be inferred from the fact that 15,300,000 people, in addition to those in the military, moved across county lines during the war. In 1939 Mobile, Alabama, had a population of 78,000. By 1943, Mobile had become a major shipbuilding center and had attracted 150,000 additional residents, mostly low-income people from small towns and rural areas of Alabama. A multitude of social problems resulted; for example, 3,000 migrant children went without schooling. The population in Norfolk, Virginia, grew from 343,000 in 1940 to almost a half million four years later. In the Detroit labor market, employment increased from 396,000 in November 1940 to 867,000 three years later.

Poor housing was not solely the lot of lower class immigrants from the South who flocked to boom towns to work in war industries. Mature, educated women who joined their husbands at military bases almost always encountered housing problems, and many tell of living in conditions so terrible that the memory of their experience caused them to shudder decades later.

Homeowners were urged to take in roomers and boarders. A government slogan encouraged people to "Protect Your Home by Sharing It with a War Worker." Income from room and board added to the family treasury, and in many cases, especially when the husband was away in the military service, the homeowner took in a guest for companionship.

Even well-to-do people took in guests. Guest houses were converted into rental property, and spare rooms were let to eager renters. It was now patriotic for private homes to take in lodgers, so families who would not have considered doing so before the war could do so without suffering social opprobrium.

In private homes, spare bedrooms that were designed for one or two persons were often rented to three or four or as many as six defense workers. As anthropologist Margaret Mead commented, young women found themselves living five or six to an apartment, sharing bedrooms with other young women they did not know; frequently they worked different shifts at factories and did not even know one another's names.

The passage of the Lanham Act in October 1940 provided $150 million to provide public housing; with amendments, the allocation had grown to $1.2 billion by early 1943, at which time nearly 2 million people were living in homes built by the government. The Lanham Act provided that 3 percent of the funds for government housing be dedicated to community facilities. In non-urban areas additional funds were provided for schools, playgrounds, child care facilities, community halls, shopping centers, nursery schools and other community needs. Much of the public housing built by the government was prefabricated and of poor quality, with tiny rooms, thin walls, poor heating, little privacy, and minimal storage space, but it was better than no housing and was even an improvement over what many of the occupants had known before the war. After *Washington Post* reporter Agnes Meyer described the housing around the Willow Run aircraft manufacturing plant near Detroit, Michigan, as a "nightmare of substandard living conditions," the government constructed 25,000 houses near the plant. But even that did not fully meet the demand of the 40,000 workers employed there in the production of B-24 airplanes and nearby in other war industries.

The housing shortage for women workers moving into Washington led President Roosevelt to direct that dormitories be built for them near their work sites. The government built some 12,000 rooms within walking distance of government offices, including some next to the Pentagon. It was not a new idea. The military had already constructed dormitories for single men and women near defense plants, particularly those located in small towns and in towns whose population had multiplied as a result of the construction of defense plants.

Prices of real estate went up faster than almost everything else, since home sales could not be regulated like commodities. Recognizing that the country faced a shortage of housing, especially in areas with defense plants, the government sought to control inflationary rental rates by imposing rent controls. On March 2, 1942, the Office of Price Administration ordered landlords to roll back rental rates to those in effect on April 1,

1941. As a consequence, rents rose only 3.5 percent during the war, at least officially. Yet landlords frequently found ways around the controlled rate by making changes that under OPA controls allowed higher rental rates, such as installing central heating, painting, or remodeling.

Prior to the institution of rent control, the cost of housing had increased sharply. From 1939 to 1942, rental rates of small houses grew by 45 percent and apartments by 31 percent; thus when rent controls came, rates of much rental housing had already risen to the market level. The demand for housing was so great that thereafter landlords were able to defer painting and repairs, in spite of numerous complaints by tenants. The government's rent regulation office in Philadelphia received 20,000 complaints in one year.

Another technique to circumvent rent control was to sell the house to the tenant, with only nominal down payment and monthly payments that exceeded the controlled rent. This practice led the government to require a minimum down payment of 33.3 percent on homes sold.

In New Jersey, workers at a shipyard banded together and bought a 500-unit apartment complex, a precursor to condominium ownership of later decades. Each cooperative included arrangements whereby a person could sell his or her equity. For the most part, however, tenants tended to be at best loosely organized, due in part to their high mobility, and they were unable to accomplish much through organized activity. Further, with the coming of the Office of Economic Stabilization in the fall of 1942, prices tended to be more stabilized and the discontent with rent control was alleviated somewhat.

Transportation

As with most other goods and services, the demand for transportation exceeded the supply and travelers became accustomed to long waits and discomfort. Trains were heavily in demand by the armed forces for movement of soldiers and shipment of goods, as well as for transporting massive amounts of raw and manufactured supplies for the defense industry. At the same time, passenger trains were the leading means of inter-city travel, especially over long distances. They were always crowded; it was not unusual to board a train and find dozens of soldiers and sailors sleeping on the floor. Any limitations on the number of passengers allowed per car were ignored, and trains accepted passengers as long as there were places for them to sit, stand or lie down. Of course, crowds and waiting lines were not unique to train travel. Everywhere people went during the war they were met with waiting lines—in restaurants, movie houses, shops, buses, trains, and nearly all other public places.

Steamships had been taken over by the government and converted to troop transports. Air travel was still new enough that not many thought of it as a travel option; besides, airlines served only larger towns, flying was expensive, and plane seats were usually preempted by government officials on war business. In addition, the AAF had put commercial airplanes to use hauling military personnel and supplies.

The manufacture of cars had been virtually halted in February 1942. In 1941, 3,779,682 cars and trucks were produced; in 1942, this figure dropped to 222,862. Only 139 were produced in 1943 and 610 in 1944, all for government use, although as late as mid-1943 there was still a stockpile of cars available from which rationing boards could make allocations to people with critical needs, such as physicians.

Gasoline and tire rationing severely restricted automobile travel. Without black market gasoline, cross country auto trips virtually disappeared, although rationing boards could authorize a special ration of gasoline to transport a car to a new location. Carpooling became commonplace; after the spring of 1942, virtually every war plant established a "share-the-ride" committee. Taxi cabs were scarce and hard to find. Inter-city buses became more heavily used than ever before. Most city transportation consisted of electric rail trolleys, and in a few areas similar trolleys—called interurbans—connected with nearby towns.

The public was asked in many ways to avoid any travel that was not necessary; signs that read "Is This Trip Necessary?" were posted in all bus and train stations. The Office of Production Management in Washington issued a booklet entitled "How to Spend a Week-end Without a Car." Yet the tourism industry continued to grow, at least for a while. In spite of the fact that the AAF had requisitioned most of the resort hotels in Miami Beach and Atlantic City for training, the tourist business there was up 20 percent in 1943.

The Press

Most people were much better able to keep up with the war on a day-to-day basis than in the previous world war. The *New York Times* carried a summary of war news every day on page two, and all newspapers attempted to report war news thoroughly. The press worked diligently to report news from all of the battle fronts.

Communication probably had more to do with the differences in the public mood in World War II as compared to World War I. People were much more aware of the ugly side of the war, thanks not only to newspapers and magazines but to radio and movies which provided extensive news not available in World War I. America had entered World War I thinking it would be over quickly and without much bloodshed; in

1941 people had a much more realistic sense of the situation. The slaughter of World War I, which had ended only 23 years before, was still clear in the minds of millions of Americans. And the United States had entered World War I voluntarily; this time it had little choice, having been attacked. There was no cheering because there was not much to cheer about. Many people had read books describing the Nazi movement and its threat to world peace and realized that if Germany were not stopped, the future of mankind was at risk. Although the Office of War Information fanned the flames of hatred toward the Japanese throughout the war, it was hardly necessary; the Japanese attack on Pearl Harbor coupled with Japanese atrocities in the Philippines, Guadalcanal, Hong Kong and Singapore early in the war inflamed America's hatred of the enemy. These feelings were exacerbated by the media's day-in, day-out depiction of the Japanese, especially their leaders, as vicious and inhuman.

Radio became a leading source of information about the war and the country during the war, serving the same purpose television news would later serve. In 1944 five times as much time was devoted to news on networks as in 1939. Between Pearl Harbor and V-J Day CBS devoted 38.7 percent of its network time to news, for example.

Each evening, regular newscasters would report news from the war fronts. Until he became head of the Office of War Information, the staccato voice of Elmer Davis was a favorite of many people. H. V. Kaltenborn also garnered a sizeable radio news audience, as did Lowell Thomas, Boake Carter, Fulton Lewis, Jr., Robert Trout, Upton Close and Earl Godwin. And the gravel-voiced Gabriel Heater always opened his evening report with, "Ah, there's good news tonight!" Edward R. Murrow, reporting live from London, became a legend during the war; his vivid accounts of the bombing of London were eagerly awaited by millions of people each evening. Murrow was the first to broadcast live from a bomber as it dropped its bombs over Berlin. George Hicks gave a vivid description of the invasion of Europe on June 6, 1944, broadcasting live from a warship just off shore.

The four radio networks and more than 550 radio stations carried the wartime morale series "This Is War" without sponsorship, underwriting the cost themselves. Some stations stayed on 24 hours a day, when that was not common in radio, bringing up-to-date news and also serving as part of the radio defense system for the AAF Fighter Command.

Despite paper shortages—by 1943, there had been a reduction in newsprint of 30 percent—newspapers continued to publish, although in abbreviated editions, and some even increased news content at the expense of advertising. The eagerness for news about the progress of the war made for large circulations. A survey of New Yorkers in July 1945 during a newspaper deliverers' strike found that 31.5 percent of the readers missed most "the news generally" and another 26.5 percent missed "war news, foreign news" most. In retrospect, it is clear that the press was not objective in its reporting during the war; there is little doubt that the press avidly supported the government and the war effort.

Official censorship of the press, except in combat zones, was minor; it was not necessary. The press voluntarily withheld information when requested by authorities or when it felt that its reporting would harm the war effort. While the press may have only rarely manufactured news, it is clear that it routinely withheld information that might have been helpful to the enemy. When the *Normandie* burned and sank in the New York Harbor, sabotage was suspected and the press did not report the incident lest it harm national morale. The press also contributed significantly to persuading people at home to conserve energy, to buy savings bonds and stamps, to donate scrap metal and scarce materials, and to join in other government projects dedicated to winning the war.

There were isolated exceptions to the withholding of news. In 1943, when General George Patton slapped a soldier in a hospital in Sicily who was suffering from battle fatigue and called him a coward, General Eisenhower, the theater commander, called reporters together and told them about the incident but asked them not to report it, in the interest of troop morale. None did, but a month later Drew Pearson, a Washington newspaper columnist, heard the story and published it. Another famous incident had to do with the announcement of the end of the war in Europe. The army brought a number of news reporters to Amiens, France, to witness the signing of the German surrender, but asked them to withhold the news so the surrender could be announced in the USA and the USSR simultaneously. Edward Kennedy of the Associated Press found a way to bypass the censor and telephoned the story to his London office, resulting in a major scoop but one that was condemned by the military and censured by fellow journalists.

Magazines, particularly pictorial magazines, flourished during the war. *Life* magazine, which had been established in 1936, was among the most popular; every week it presented news of the war in pictures and frequently ran stories about life in wartime America. *Collier's*, which was primarily a feature rather than news magazine, had full-time reporters in war zones; Quentin Reynolds, a celebrated newsman, reported for the magazine from London, providing some of the most insightful stories of the war.

Entertainment

One might assume that because of the grim news that came through the media daily, people would have sat out the war in solemnity, awaiting its end. Quite the opposite was true; in fact, the pursuit of diversion was almost frenetic. Many people had more money than they had ever had and were eager to spend it, with the result that many lived as if there were no tomorrow.

The most popular entertainment during the war was movies. Attendance increased 50 percent in 1942 alone, for several reasons including the fact that movie houses were air conditioned—still a rarity in private homes—and provided a respite from the heat on summer evenings. Movies were an escape from reality, but they were also a major medium for building support for the war effort. Many young people went to movies every week, some two or three evenings a week. Admission at movie houses in small towns cost 25 cents—occasionally as little as 15 cents—and provided one of the few opportunities for an inexpensive date, given the social mores of the day. Movie houses changed the offerings often to accommodate the frequent moviegoer, which kept Hollywood busy turning out an abundance of films.

During the war years, movie houses interspersed news reels between feature films, providing the only movie pictures of the war. The news reels made no attempt to be objective but instead were dedicated to building morale and enthusiasm for the war effort. Movies were propaganda; they taught people to hate the "Japs and the Nazis." In addition, short films of five to ten minutes were shown, often patriotic accounts of war production achievements or documentaries about airplane plants. In this period when virtually everyone was unabashedly patriotic, no one seemed offended by propaganda in films, magazines, and newspapers. The Office of War Information often issued biased news reports about the war and the home situation, but few thought of it as such and if so they were not much concerned about it.

Much of the movie fare consisted of war pictures, although in the first year of the war many of the movies were pure entertainment unrelated to the war, including *Woman of the Year, Road to Morocco,* and *The Man Who Came to Dinner.* In 1943, there were more pictures about the war, such as *Sahara, Guadalcanal Diary,* and *The Moon Is Down;* these were all serious films, but there were also war-related films such as *This Is the Army* and *Stage Door Canteen* that were highly patriotic but showed none of the gore of combat. Then there was the box office bomb *Mission to Moscow,* based on the book by former Ambassador Joseph E. Davies, which was blatant propaganda on behalf of the Soviet Union. The war movies were, of course, propagandistic in that the Americans almost always won and usually included some philosophic discourse on the morality of the American position. When Americans lost, the films emphasized the courage of the American survivors.

Hollywood was able to get away with making some terrible movies, such as *Four Jills in a Jeep* and *Hollywood Canteen,* by giving them a patriotic focus. Many films were apparently aimed at the lowest intelligence level, as frequently revealed by their portrayal of the Japanese and Germans. Producers apparently took to heart H. L. Mencken's statement that you could never go broke underestimating the intelligence of the American people. It should be noted that exhibitors kept telling Hollywood that "the public is fed up with war films," which was not altogether true, as demonstrated by the success of many war films.

Motion picture producers, distributors and exhibitors voluntarily formed the Motion Picture Committee Co-Operating for National Defense, which after the attack on Pearl Harbor was renamed the War Activities Committee of the Motion Picture Industry. At the request of the committee, a government representative was appointed to counsel the industry on how best to serve the country. The representative, Lowell Millett, was assigned to the Office of War Information, but the post was eliminated in 1943 when Congress gutted the domestic branch of the OWI. Thanks to the War Activities Committee, more than 100 government produced or sponsored documentary and combat films, including *The Memphis Belle, The Battle of Midway,* and the *Why We Fight* series of films, plus several documentaries made by the governments of Britain and the Soviet Union, were shown in movie houses all over the country.

The Writers' War Board, which functioned largely on the East Coast, and the Hollywood Writers' Mobilization unabashedly promoted support for the war through their articles, by selling war bonds, and by writing radio and movie scripts and plays for the armed forces. Effort from Millett to promote support for the war in movies was unnecessary; the producers, directors, and writers were all too well disposed to do so on their own, which they had done before Millet was appointed and continued to do after his post was abolished. Major movie houses in large cities supplemented films with live entertainment—bands and singers—so when people attended the movies they often saw live performances by Frank Sinatra, Dinah Shore, the Dorsey Brothers band, and dozens of other big name bands and singers of the day, all for the price of the movie ticket.

While radio news increased sharply during the war, radio remained a major medium of entertainment. Mystery plays, particularly serials of radio sleuths, were very popular: *The Saint, Bulldog Drummond, Ellery Queen, Charlie Chan, Sherlock Holmes, Hercule Poirot, Perry Mason, Crime Photographer, Dick Tracy,* and *The Thin Man.* Comedy was even more popular. Leading comics were Bob Hope, Fred Allen, George Burns and Gracie Allen, and Edgar Bergen and his dummies.

Nightclubs became even more popular than before the war, and the proliferation of name bands made them an even greater attraction.

Glenn Miller and his band had joined the Army Air Forces and many bands lost some of their best musicians to the military services, yet the bands flourished during the war. Nightclubs did a booming business and were always crowded. Almost a year to the day after the attack on Pearl Harbor, 800 revelers at the Coconut Grove nightclub in Boston were caught in a panic when a busboy accidentally set fire to an artificial palm tree and the blaze turned into a conflagration, killing 480 people. In May 1944, the government put a 30 percent tax on cabarets in an attempt to dampen what appeared to be excessive revelry but later removed it upon discovering that the tax fell most heavily on servicemen.

The teen idol was young Frank Sinatra, whose bobby-soxer fans presaged the emotional outpourings of Elvis Presley fans 15 years later. Some of the most popular songs of the twentieth century either were written or gained widespread popularity during the war. Movies, songs and novels tended to be sappy during the war years because that was the mood of the country, a time of sentimentality. The musical play *Oklahoma!* opened on Broadway and was a smash, perhaps because it reflected a wholesomeness about America that everyone wanted to believe and presented spontaneous gaiety and a "happy face."

The sale of books rose during the war. The paper shortage dictated thinner paper, narrower margins and smaller type, but the number of copies sold jumped. The number of titles published was smaller than before the war, but sales of the most popular titles were phenomenal—sales of 1 to 2 million copies were not unusual. By the end of the war, the number of titles published was about half that of four years earlier, yet the number of copies sold was much greater. Wendell L. Willkie, the 1940 Republican presidential candidate, took a trip around the world after losing the election and wrote a small book entitled *One World* that sold more than 2 million copies in less than two months and remained at the top of the best-seller list for 16 consecutive weeks.

Books, like newspapers and magazines, supported the war and America's rightness about it, but like the movies, there were war books and there were books written purely to entertain. In his book *Men on Bataan,* John Hersey found more nobility and honor among the men than they themselves would have suggested since they were simply trying to stay alive and worried less about noble principles than did the author. William L. Shirer's *Berlin Diary* became a best-seller because it helped people to understand what had happened in Germany up to America's entrance in the war. Ernie Pyle's newspaper columns from North Africa relating the experiences of ordinary soldiers doing a dirty job under miserable circumstances were so popular that they were reissued as books. William L. White's *They Were Expendable* about PT boats related true stories of heroism among Americans in defeat and quickly became a best-seller. Richard Tregaskis's *Guadalcanal Diary* portrayed the war in the Pacific most gruesomely, but since it was the story of Americans winning battles, after so many months of defeat, it too became a best-seller. The most "sophisticated" books about the period, such as Norman Mailer's *The Naked and the Dead,* Herman Wouk's *The Caine Mutiny,* and James Jones's *From Here to Eternity,* did not appear until after the war.

But it was not all serious reading. Bob Hope's *I Never Left Home* was pure Hope. Then, in late 1942, *See Here, Private Hargrove,* a lighthearted depiction of what life was like in the army for the lowly private, swept the best-seller lists. *Up Front,* by Bill Mauldin, the cartoonist laureate of the war, came out in 1945, giving the reader a humorous description of the war from the viewpoint of two cynical, battle hardened infantrymen, augmented by some of Mauldin's best cartoons from the GI newspaper *Stars and Stripes* and *Yank* magazine.

A half century later, the World War II generation seemed innocent, but in fact there was plenty of cynicism. Soldiers in combat and even in the States expressed little of the maudlin patriotism found in war movies, and many of the novels dealt with the raw side of life. The author Philip Wylie, the supreme cynic, set off a nationwide protest when he wrote in *Generation of Vipers* that "Mom is a jerk."

Sports

The search for entertainment and escape gave a boost to sports, particularly those that suffered least from the war effort. Many people who had endured the Depression and for the first time had money to spend began to attend sports events.

Baseball, which had been declared nonessential in 1918, cutting short the season by one month, was played throughout World War II. On January 15, 1942, in response to a plea by baseball Commissioner Kenesaw Mountain Landis, President Roosevelt agreed that baseball was important to the country's morale and said it should continue. By implication, the president authorized continuation of all team sports for the duration. On July 8, 1942, however, automobile and motorcycle racing were banned for the remainder of the war.

Travel restrictions and curbs on night games inhibited the game, but baseball remained popular and well attended. Night games were curtailed in 1942 and banned on the East Coast in 1943, but resumed in 1944. Crowded parking lots at baseball stadiums were attributed by some people to black market gasoline; later in the war, some parking lots were closed to discourage fans from driving automobiles to the games. Due to travel restrictions, spring training was held in locations close to the teams' home cities rather than in warmer climes, as before the war.

More than 4,000 professional baseball players joined the military services, but the fans were less than sympathetic towards the most famous players who took advantage of legal deferments. Before he was drafted in the spring of 1943, the all-time hero of baseball, Joe DiMaggio, who had been deferred because of his wife and son, was booed from the stands. Ted Williams, who batted .406 for the Boston Red Sox in 1941, was deferred because he supported his mother, but he joined the Marine Corps in 1942 and became a fighter pilot, serving three years in World War II, then another two years in the Korean War. Stan Musial, the hitting genius of the St. Louis Cardinals, was deferred because of responsibility for his parents, wife and child, but was drafted and entered the navy in early 1945. Bob Feller joined the navy three days after Pearl Harbor. Hank Greenberg of the Detroit Tigers had been drafted earlier and got out of the army in early December 1941, but, as sports writer Gregory Lalire points out, Greenberg re-enlisted days after the attack on Pearl Harbor and ended up spending four and one-half years in the service.

Other players took a good deal of criticism from the stands because they were not in military service, yet servicemen overseas were less critical, for they were happy to be able to tune in to games by shortwave radio. The 1,700 active baseball players did not compare in talent with the 4,000 who were in the military services, but they kept the sport alive and the public interested.

In spite of limitations, horse racing continued throughout the war, and gambling on the horses was at an all-time high. On opening day of racing at Hialeah Race Track in Florida in 1944, the amount of money bet was almost 50 percent higher than on any previous opening day. When the final figures for 1944 were in from the 17 states where racing was legal, they showed that racing enthusiasts had bet more than $1.1 billion that year. As one writer noted, there is something about a war that makes people reckless about gambling. But the government discovered that absenteeism in war plants and the heavy attendance at race tracks were related, and on January 3, 1945, race tracks were closed until further notice. The ban on racing lasted only until May 9, being lifted essentially concurrently with the end of the war in Europe.

Notwithstanding the loss of important players to the military services, ice hockey and professional football continued to be played. Sports writer Ron Fimrite says 638 players in the National Football League served in World War II, including two who won the Congressional Medal of Honor.

Victory Gardens

The U.S. Department of Agriculture, along with state agricultural extension services, promoted the planting of Victory Gardens, and by the end of the war Victory Gardens numbered in the millions. They were located in back yards, on the roofs of apartment buildings, in baseball fields, city parks, and almost any place where spare land could be found. In Arkansas the governor proclaimed February 8, 1943, Victory Garden Day and urged people to plant gardens on vacant lots and other vacant spaces. It was patriotic to grow a Victory Garden, it provided exercise and recreation, and also meant that a family might have vegetables that could not be bought, either fresh or canned, at the grocery store. Frozen foods were then still a novelty unknown to most shoppers.

Almost every activity associated with the war effort was organized, including the Victory Garden movement. By 1942, New York State had Victory Garden Councils in 55 counties, and in January 1943 the program was extended to towns and cities; it was estimated that 1.5 million gardens were planted in the state that year on some 200,000 acres. Across the country in the least populous state of Wyoming, 17,000 Victory Gardens were planted in 1943. In Illinois, 600,000 urban and 150,000 farm Victory Gardens were planted in 1942, and in 1943 a total of 1,151,000 Victory Gardens were planted, including 145,000 in the city of Chicago. The Ohio Agricultural Extension Service reported that 865,454 were planted in Ohio in 1944-45. The U.S. Department of Agriculture estimated that Victory Gardens produced 40 percent of the vegetables grown during the war. A Gallup poll in January 1943 found that 75 percent of those queried said they had canned food for the year, in spite of the fact that the preserving of fruit was inhibited by the shortage of sugar.

Epilogue

The period of the Second World War, with the intense nationwide push for rapid mobilization, was a time never to be forgotten by those who lived through it. Spurred to a fever pitch of patriotism by an eloquent president and a proactive press and other media, the entire country mobilized with a fervor, optimism and unanimity of resolve never exhibited before or since. With the exception of a relatively few, notably the interned Japanese Americans, people felt good about themselves and their contributions to the war effort. War Loan drives, Victory Gardens, scrap metal collections, blood drives, and volunteer entertainment of men and women in uniform all engendered feelings of satisfaction.

To be sure, it *was* war, with all its fear and heartache, death and suffering. Still, people felt the war was justified because they were convinced its purpose was noble. Daily news reports kept the populace mindful of the enormities of Hitler's aggression, and there is no unifying force like a common enemy.

Adding to the upbeat tenor of the times was the very significant reality of increased income and improved living conditions for many who had struggled through lean Depression years. Even though many consumer goods were not available and others were in short supply, consumer purchases in 1944 exceeded those of 1939 by 12 percent, in contrast to Great Britain where consumer purchases of goods and services *declined* 22 percent between 1938 and 1944. Many Americans had money for the first time in a decade or more and bought what was available. They ate better, had money for recreation, and generally enjoyed more physical amenities. Writer William Manchester, who served as a marine sergeant in the Pacific during the war, contends that the United States was the only country involved in World War II whose citizens lived better during the war than before.

There was, of course, another side to the story. Families whose sons, fathers, or husbands were killed in the war or returned physically or psychologically maimed, and couples who grew apart from living apart, saw it differently. So did most young men who lost as much as four or five years from the prime of their lives and bore for life emotional scars of the war, from which many would never recover. Some lost their businesses and others never regained the business or professional momentum that they had built before the war. There was sadness, loneliness, discomfort, and privation; there was anxiety, pain, and sacrifice of life.

But human memory tends, decades later, to emphasize the positive, exciting aspects of past experiences rather than the negative. Thus a vast number of Americans remembered the years 1941 through 1945 as the most interesting time of their lives. Many were the unsophisticated GIs whose world view was broadened by service overseas, and many were civilians who experienced new adventures they would not have had otherwise. The urgency of the war effort and the accompanying mobility tended to break down barriers of reserve: people were more open, and strangers talked to strangers, exchanging comments on the latest news of fighting, telling about their sons or brothers who were over there. In unity of purpose there was a bond. That ineffable spirit, so hard to put into words, so elusive of recapture, crowned the years of World War II.

Abbreviations

AAF	Army Air Forces
ACLU	American Civil Liberties Union
AFL	American Federation of Labor
AGF	Army Ground Forces
ASF	Army Service Forces
BLS	Bureau of Labor Statistics
CAP	Civil Air Patrol
CDA	Committee to Defend America by Aiding the Allies
CIA	Central Intelligence Agency
CIO	Congress of Industrial Organizations
CMTC	Citizens Military Training Camps
CO	conscientious objector
COL	Cost of Living Index
CPS	Civilian Public Service
CPT	Civilian Pilot Training Program
FDR	Franklin D. Roosevelt
FEPC	Fair Employment Practices Committee
JACL	Japanese American Citizens League
MCWR	Marine Corps Women's Reserve
NAACP	National Association for the Advancement of Colored People
NDAC	National Defense Advisory Commission
NHA	National Housing Agency
NLRB	National Labor Relations Board
OCD	Office of Civilian Defense
OCS	Officer Candidate School
ODT	Office of Defense Transportation
OEM	Office of Emergency Management
OES	Office of Economic Stabilization
OFF	Office of Facts and Figures

OPA	Office of Price Administration
OPACS	Office of Price Administration and Civilian Supply
OPM	Office of Production Management
OSRD	Office of Scientific Research and Development
OSS	Office of Strategic Services
OWI	Office of War Information
OWM	Office of War Mobilization
OWMR	Office of War Mobilization and Reconversion
PAW	Petroleum Administrator for War
PWA	Public Works Administration
RFC	Reconstruction Finance Corporation
ROTC	Reserve Officers Training Corps
SPAB	Supply Priorities and Allocations Board
SPARS	Coast Guard Women's Reserve (from the motto *Semper paratus*)
UAW	United Automobile Workers
USDA	United States Department of Agriculture
USES	United States Employment Service
USO	United Service Organization
V-E Day	May 10, 1945, end of the war in Europe
V-J Day	August 14, 1945, end of the war with Japan
VOC	Volunteer Officer Candidates
WAAC	Women's Army Auxiliary Corps
WAC	Women's Army Corps
WAF	Women in the Air Force
WASP	Women's Airforce Service Pilots
WAVES	Women Accepted for Volunteer Emergency Service
WFA	War Food Administration
WLB	National War Labor Board
WMC	War Manpower Commission
WPA	Works Progress Administration
WPB	War Production Board
WRB	War Resources Board
WSA	War Shipping Administration

Bibliography

Allen, Frederick Lewis. *Since Yesterday: The Nineteen-Thirties in America, September 3, 1929–September 3, 1939.* New York: Bantam, 1965.

Anderson, Elaine. "Consumer Rationing in Lucas County During World War II." *Northwest Ohio Quarterly,* 4:3 (1975), pp. 79–89.

Ano, Masaharu. "Loyal Linguists: Nisei of World War II Learned Japanese in Minnesota." *Minnesota History,* 45:7 (Fall 1977), pp. 273–287.

Bacon, Edmund N. "Wartime Housing." *Annals of the American Academy of Political and Social Science,* 229 (September 1943), pp. 128–137.

Baxter, James Phinney III. *Scientists Against Time.* Cambridge, MA: MIT Press, 1946.

Best, Gary Dean. *Pride, Prejudice, and Politics: Roosevelt Versus Recovery, 1933–1938.* New York: Praeger, 1991.

Blum, John Morton. *From the Morgenthau Diaries: Years of War, 1941–45.* Boston: Houghton Mifflin, 1967.

________. *V Was for Victory: Politics and American Culture in World War II.* New York: Harcourt, Brace and Jovanovich, 1976.

Brinkley, David. *Washington Goes to War.* New York: Knopf, 1988.

Brody, David. "The New Deal and World War II." In John Braeman, Robert H. Bremner and David Brody, eds., *The New Deal: The National Level,* vol. 1. Columbus: Ohio State University Press, 1975.

Brown, DeSoto. *Hawaii Goes to War: Life in Hawaii from Pearl Harbor to Peace.* Honolulu: Editions Limited, 1989.

Brown, Francis J. *Higher Education in the National Service.* Washington, DC: American Council on Education, 1950.

Buchanan, A. Russell. *The United States and World War II.* 2 vols. New York: Harper and Row, 1964.

Campbell, D'Ann. *Women at War with America: Private Lives in a Patriotic Era.* Cambridge, MA: Harvard University Press, 1984.

Cantril, Hadley, and Mildred Strunk. *Public Opinion, 1935–1940.* Princeton, NJ: Princeton University Press, 1951.

Cardozier, V. R. *Colleges and Universities in World War II.* Westport, CT: Praeger, 1993.

Caro, Robert A. *The Years of Lyndon Johnson: The Path to Power.* New York: Vintage Books, 1983.

Cavness, Max Parvin. *The Hoosier Community at War.* Bloomington: Indiana University Press, 1961.

Chadwin, Mark Lincoln. *The Hawks of World War II.* Chapel Hill: University of North Carolina Press, 1968.

Chafe, William H. *The American Woman: Her Changing Social, Economic, and Political Roles, 1920–1970.* New York: Oxford University Press, 1972.

Chandler, Lester V. *Inflation in the United States, 1940–1948.* New York: Harper and Brothers, 1951.

Clive, Alan. *State of War: Michigan in World War II.* Ann Arbor: University of Michigan Press, 1979.

Cohen, Stan. *V for Victory: America's Home Front During World War II.* Missoula, MT: Pictorial Histories Publishing Co., Inc., 1991.

Cole, Wayne S. *America First: The Battle Against Intervention, 1940–41.* Madison: University of Wisconsin Press, 1953.

Conner, William H., and Leon de Valinger, Jr. *Delaware's Role in World War II.* Dover, DE: State Archives Commission, 1955.

Correspondents for *Time, Life* and *Fortune. December 7: The First Thirty Hours.* New York: Alfred A. Knopf, 1942.

Corwin, Norman. "The Radio." In Jack Goodman, ed., *While You Were Gone.* New York: Simon and Schuster, 1946.

Cravens, Wesley Frank, and James Lea Cate, eds. *The Army Air Forces in World War II,* vol. 7. Washington, DC: Office of Air Force History, reprint 1983.

Crossland, Richard B., and James T. Currie. *Twice the Citizen: History of the United States Army Reserve, 1908–1983.* Washington, DC: Department of the Army, 1984.

Cuff, Robert D. "U. S. Mobilization and Railroad Transportation: Lessons in Coordination and Control, 1917–1945." *Journal of Military History,* 53:1 (January 1989), pp. 33–50.

Culley, John J. "The Santa Fe Internment Camp and the Justice Department Program for Enemy Aliens." In Roger Daniels, Sandra C. Taylor and Harry H. L. Kitano, eds., *Japanese Americans: From Relocation to Redress.* Seattle: University of Washington Press, 1991.

Daniels, Roger, Sandra C. Taylor and Harry H. L. Kitano, eds. *Japanese Americans: From Relocation to Redress.* Seattle: University of Washington Press, 1991.

Director of Selective Service. *Selective Service in Wartime.* Washington, DC: Government Printing Office, 1943.

Ellis, John. *The World War II Data Book: The Essential Facts and Figures for All the Combatants.* London: Aurum Press, 1993.

Fairchild, Byron, and Jonathan Grossman. *The Army and Industrial Manpower.* Washington, DC: Department of the Army, 1959.

Federal Records of World War II: Civilian Agencies, vol. 1. Washington, DC: Government Printing Office, 1950.

[Fesler, James P., ed.] *Industrial Mobilization for War: History of the War Production Board and Predecessor Agencies, 1940–1945.* vol. I: Program and Administration. Washington, DC: Government Printing Office, 1947.

Fimrite, Ron. "Call to Arms." *Sports Illustrated,* 75:18 (February 1991), pp. 100, 102, 104, 106, 108.

Fox, Stephen. *The Unknown Internment: An Oral History of the Relocation of Italian Americans During World War II.* Boston: Twayne Publishers, 1990.

Furer, Julius Augustus. *Administration of the Navy Department in World War II.* Washington, DC: Department of the Navy, 1959.

Fussell, Paul. *Thank God for the Atomic Bomb.* New York: Summitt Books, 1988.

Gallup, George A. *The Gallup Poll: Public Opinion, 1935–1971.* New York: Random House, 1972.

Gelb, Norman. *Dunkirk: The Complete Story of the First Step in the Defeat of Hitler.* New York: William Morrow, 1988.

Godson, Susan H. "The Waves in World War II." *Naval Institute Proceedings,* 107 (December 1981), pp. 46–51.

Goldberg, Alfred, ed. *A History of the United States Air Force, 1907–1957.* Princeton, NJ: D. Van Nostrand Company, Inc., 1957.

Goodman, Jack, ed. *While You Were Gone: A Report on Wartime Life in the United States.* New York: Simon and Schuster, 1946.

Greenfield, Kent Roberts, Robert R. Palmer, and Bell I. Wiley. *The Organization of Ground Combat Troops, United States Army in World War II.* Washington, DC: Historical Division, Department of the Army, 1947.

Grover, David H. *U.S. Army Ships and Watercraft of World War II.* Annapolis, MD: Naval Institute Press, 1987.

Hancock, Joy Bright. *Lady in the Navy: A Personal Reminiscence.* Annapolis, MD: Naval Institute Press, 1972.

Hansen, Willard W. "History of Military Training: Reserve Officers Training Corps and the 55C Schools, 1939–1944." Unpublished manuscript, Headquarters, Army Service Forces, 1 April 1945 (on file, Center of Military History, Washington, DC).

Hartmann, Susan. *The Homefront and Beyond: American Women in the 1940s.* Boston: Twayne Publishers, 1982.

Hartzell, Karl Drew. *The Empire State at War: World War II.* Albany: State of New York, 1949.

[Herring, Pendleton, ed.] *The United States at War: Development and Administration of the War Program by the Federal Government.* Washington, DC: Bureau of the Budget, 1946.

History Commission, World War II, of Newport News. *History of the City of Newport News, 1941–1945.* Richmond, Va: The Baughman Co., 1949.

Hoehling, A. A. *The Week Before Pearl Harbor.* New York: Norton, 1963.

Holley, Irving B., Jr. *Buying Aircraft: Matériel Procurement for the Army Air Forces.* Washington, DC: Department of the Army, 1964.

Ickes, Harold L. *The Autobiography of a Curmudgeon.* New York: Reynal and Hitchock, 1943.

Jamieson, John. *Books for the Army: Library Service in the Second World War.* New York: Columbia University Press, 1950.

Janeway, Eliot. *The Struggle for Survival: A Chronicle of Economic Mobilization in World War II.* New Haven, CT: Yale University Press, 1957.

Jeanes, William. "Baseball in World War II." *Sports Illustrated,* 75:9 (August 26, 1991), pp. 5, 7.

Johnson, Marilynn S. "Urban Arsenals: War Housing and Social Change in Richmond and Oakland, California, 1941–1945." *Pacific Historical Review,* LX:3 (August 1991), pp. 283–308.

Jones, Alfred Haworth. "The Making of an Interventionist on the Air: Elmer

Davis and the CBS News, 1939-1941." *Pacific Historical Review,* 42:1 (February 1973), pp. 74–93.

Kalisch, Beatrice J., and Philip A. Kalisch. "Nurses in American History: The Cadet Nurse Corps in World War II." *American Journal of Nursing,* 76:2 (February 1976), pp. 240–242.

King, Ernest J. *U.S. Navy at War, 1941–1945: Official Reports of the Secretary of the Navy.* Washington, DC: Department of the Navy, 1946.

King, Spencer Bidwell. *Selective Service in North Carolina in World War II.* Chapel Hill: University of North Carolina Press, 1949.

Kitagawa, Daisuke. *Issei and Nisei: The Internment Years.* New York: The Seabury Press, 1967.

Knight, Douglas M., ed. *The Federal Government and Higher Education.* Englewood Cliffs, NJ: Prentice-Hall, 1960.

Koistinen, Paul A. C. "Mobilizing the World War II Economy: Labor and the Industrial-Military Alliance." *Pacific Historical Review,* 42:4 (1972), pp. 443–478.

Kreidburg, Marvin A., and Morton G. Henry. *History of Military Mobilization in the United States Army, 1775–1945.* Pamphlet No. 20-212. Washington, DC: Department of the Army, 1953.

Lalire, Gregory. "With the World at War, the Game of Baseball Contributed to the Final Victory in Its Own Way." *World War II,* 8:3 (September 1993), pp. 64, 66, 68, 70.

Langer, William L., and S. Everett Gleason. *The Undeclared War, 1940–1941.* New York: Lippincott, 1953.

Larson, T. A. *Wyoming's War Years, 1940–1941.* Cheyenne: University of Wyoming Press, 1954.

Lautere, Louis. "Side Lights on the Negro and the Army." *Opportunity: A Journal of Negro Life* (Winter 1944), p. 7.

Lebergott, Stanley. *Manpower in Economic Growth: The American Record Since 1800.* New York: McGraw-Hill, 1964.

Lichtenstein, Nelson. "The Making of the Postwar Working Class: Cultural Pluralism and Social Structure in World War II." *The Historian,* LI:1 (November 1988), pp. 42–63.

Lingeman, Richard R. *Don't You Know There's a War On? The American Home Front, 1941–1945.* New York: Putnam, 1970.

Lohman, J. D. "Are We Wasting 200,000 Soldiers." *Saturday Evening Post,* CCVI (1953), pp. 51–60.

Lydgate, William A. *What America Thinks.* New York: Thomas Y. Crowell, 1944.

Lyons, Gene M., and John W. Masland. *Education and Military Leadership.* Princeton, NJ: Princeton University Press, 1959.

McMinn, John H., and Max Levin. *Personnel in World War II.* Washington, DC: Office of the Surgeon General, Department of the Army, 1963.

Mahon, John K. *History of the Militia and the National Guard.* New York: Macmillan, 1983.

Manakee, Harold R. *Maryland in World War II,* vol. I, "The Home Front Volunteer Services." Baltimore: Maryland State Historical Society, 1958.

Manchester, William. *The Glory and the Dream: A Narrative History of America, 1932–1970,* vol. 1. Boston: Little, Brown, 1973.

Mead, Margaret. "Women in the War." In Jack Goodman, ed., *While You Were Gone*. New York: Simon and Schuster, 1946.
Meyer, Agnes. *Journey Through Chaos*. New York: Harcourt, Brace and Co., 1944.
Miller, Frances S. "I Deserted to the Navy." *AAUW Journal* (Fall 1945), pp. 12–14.
Millett, Allan R., and Peter Maslowski. *For the Common Defense: A Military History of the United States*. New York: The Free Press, 1984.
Millett, John D. *The Organization and Role of the Army Service Forces, United States Army in World War II*. Washington, DC: Government Printing Office, 1954.
[Millis, Walter, ed.] *The War Reports*. New York: Lippincott, 1947.
Milner, Lucille. "On the Civil Liberty Front." *New Republic*, v. 110, no. 26, June 26, 1944, pp. 839–840.
Mitchell, Donald W. *History of the Modern American Navy: From 1883 through Pearl Harbor*. New York: Knopf, 1946.
Myer, Dillon S. *Uprooted Americans: The Japanese Americans and the War Relocation Authority During World War II*. Tucson: University of Arizona Press, 1971.
Nash, Gerald D. *The Great Depression and World War II: Organizing America, 1933–1945*. New York: St. Martin's, 1979.
Nelson, Donald M. *Arsenal of Democracy: The Story of American War Production*. New York: Harcourt, Brace and Company, 1946.
O'Leary, Paul Z. M. "Wartime Rationing and Governmental Organization." *American Political Science Review*, XXXIX (December 1945), p. 1090.
Osborn, Richard C. "Corporate Profits: War and Postwar." Bulletin No. 77, Bureau of Economic and Business Research, University of Illinois, 1954.
Palmer, Robert R., Bell Wiley and William R. Keast. *The Army Ground Forces: The Procurement and Training of Combat Ground Troops*. Washington, DC: Department of the Army, 1948.
Parks, Robert J. *Medical Training in World War II*. Washington, DC: Department of the Army, 1974.
Pelz, Stephen E. *Race to Pearl Harbor: The Failure of the Second London Naval Conference and the Onset of World War II*. Cambridge, MA: Harvard University Press, 1974.
Perrett, Goeffrey. *Days of Sadness, Years of Triumph, The American People, 1939–1945*. New York: Coward, McCann and Geoghegan, 1973.
Phillips, Caleb. *The 1940s: A Decade of Triumph and Trouble*. New York: Macmillan, 1975.
Polenberg, Richard, ed. *America at War*. Englewood Cliffs, NJ: Prentice-Hall, 1968.
________. *War and Society: The United States, 1940–1945*. New York: Lippincott, 1972.
Pollard, James E. *History of the Ohio State University: The Bevis Administration, 1940–1946*. Columbus, OH: Ohio State University Press, 1967.
Pringle, Henry. "The War Agencies." In Jack Goodman, ed., *While You Were Gone*. New York: Simon and Schuster, 1946.
Provinse, John H. "Relocation of Japanese-American College Students: Acceptance of a Challenge." *Higher Education*, 1:8 (April 16, 1945), pp. 1–4.
Quick, Paddy. "Rosie the Riveter." *Radical America*, 9 (1975), pp. 115–121.
Reserve Officers of Public Affairs Unit 4-1. *The Marine Corps Reserve: A History*. Washington, DC: Government Printing Office, 1966.

Robinson, Edgar Eugene. *The Roosevelt Leadership, 1933–1945*. New York: Lippincott, 1955.
Salmond, John A. *The Civilian Conservation Corps, 1933–1942: A New Deal Case Study*. Durham, NC: Duke University Press, 1967.
Satterfield, Archie. *The Home Front: An Oral History of the War Years in America, 1941–45*. Chicago: Playboy Press, 1981.
Schaffter, Dorothy. *What Comes of Training Women for War*. Washington, DC: American Council on Education, 1948.
Schlegel, Marvin Wilson. *Conscripted City: Norfolk in World War II*. Richmond, VA: Norfolk War History Commission, 1951.
_______. *Virginia on Guard: Civilian Defense and the State Militia in the Second World War*. Richmond: The Virginia State Library, 1949.
Schuler, Edgar A. "V for Victory: A Study of Symbolic Social Control." *The Journal of Social Psychology*, 19:22 (1944), pp. 283–299.
Shannon, David A. *Between the Wars, 1919–1941*. Boston: Houghton-Mifflin, 1979.
Sherwood, Robert E. *Roosevelt and Hopkins: An Intimate History*. New York: Harper and Bros., 1949.
Shindler, Colin. *Hollywood Goes to War: Films and American Society, 1939–1952*. London: Routledge and Kegan Paul, 1979.
Sibley, Mulford Q., and Philip E. Jacob. *Conscription of Conscience: The American State and the Conscientious Objector, 1940–1947*. Ithaca, NY: Cornell University Press, 1952.
Smith, C. Calvin. *War and Wartime Changes: The Transformation of Arkansas, 1940–1945*. Fayetteville: University of Arkansas Press, 1986.
Somers, Herman Miles. *Presidential Agency: OWMR, Office of War Mobilization and Reconversion*. New York: Greenwood Press, 1950.
Spicer, Edward H., Asael T. Hansen, Katherine Luomala, and Marvin K. Opler. *Impounded People: Japanese-Americans in the Relocation Centers*. Tucson: University of Arizona Press, 1969.
Stokes, Thomas L. "The Congress." In Jack Goodman, ed., *While You Were Gone*. New York: Simon and Schuster, 1946.
Stone, I. F. *The War Years, 1939–1945*. Boston: Little, Brown, 1988.
Stouffer, Samuel A., Edward A. Suchman, Leland C. Devinney, Shirley A. Star, and Robin M. Williams, Jr. *The American Soldier: Adjustment During Army Life*, vol. 1. Princeton, NJ: Princeton University Press, 1949.
Sundquist, Eric J. "The Japanese-American Internment: A Reappraisal." *American Scholar*, 57:4 (Autumn 1988), pp. 529–547.
Tanner, Doris B. "Cornelia Clark Fort: A WASP in World War II." *Tennessee Historical Quarterly*, 40:4 (Winter 1981), pp. 381–394, and 41:1 (Spring 1982), pp. 67–80.
Terkel, Studs. *The Good War: An Oral History of World War II*. New York: Pantheon, 1984.
Thomas, Mary Martha. *Riveting and Rationing in Dixie: Alabama Women and the Second World War*. Tuscaloosa: University of Alabama Press, 1987.
Thomas, R. J. "What Labor Did." In *While You Were Gone*. Jack Goodman, ed. New York: Simon and Schuster, 1946.
Thompson, George Raynor, Dixie R. Harris, Pauline B. Oakes, and Dulany Terret. *The Signal Corps: The Test*. Washington, DC: Department of the Army, 1957.

Treadwell, Mattie E. *The Women's Army Corps*. Washington, DC: Department of the Army, 1954.

Turner, E. S. *The Phoney War*. New York: St. Martin's, 1961.

U.S. Army Service Forces: Annual Reports, 1941–45. Washington, DC: Government Printing Office, 1941–45.

"U.S. Naval Administration in World War II: Women's Reserve." Unpublished manuscript, Historical Section, Bureau of Naval Personnel (Microfiche on file, Navy Department Library, Washington Navy Yard).

Verges, Marianne. *On Silver Wings, 1942–1944: Women's Airforce Service Pilots of World War II*. New York: Ballantine, 1991.

Walton, Francis. *Miracle of World War II: How American Industry Made Victory Possible*. New York: Macmillan, 1956.

Watson, Mark Skinner. *The United States Army in World War II: Chief of Staff and Pre-War Plans*. Washington, DC: Historical Division, Department of the Army, 1950.

Watters, Mary. *Illinois in the Second World War: Operation Home Front*, vol. 1. Springfield: Illinois State Historical Library, 1951.

Weatherford, Doris. *American Women and World War II*. New York: Facts on File, 1990.

Wilcox, Walter B. *The Farmer in the Second World War*. Ames: Iowa State University Press, 1947.

Wittner, Lawrence S. *Rebels Against War: The American Peace Movement, 1941–1960*. New York: Columbia University Press, 1969.

World War II from an American Perspective: An Annotated Bibliography. Santa Barbara, CA: ABC-Clio, 1983.

Index